suede
love&poison

suede

love&poison

the authorised biography

David Barnett

André Deutsch

First published in 2003 by
André Deutsch Ltd
an imprint of the
Carlton Publishing Group
20 Mortimer Street
London W1T 3JW

A catalogue record for this book is available from the British Library

ISBN 0 233 00047 X

The publishers would like to thank the following sources for their kind
permission to reproduce the pictures in this book:

Brett Anderson
Peter Anderson
Alan Fisher
Justine Frischmann
Simon Gilbert
Phillip Williams
Iain Williams
John Cheves
Mitch Ikeda
Sam McCormick
David Fraser
Petra Lohner
Mat Isepp
Chris Lopez
Tom Sheehan

Every effort has been made to acknowledge correctly and contact
the source and/or copyright holder of each picture, and André Deutsch
Limited apologises for any unintentional errors or omissions which will
be corrected in future editions of this book.

Typeset by E-Type, Liverpool
Printed and bound in Great Britain
by Mackays

contents

acknowledgements

This book would not have happened without the enthusiasm and encouragement of Brett Anderson, whose candid and revealing interviews form the backbone of this story. Mat Osman, Simon Gilbert, Richard Oakes and Alex Lee have all been similarly enlightening in providing their own individual perspectives and their frankness at times has been astonishing. Wonderful All Times. Extra special thanks must go to the former members of the band, Justine Frischmann, Mike Joyce and Neil Codling whose co-operation has gone well beyond anything I could have expected. Although Bernard Butler ultimately declined the opportunity to be give his side of the story, the meeting I had with him to discuss his concerns is hugely appreciated. While never shying away from the madness and extremity of the whole affair, I hope I've shown some understanding of the behaviour of both sides. Offering their own illuminating insights, the key peripheral players, Peter Anderson, Alan Fisher, Jon Eydmann, Phill Savidge, Saul Galpern, Victor Aroldoss, Peter Sissons, Ricky Gervais and Tony Hoffer have been vital in untangling the web of rumour and intrigue. Equally essential on the fringes are Chris Mackay, Stewart Furini, Alison Hale, Malcolm Dunbar, Mike Smith, Sheri Friers Sam McCormick, Peter van der Velde, Ali Lush and Nathalie Fraser. For much appreciated advice and support above and below the call of duty, three hearty cheers to: Ben Lurie, Bennie Brongers, Jane Glover, Phyl Sprigg and Richard Kiernan at Interceptor, Lucia Burghi Gonzalez, Jo Reilly, Jodie Banaszkiewicz, Ricky Coffey, Penny Humphreys, Kimble Garcia, Mike Gourlay, Janet Choudry, Erol Alkan, Lucy Madison, Matty Wall, Mike Christie, Vanessa Saunders, Claire Grainger, Nadine McBay, Lucy Cane, Fraser Thomson, Mat Everitt, Anissa Mangen, Alex Croft, Sam Cunningham, Jeremy Allen, Soraya Syed, Kas Syed, Jim and Alan, Michelle Kerry, Brychan Todd, Sarah McGiven, Jaci Spode, Simon Hobart, Peter Stewart, Robert

Hayden, Erin Dineen, Charlotta Waggert, Iona Ogilvie, John Brandham, Sarah Bee, Jose Contreras Ramis, Peter Crompton, Max and Jack, David Gejlemo, Claudia Pramono, John W. Lucey, Baxendale, Arse, Mark Galer, Charlie Myatt, Davis Wilkie, Goth, Jessica Appla, Martin Wallace, that bloke who mistook me for Alex James at Reading, David A Smith, the Mackays, Joanne Boyle and above all Andy, Kate, Oscar, Sam, mum and my two dads. There are undoubtedly legions of others I've missed out to whom I can only say buy enough copies of this book to ensure a revised edition. Special mention must go to Simon Price for invaluable help in the initial interviews and conception of this project. Similarly effusive thanks to my editors Ian Gittins and Mike Flynn, Miranda Filbee and all at André Deutsch. And Brobdingnagian gushes of gratitude to Charlie Charlton for proving, as Gabriel pointed out, that dreams can indeed come true. It's been a blast. Nam Myoho Renge Kyo. Everything Will Flow.

David Barnett, August 2003

preface

The last night of the Phoenix Festival, Stratford-upon-Avon, July, 1995.

Back at the cosy Shakespeare Hotel an orgy of Bacchanalian proportions ensued. An argument about the merits or otherwise of Pulp's "Underwear" finally drove Brett and Mat from the festivities and at some point in the evening Charlie finally offered me a post at Suede HQ. I accepted with the caveat that under no circumstances did I wish to be involved in these so-called drugs of which Suede were so fond. When the concept of sleep dissolved in a fog of artificially induced enthusiasm for the lyrics of Jarvis Cocker, a trip to the local tavern prevailed. Several ales later we hastened back to our lodgings only to find a cordon of Her Majesty's constabulary ringing the building. "Here, take this," spake Charles, thrusting a curious miniature origami-style package into my sweating palms, before darting into the foyer. It was at this point that m'colleague turned a worryingly unnatural shade of grey. Charlie returned to aid and abet said colleague up the recently refurbished stairs. As a curious gagging and spluttering emanated from m'trusted colleague, the young bastard of an uppity Hitler – or hotel manager as officialdom would have it – became unnecessarily interested. "Shall I call a doctor?" he cuntingly enquired. "Not necessary," responded Charlie, hurling the wreck of my accomplice into the nearest room. A moist re-enactment of a particularly colourful fireworks display erupted, accompanied by much slamming of doors and hollers of "We've just had this fucking place redecorated!" from the young Adolf. The next half an hour was spent paranoidly picking wraps and reefer butts from the room's wastepaper baskets between vague fits of concern that my chum may have fatally overdosed on Suede-subsidised lager.

Finally, groggily, absolutely, I had arrived.

introducing the band

"THERE'LL BE BLUE SKIES OVER...the white cliffs of Dover." Dame Vera Lynn's voice floats incongruously across the tiny church hall as red lighting and hissing dry ice turn the venue into a steaming brothel. The audience, comprised largely of freaks and misfits, are pressed hard against the stage, temperatures rising. A shadowy, spiky-haired figure creeps surreptitiously from behind the velvet curtains on to his drum stool as the opening strains of "Pantomime Horse" shimmer forth, the players still waiting in the wings. The court jester slithers on, sits like a man and smiles like a reptile, his clinging garb a second skin waiting to be shed. Ethnic talismans dangle from his neck and wrists, complementing his hypnotic, almost satanic movements. As the music spirals upward, this snake-charming man stretches his back into erotically contorted shapes, chameleon, Corinthian and caricature. "Have you ever tried it that way?" From either side of the stage the bass player and guitarist waltz into view like sentinels, sending the song spinning through several crescendos before it finally crashes earthward like a mortally wounded beast. Before the sweat-drenched audience can recover, the band rip through two furious new numbers, rife with spit and swearing. Brett seems to be shouting "shit sucker!" and "rescue me from this horrible life". Then it's The Hit. Pandemonium breaks out. Bruised shins and crushed ribs. The singer and guitarist exchange angry glances, the crowd encourages them like it's an illegal boxing match. Is this for real or just part of the show? There's a guitar change for one of the slower songs but something's not right. Brett hurls his microphone to the ground in disgust and storms off. Bernard follows him. The crowd gets restless and some of those on the balcony start chanting, "There's only one Simon Gilbert!" Brett's back. He joins in with the singalong, then adds, "Thank fuck for that!" No one's quite sure if he's joking or not. Bernard's returned too, for his showpiece

"He's Dead". Tonight it seems like one incredible guitar solo with Brett reduced to accompanying go-go dancer. Toward the end the guitarist picks out a few notes of "Loch Lomond". Not to be outdone, Brett joins in, "…I'll be in Scotland afore ye". The Edinburgh crowd think he's taking the piss. "Patronising cunts!" More catcalls follow an aborted intro to "Metal Mickey". "What are you wearing?" Another guitar change, another technical hitch. Somebody's going to hit someone any minute. By the final song, the tension and danger are almost overwhelming. It makes for a fantastic show. "Stay Together" isn't in the shops for another couple of days, but this paranoid racket bears little resemblance to the polite version the fans have been hearing on the radio. Bernard's guitar is like a squealing sacrifice, squirming in his hands. Brett is screaming "Whipping up a storm like a fucker from the dead!" over and over again until he exits without warning, leaving the others to finish the song without him. Finally, only Bernard remains, centre stage, his "Remember Elvis" T-shirt sodden. His left hand squeezes the last drops of life from his guitar while he gives a triumphant salute with the other, a perverse cross between Benny Hill and the lone victor in a fight to the death. This is Bernard Butler's last public performance with Suede.

Five months later, in the first interview since Bernard's departure, Brett Anderson told the *NME*: "The history of this fucking band is ridiculous. It's like Machiavelli rewriting *Fear And Loathing In Las Vegas*. It involves a cast of thousands. It should star Charlton Heston…it's like a pram that's just been pushed down a hill. It's always been fiery and tempestuous and really on the edge and it never stops. I don't think it ever will. It would make a fucking good book."

That was back in August 1994, though the quote could just have easily have come from almost any point in the band's tumultuous career. For the story of Suede is one of extremes. Of dizzying heights and desperate lows. Of times when they seemed to have the world at their feet and other periods where it seemed impossible to continue.

Suede's detractors have often pegged the band as cold, cynical, pretentious and, most damning of all, humourless. The very opposite is the case. Suede are all too human. Their songs are tragic-comic dramas about real people and real lives. Or as Brett once put it, "about the used condom under the bed". Their story – without wishing to sound too cynical, humourless or (God forbid) pretentious – is a testament to the power of the human spirit. And, hopefully, it will make a fucking good book.

where the pigs don't fly

IT WAS THE YEAR OF *Sergeant Pepper* and the Summer of Love: 1967. It was a time of cultural revolution. Music was changing. Drugs were changing. Attitudes were changing. And Britain was swinging, still celebrating England's World Cup victory the previous year. The Labour party was back in power, re-nationalising industries and passing pro-abortion legislation which some saw as liberation for women and others as symptomatic of a new permissiveness. Joe Orton was outraging and delighting West End audiences in unequal measure with farces daring to admit that, yes, people nowadays did sometimes have sex out of wedlock and, no, it didn't necessarily need to be with someone of the opposite gender. Then Joe's boyfriend got jealous of all this success and battered him to death with a hammer. This was a shame since he was in the middle of writing a screenplay for the Beatles which would have seen them all jump into bed with the same woman. The Fab Four, meanwhile, along with the Stones, the Kinks and others were busy making the best music in the world. The very day after Brett was born, BBC Radio 1 began broadcasting for the first time – the establishment's answer to pirate pop stations like Radio Caroline.

Yet for all the youthful *zeitgeist*, many remnants of a bygone age clung on. The death penalty was still in place, voting was strictly for over-21s only, homosexuality was illegal and television was broadcast in black and white. LSD didn't just stand for the latest drug of choice or "Lucy in the Sky with Diamonds"; it also represented a ridiculously antiquated monetary system that made a simple shopping trip a mathematical nightmare. Dwarfing all of this, however, was the very real spectre of nuclear destruction. The Cuban missile crisis was an all too recent memory and Britain had just launched her first Polaris submarine. The

Vietnam War was already officially two years old and, with growing American involvement, escalation to a worldwide conflict seemed just round the corner. This was the world that greeted Brett Lewis Anderson. "I was a very timid child…there seemed a lot to be frightened of. There was the threat of nuclear war, the fear of your parents dying of aerosol poisoning. It was dreadful."

"We are all in the gutter, but some of us are looking at the stars," declared some old Irish queen or other. It's well known that Brett Anderson's particular gutter was the anonymous commuter town of Haywards Heath. Well known, however, doesn't necessarily mean true. Brett in fact hails from the neighbouring village of Lindfield, winner of "Best Kept Village in Sussex" umpteen times and country retreat of Henry VII and Charles Dickens. The larger town was actually born when Lindfield's Victorian residents refused to have their picturesque neighbourhood sullied by those new-fangled steam trains. The local railway station was consequently built on the heath (open, common land of poor soil) a few miles away and the houses springing up around the railway line eventually became a new town, soon overtaking Lindfield in size, if not character. Brett's father, Peter Anderson, still bemoans his son's claim to come from Haywards Heath. "It's a horrible place," says Peter. Neither is he too enamoured with Brett's public image. "He adopts this cockney-style accent at times and gives the impression he's terribly hard and a bit common. But he's very well educated and kind hearted. He's not hard man of rock. He's concerned about things, he loves his cats, he's extremely kind-hearted. His mother would have been proud of him and I'm sure he'd like to have seen her at one of his gigs. In fact I know he would."

The Anderson clan were originally of military stock. "My grandfather was in the army. He was in the Royal Scots Fusiliers," explains Brett. "He was actually a drummer. He was a bit of a rogue, a bit of a wild card. He'd knock his family about. He ended up dying on a park bench."

This ancestry perhaps explains some of Peter's tastes which, for an unemployed ice cream vendor, could fairly be described as eccentric at least. He was and still is a fanatical fan of classical music for starters.

"My whole memory of my dad when I was growing up was that he had a different job every week," Brett remembers. "He trained as a chef and worked as a chef for a couple of weeks before I was born. I don't have any memory of him working as a chef. He was an ice cream man, he was a window cleaner, before he became a taxi driver. The most

embarrassing job he ever had, though, was as a swimming pool attendant at the local swimming pool that our school was forced to go to
every Tuesday. He never worked in an office. It was always just a matter
of scraping a living somehow. He was always very devoted to his family.
I think he considered success in life as being the father of a family." Peter
Anderson remains a taxi driver to this day, his cab decorated with Suede
memorabilia.

Brett's mother, Sandra Farrow, was similarly cultured in a stereotype-
busting manner. A talented painter, she was a fan of Gustave Klimt and
the Mexican artist Frida Kahlo. Frida's tragic story made a lasting
impression on the young Brett. After contracting polio at the age of six,
she suffered a horrific bus accident as a teenager. Hurled from the
vehicle, she was impaled on an iron pole which pierced her through the
womb. Surviving but unable ever to have children, she embarked on a
fiery affair with the exiled Leon Trotsky but was frequently beaten by
her husband. Her paintings reflected her painful life, particularly her
numerous self-portraits which hugely exaggerated her moustache and
eyebrows, giving the impression of a man trapped in a woman's body,
an image echoed in many a Suede lyric.

"My mum's family were very rustic," Brett remembers. "She used to
be a dress maker, posh women would come over and rip her off. She
never really had much of a sense of her own worth. It was like a do-it-
yourself sort of house. It's not an easy cliché for a kid from Sussex. I
wasn't born down a mine but we were very poor. We actually used to do
things like go to the fields to pick mushrooms to make soup out of. There
was never any money around. My family was always worrying about
money. That background probably gave me a lot of drive to make something happen in my life. Subconsciously, it made me quite ambitious in
lots of ways. She nurtured an artistic sensibility in me, just by being who
she was, I suppose, by loving music and painting."

"The thing about Brett's mum was that she had that thing that I didn't
know about anyone else," remembers Brett's longest serving collaborator, Mat Osman. "She was a very natural artist. She painted and drew
stuff and didn't see anything odd in that. And we came from the sort of
town where people don't do that. You have painters and popstars, and
I'd not really come across a family before where everyone drew and
decorated their room and stuff."

The Andersons lived at the very end of the only row of council houses
in Lindfield, next to a small wood with a rubbish tip that grew to

become an enormous sprawling dump. "It was like some kind of Victorian house," recalls Brett. "My dad had Hector Berlioz blasting down the stairs and we had Aubrey Beardsley pictures on the wall."

Peter's favourite composer, however, was Franz Liszt, the flamboyant Hungarian piano virtuoso and old romantic. The first of the international playboys, Liszt was a nineteenth century popstar whose love life was as passionate as his music. He left a trail of broken hearts across Europe, not least those of Princess Carolyne von Sayn Wittgenstein and Countess Marie d'Agoult, before giving up the highlife to become a priest. Peter made several pilgrimages to Liszt's birthplace, returning with soil as a souvenir. When the Andersons had their first child in 1963, Peter named her after Liszt's own daughter, Blandine. "She unfortunately got named by my dad," laughs Brett. "Luckily, I got named by my mum."

It must have seemed like divine intervention when the Andersons' second child, a boy this time, was born on the birthday of Peter's other great hero, Viscount Horatio Nelson, on September 29, 1967. To celebrate this uncanny coincidence, Peter would insist on raising the Union Flag in the family's garden every year. He still does. "It used to bug the shit out of me as a kid, but now I think it's one of the greatest things ever."

Brett believes he was named after Roger Moore's character, Lord Brett Sinclair, from the TV show *The Persuaders*. "That's what my mum told me. He was one of these gentleman-type private detectives. I always thought that was quite cool."

Mat Osman remembers the Andersons as being truly out of step with the local community. "Haywards Heath is a fairly rich area and Brett was easily the poorest person I knew," he confirms. "His family were truly eccentric. Everyone's exactly the same, everyone's earning the same amount and doing the same job, and suddenly you went round to Brett's house and his mum was painting and riding around on a tricycle and his dad was doing archery and conducting classical music in the living room. They were genuinely unusual and genuinely poor. They were the poorest people I knew."

Brett credits his older sister, now a ceramic artist, with introducing him to his life-long love affair with music. "I really looked up to her. Blandine was always quite a cool person to me. She played me David Bowie and bought me Beatles albums for my birthday. When she left home at 15 she left all her records. She's a very intelligent, warm person, very honest about stuff, very plain talking, never been interested in glitzy lifestyles. She lives in a house on a hill in Devon. She had this vision of me being into Sweet and Elton John. There's actually pictures of me with these Elton John glasses when I'd pretend to play 'Crocodile Rock'."

From a very early age Brett discovered he had a gift to create rather than just replicate musically. "I have a vivid childhood memory of lying in my parents' bedroom and actually humming to myself and being aware that I was actually able to make a tune up," recalls Brett. "And I remember it suddenly dawning on me that it was the sort of thing I could do, rather than something that only other people could do."

From that point his only ambition was to be a musician. "When people asked me, 'What do you want to do when you grow up?' I used to say, 'I don't wanna tell you, because it sounds corny'. It was always what I was determined to do."

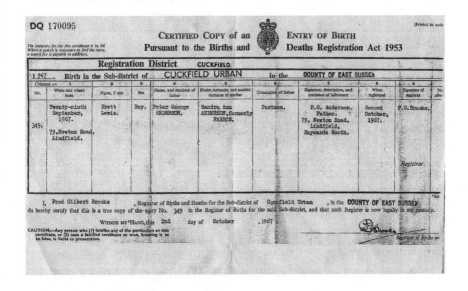

It was thanks to Blandine, too, that Brett first picked up a guitar. "She was at art college and I went down to visit her when I was about 13. She had an acoustic guitar and I just picked it up and started playing Bob Dylan things and really simple singer-songwriter stuff, 'Leaving On A Jet Plane', 'Kumbaya', very simple chords. That was it really."

He bought his first electric guitar, a red Westone, for £40 soon afterward.

"He always used to sing with a guitar and used to write some bits and pieces with his friends and they used to sing cover versions," remembers Peter Anderson. "He was very keen on the Beatles' stuff and Morrissey and the Smiths he liked, that was their band. David Bowie, Elton John's early stuff, Billy Joel, Sex Pistols he liked. I remember him going to school and swapping something for it and he was very proud of his Sex Pistols album that he brought home."

The Sex Pistols and punk rock in general would be a huge influence on the young Brett. He became obsessed with the anarcho-pacifist punk collective Crass, and wore one of their song titles, "Nagasaki Nightmare", on the back of his jacket, a nod to the nuclear paranoia endemic in the '80s, a theme which would resurface in many of Suede's lyrics.

"I was officially a punk, 'cause in those days you had to be in a gang," says Brett. "There were punks and there was ska-boys and head-bangers. I had a friend who was a punk and I remember going round to his house and he said, 'Oh, by the way, I'm becoming a head-banger'. And within the next couple of days he'd sold me all of his punk records, bought a denim jacket and started growing his hair! I suppose it was a reaction to my dad who's a massive, massive classical music fan. Telling me this is genius. And I hated the pomposity of it. It'd be like a battle between my dad's stereo and my record player. If you'd sit somewhere on the stairs you'd get this bizarre combination of Steve Ignorant and Tchaikovsky! I loved the rawness and the animal energy of punk."

Yet despite these rebellious leanings, it appears that Brett was something of a swot throughout his years at school, earning glowing reports and ultimately becoming a prefect. His fear of the big bad world was expressed in a prize-winning school essay he wrote at the age of seven, later reproduced in the local newspaper, much to his embarrassment:

"I have lived in Lindfield all my life. I like living in Lindfield because it has lots of trees and fields. But I would like to see people building not in Lindfield but in big towns where there are slums that are not used. They could be built on. I like Lindfield very much because it has lots of farms and on one of them there are some goats in a field. I think some people should be put in prison because they break down trees and it's all done by teenagers because they think they are so great. I would like only cars to come into Lindfield and no lorries at all. Lorries make Lindfield look horrid because they are so big and smoky and smelly and they make a big noise. I would like the toll gate put back. I would like all the rubbish in the woods to be cleared out and rubbish not to be dumped in the wood. People chop down trees in the wood and I would like that to be stopped."

Both he and Blandine had been encouraged by their parents to learn to read and write long before their first day at Lindfield Primary. "I actually really liked school," he admits. "The two things I enjoyed were learning about stuff and sport, I loved both. I was quite academic, I was very good at science. If there was a bright kid they'd be pushed into physics and maths, so I enjoyed that."

"I first remember Brett at Lindfield Primary School, when I moved into Miss Holden's class aged nine," recalls Alison Hale, a Suede fan who still can't quite believe that the Brett Anderson she went to school with went on to become one of her favourite pop stars. "They had two years in one class so he was a fourth year, aged ten, when I was a third year. Miss Holden was the nastiest, most fierce and hated teacher in the entire school. I was gutted and really scared going into her class. Brett and his friend Barry Davies were her favourites because they were the brightest. She was horrible to all the others but called Brett her 'little mathematician' and would get him to work stuff out on the blackboard. I couldn't believe it when he became a rock star. I remember phoning up my friend and going, 'Oh my god, Brett Anderson's the singer in Suede!' and she was like, 'I know, and Mat Osman's the bass player!' We all thought Brett was going to be a rocket scientist or something."

Confounding the popular notion of Brett as some kind of limp-wristed, flower-arranging fop, he was in reality a star sportsman, becoming captain of his school football team at Oathall Secondary in Haywards Heath and playing several games for Sussex County. "He was very good at cross-country running and football," beams Peter Anderson proudly. "When he was at Oathall he used to do a paper round and he'd always get up about an hour before his paper round and run all round the block. He got chosen for the cross-country team at Oathall and would go into these competitions with other schools and he'd nearly always be the first one. It was great to see him coming up the hill first. But he packed it in because he used to get terrible stomach cramps."

"I wish I'd paid more attention to him at school," sighs Alison Hale. "I remember he used to carry a comb in his back pocket and preen himself a lot. Always flicking his hair about. His hair was lightened then à la David Bowie, but he still had that same floppy fringe. We all used to think he was a poser. We followed him around a bit because my friend fancied his mate, Simon Cambers."

Brett's dress sense during his final days at Oathall was more than a little eccentric for a small town boy, no doubt influenced by Bowie's *Let's Dance* look, complete with a canary suit. "He used to have bleached hair and that yellow jacket, he did dress Bowie-esque," agrees Peter Anderson. "But I think he was just trying to emulate popstars that he admired at the time. He looked quite elegant. He looked great!"

Not everyone agreed, particularly Haywards Heath gangs like the Bentswood Boot Boys from Bentswood Road, an area he had to navigate carefully *en route* to Oathall. "No doubt the local lads gave him some grief," reckons Alison Hale.

"Throughout the whole of growing up there was a very vivid undercurrent of violence," Brett agrees. "They always called me queer. I quite liked it, actually, because when you're insulted by someone you consider a complete piece of shit, how can it be an insult? There was a really violent element to the school I went to. I remember once this boy got lifted up by these two older kids with a huge iron bar, which they put under his crotch and bent around him. He had to go to hospital to get his balls extracted. I kind of avoided trouble because I was good at sport."

Brett would later immortalise these teenage years in the song "Bentswood Boys", which also name-checks his very first girlfriend, Tina Harvey. "She lived in Bentswood Road and inevitably ended up the duff early."

Brett enjoyed, or endured, his first sexual encounter when he was 15. "It was a bit of a let-down," he admits. "It was quite dull. I think you have to learn to enjoy sex, really, it's one of those things you have to wrestle with and turn into something you can deal with. It's like olives. When you first have an olive it's like, 'What's this, it's weird?' Now I love them, I can't keep my teeth out of them."

Peter Anderson remembers his son being quite the ladies man. "I think he had one or two. There was a girl called Alex used to come round and then she went out with Simon, one of his friends. I think that was what you would call his first steady girlfriend, before that most of them were just friends, but there were a few parties. Justine came down once, quite an attractive girl. But I only saw her a couple of times and then they split up."

Sexual liaisons aside, Haywards Heath offered precious little in the way of excitement for those below pub-going age. Brett and his friends had to make their own entertainment. "Me and Simon Cambers did do a lot of stupid things like busk Bob Dylan songs and do improvised scenes from *Dirty Harry* in Haywards Heath High Street," he remembers. "We'd go out busking and it would be literally me and my mate singing these really off-key Bob Dylan songs. I'd actually like to get a time machine and go back and watch some of these things. One person would walk past laughing and we'd be proud that we'd done it. It was always about taking the piss out of this place for being so straight."

Further thrills were to be had when Brett bought a Yamaha GT50 motorbike, paid for by the money he earned scrubbing toilets and doing various tedious office jobs, the details of which he has since burnt from his memory. "I'd drive around Haywards Heath with my friend who had a Mr T mask and me with a Spiderman mask and we'd just drive around until occasionally people would notice us and nearly crash their cars."

Peter Anderson remembers Brett's motorcycling antics none too fondly. "That lasted about a year, then he smashed it up coming back from school and said, 'That's enough of that!' We were very pleased about that. But that was his first and last venture into driving. I don't think he's got any intentions of learning to drive even now."

The best time of the year, as far as Brett and his friends were concerned, was magic mushroom season. "Literally, what we'd do all the time was go and make mushroom tea and just walk around this place, literally off our nuts. I used to love the juxtaposition of it, because Haywards Heath's quite a safe little place and we'd be walking around it tripping off our tits. 'Where The Pigs Don't Fly' was inspired by the acid trips me and my friends would take there, watching all the nine-to-fivers running around unaware of the planet we were really on. People used to smoke dope and take mushrooms and occasionally people would get hold of acid. We didn't even know what coke was then. Didn't even have speed."

Brett's parents remained blissfully unaware of their son's extra-curricular activities. To them he was a model pupil. "He was extremely keen, he never gave us any trouble," agrees Peter Anderson. "Of course, you don't always know what he was getting up to outside the house, but it never came back to us. It was only a thing that came out later that he went to pick his magic mushrooms. I'm not particularly keen on watching him sniff stuff, but he's over 21 and therefore it's no longer up to me. I don't think it's particularly necessary. He would like to see it all legalised and that sort of thing. We differ on those views, but there you go."

Despite this healthy interest in sex and drugs, it was rock'n'roll that remained Brett's prime passion. He had been taking guitar lessons from his uncle, who was a semi-professional player in a band called the Deputies. "I think they were a kind of version of Joe Brown and the Brothers, sort of '50s thing," says Brett. "He'd come round and give me a lesson every week and I'd give him a fiver. The whole thing started with me wanting to be a guitarist, not a singer. I spent a lot of time bashing around in my bedroom. I had 'kind of' bands...before I met Mat."

These early ventures included Suave & Elegant (a name that would resurface when the embryonic Suede were searching for a name) and the Pigs, whose only claim to fame was their theme song "We Are The Pigs", which would later lend its title to the lead single from *Dog Man Star*.

"When I say bands, I mean two people in a room with a guitar," admits Brett. "Me and my friend Simon Holbrook used to get together. We had this hippy band and we used to have songs with titles like 'String The Years Together Like Beads' and we had a song called 'Homage To The Beatles'."

The latter's chorus went something like this:

> "Homage to the Beatles, homage to those guys
> Homage to the Beatles and Paul McCartney's eyes."

"It sounds hilarious now," laughs Brett, "but it was incredibly serious."

Brett's first musical mentor was Simon Cambers, another friend from Oathall. "He was a drummer in loads of bands. He played in Saudi Arabia. He's a really good musician." But it wasn't until moving to Haywards Heath Sixth Form College in the summer of 1984 that Brett met the player who would prove to be his longest running musical collaborator. At six feet five, with his long black coat, long hair and distinguished profile, Mathew David Osman appeared to Peter Anderson as nothing less than the living reincarnation of Franz Liszt. The Andersons' living room retains a large painting of Liszt where the composer does indeed bear an uncanny resemblance to Suede's bass player.

"I think Mat had started a Goth band," recalls Peter. "And his first meeting with Brett was, 'D'you wanna join a band?' That's how they got together."

"I already knew about Brett. He was pretty well known," Mat remembers. "You know what it's like in a small town. Anyone who's not the most normal person is pretty much a legend. He was dressed like Tommy Steele playing a young stockbroker, with a yellow tie and a tie pin. And anyone in Hayward's Heath who's not exactly the same as everyone else might as well have two heads."

Born in Welwyn Garden City on October 9, 1967, Mat grew up in the Home Counties, "where most people live, anywhere that's an hour from London by train". His mother, Brenda, was a supply teacher. His father, a businessmen who worked for companies like Dunlop and American Express, left when Mat was ten years old. Neither of his parents were huge music fans and he was brought up on a strange collection of hand-me-down records by bands such as Showaddywaddy. The first band he remembers liking for himself was Abba. He bumped into Brett busking Beatles songs at college.

"I absolutely hated the Beatles at the time. I had no idea of musical history pre-1974, before that it was in black and white. He was playing Beatles songs, I don't know why. It wasn't normal in any way, he'd just decided to do it. And literally the first thing I said to him was 'D'you wanna be in a band?' because he was a guitarist who wasn't an idiot. He was the first person I knew who was cool and could play an instrument."

Before sixth form Mat had attended Warden Park near Cuckfield. "It was a slightly posher version of Brett's school," says Mat. The two schools were regularly embroiled in huge organised gang fights. "All of that gang culture is about the right detail," says Mat. "When casuals were really big, the designers they were into would change week by week so you could get beaten up for wearing a Pringle shirt rather than a Fred Perry. I think the reason so many people were mods was that the school uniform was kind of made for it. A mod at our school didn't have a parka or anything, you just tucked the end of your tie in!"

Like Brett, Mat had been obsessed with music for as long as he could remember. His original desire to become a guitarist was thwarted due to his ungainly height. "My best friend at school had a guitar and I tried it on and it looked like a ukulele," he laughs. "So I went down to Impact Music and bought a bass there. It was £89, which was quite a lot in those days, but I was working a lot. The only reason you get into the bass really is because you want to be in a band. I always wanted to be in a band; it seemed to be the highest realm of human existence."

Brett and Mat's first musical venture was a band called Paint It Black, which briefly included a friend of Mat's called Stewart Avery, now Stewart Furini. "At the end of the first year Mat lent me an electric guitar and an amp, which I wasn't very good at playing but it was fun anyway," remembers Stewart.

Stewart and Mat bonded after bunking off a school project to which they'd both been assigned. "We didn't bother going into college. Instead, we went to Mat's house and played bass and guitar all morning. Mat had an old tape echo unit which we mucked around with."

The two bought a bottle of vodka to liven the proceedings and in typical teenage form Stewart soon became violently sick. "Mat had to nurse me back to his house and I had to stay the night there. He played me loads of his records. Until I met Mat I had no interest whatsoever in music but he introduced me to Lou Reed and Talking Heads and I spent the next five years listening to nothing else."

Mat soon introduced Stewart to Brett, whom he explained he was starting a band with. Stewart was immediately struck by Brett's unorthodox appearance. "His hair was always styled and he definitely cared about what he wore," remembers Stewart. "I was a scruffy, grungy kind of dresser and felt that I didn't really match up to Brett in any way."

Such was the shortage of musicians in the Haywards Heath area that Brett and Mat – hardly virtuosos themselves – invited Stewart to join the fledgling group. "I was certainly right on the edges of this," he admits, "though the story brought me a lot of credibility when I started teaching! I remember perhaps two or three rehearsals at which I was easily the worst guitarist to play in a band."

Paint It Black made their first and last performance in Brett's bedroom in Lindfield, which was adorned with a mural of Pink Floyd's *The Wall*. "I sat on Brett's bed and played a borrowed guitar," says Stewart. "There was a small group of friends as the audience. I remember another singer joined us called Gareth who did a lot of singing and dare I say posing? Brett did some of the singing. I've got very hazy memories of a song with a chorus along the lines of 'How does it feel to have a rich father, red make of car…baby, I don't care'. This was sung by Brett and written by him, I think." Stewart remembers the band also trying to play either "Heroin" or "Venus In Furs" as well as original stuff.

"Brett actually took over from me as editor of the college magazine that was put together by students," reveals Stewart. "It was called various names in the year that we were involved in it: *Close To The*

Kremlin, Close To The Heart, Close To The Bone, or some such variations. I think Brett actually edited the last issue."

The magazine in question included a "Farewell to the Class of 86" feature. Brett's entry had him nicknamed "Valentino" Anderson:

"A stressful year for Brett. He has faced being given away as a prize, being immortalised in his own cartoon-strip and being the butt of jokes in every issue. A passive contributor but as indispensable as toilet paper. Good points: good humoured; tolerant. Bad points: promises much, but delivers little. Brett would make a packet as a *Jackie* cover-model or should consider opening a hairdressing salon."

"They'd probably been a success for about a year or so before I heard about them and then realised who the two of them were," says Stewart. "I was really pleased for them. I never really got to know Brett but Mat was a good mate and he'd always given the impression that all he wanted to do was be successful with music."

The Haywards Heath Class of '86 staged an end of term production called Grunge Aid on July 19. "I'm certain about a *Monty Python* sketch Brett and Simon Cambers and some others did," remembers Alison Hale, "they were all sat in chairs in pinstripe suits. It was that famous sketch 'When I was a lad…', you know the one. I remember it being very professional and more sophisticated than all the others."

"I do remember some trite, studenty bullshit thing involving *Monty Python*," Brett admits ruefully, "but we've all done things we'd rather forget."

With college over and Stewart now out of the equation, Paint It Black evolved into a new outfit called Geoff, the only one of Brett and Mat's pre-Suede ventures to approach anything remotely resembling a real band. Gareth Perry relished the role of frontman, Brett stuck to guitar and backing vocals. Mat played bass and a drummer by the name of Danny Wilder was recruited. "I don't think we ever played with him and his drums," says Mat, "he just used to hit stuff."

Alison Hale remembers Danny playing in a local pub called The Pilgrim with another band around the same time. "I had a big crush on him at the time and he was wearing nothing but white boxer shorts with red hearts on!"

Gareth was even more of a local heart-throb. "He was a kind of a Haywards Heath…dish," grins Brett. "The sort of local celebrity guy who thought he was a cross between George Michael and Sid Vicious. He had a really good voice and there were some good songs but Gareth never really came from the same school as me and Mat. It was just the fact that we were all interested in music."

The singer's celebrity status was no doubt influenced by his brother's success as a male model – immortalised in the classic Athena poster as the '80s "New Man" holding a baby (later brilliantly parodied with the baby declaring, "You're not my dad!").

"Gareth's older brother, Adam, was impossibly glamorous," confirms Mat. "There was an article about him in the *Daily Mail* saying, 'I've slept with 1,000 women'. So he had a big record collection and had a lot of stuff that I didn't know, like Kraftwerk and Simple Minds and stuff. I did go through that thing of discovering records through other people. I was probably a bit of a prick. I was a music snob."

Brett laughs at this admission. "I really liked Lloyd Cole and Mat said it was a complete rip off of the Velvet Underground!"

"Most of the records I found out about through the music press," continues Mat. "There was never this whole *Mojo* culture then. When I was discovering about music made before I was born, it was like being an archaeologist."

While Brett and Mat became more and more excited by alternative music, Gareth's tastes remained far more conservative. "Me and Mat were getting into the more studenty vibe like the Housemartins and the Smiths and all that kind shambling C86 thing and Gareth wanted to do more mainstream stuff," confirms Brett.

As a result of the musical divide, Brett started to bring completed songs with words as well as music. "That was kind of the turning point," he says. "Occasionally, I'd write a song and bring it to the band and say, 'What do you think of this?' They were pretty derivative, very Beatles inspired. But I did start to write. There was a song called 'Red Ferrari' and 'Positively Negative', that was one of mine. They really weren't very interesting, it was just learning how to do it."

Geoff made their worldwide debut at Haywards Heath's Clair Hall. "We played literally one gig in our whole history, which wasn't even the four members of the band," laughs Brett. "Mat couldn't be bothered to turn up. He had a job at Gatwick Airport and he had to work that night. So me and Gareth decided we'd do it with me on acoustic guitar and him singing. It was probably one of the most inept pieces of music-making ever. Like the Proclaimers but much, much worse."

"I used to work cleaning aeroplanes," adds Mat. "I was probably pulling sick bags out as they played!"

Geoff got as far as recording a couple of demos including "Breathless" and an instrumental called "Murder Most Fiddly". But the band's death warrant was effectively signed when university beckoned. Danny continued as a professional drummer while Gareth landed a plush job in Virgin retail. Ever sensible, Mat headed for the London School of Economics to pretend to study politics. "You've got to remember there were student grants," he explains, "so for most people, if you could get into university, it was minimum wage. It was great, you got paid for it. I know there must have been some people who had some interest in the subject but I didn't know any of them. We were all just, where's a cool city to go?"

Brett, meanwhile, nursing a romantic vision of a musical Mecca where Rusholme Ruffians hung out at the Salford Lads Club, hit the North.

just a girl

STRANGEWAYS HERE WE COME. In the late summer of 1986 Brett climbed into the passenger seat of his father's silver blue Austin Allegro taxi and set off for Manchester University, ostensibly to study Town and Country Planning. "Really, it was just to sponge some money off the government and meet some girls."

Sporting a quiff, Doctor Martens and baggy jeans, it's probably fair to say that the starry-eyed Brett saw Manchester as a kind of musical menagerie where he would find the Marr to his Morrissey. The reality of student life at Owens Park Halls of Residence, with its wacky pranks and stolen traffic cones, was disappointingly different. "I went up there, I suppose, on some kind of romantic whim that because so many of the bands I loved came from there, I would somehow connect with it as a city. I love the city and I've still got a soft spot for it, but the student lifestyle, I just couldn't stick it. There was something incredibly fucking annoying about all these twats running around. I was there for a year and I really hated it. I found it quite depressing."

He applied for a transfer down south, aiming to hook up again with Mat, who was now studying Politics at the London School of Economics, and take up where Geoff had left off. As it turned out, an immediate transfer wasn't possible and Brett was forced to take a year out. He decided to give Manchester another go. Browsing the ads in the local job centre he saw a vacancy for a DJ to play records at a club called the Cyprus Tavern. Although he'd never touched a set of decks before in his life, he figured it was at least still connected with music and anyway, it couldn't be too difficult, could it?

And so Brett began his little-known year-long career as a professional DJ. "When I say DJ, it wasn't like Paul Oakenfold or anything like that, it was literally requests in this really hard club which was a kind of hang out of lots of shady characters."

On his first night the bouncers explained to their new DJ that the moment he saw any hint of aggro – which he could expect on a fairly regular basis – he should simply cut the music and they'd rush on to the dancefloor and sort out the troublemakers.

"And of course, because I was completely inept, at the end of *every* song all these bouncers would be running on to the floor, because of all the gaps. I'd be going 'sorry, sorry'. I don't know how I kept the job actually."

Occasionally, the trouble spilled further than the dancefloor. The regulars expected their requests for Motown and the '80s pop-soul of the day to be adhered to and didn't take too kindly to this skinny southerner trying to slip in something like the Smiths alongside Joyce Simms or Chaka Khan. On more than one night Brett risked getting a good kicking from the Manchester soul boys for refusing to play the songs they wanted to hear.

"I remember one night this gang of boys chased me home and tried to beat me up. I didn't live that far away. I was living with this girl called Emily that I met at university. I was walking back to our house and suddenly I had this car behind me, and they were suddenly up on the pavement, trying to run me down 'cos I wouldn't play the music they wanted me to play!" Brett saved his neck by taking refuge in the bins of the local school. "It was all quite fun, though, a very colourful atmosphere."

Although the original plan to meet like-minded individuals and form a band had come to naught, Brett persevered with his songwriting, knocking together the odd demo which he'd post down to Mat in London for his valued opinion. "It was quite funny actually. He'd write back with a criticism of them, almost as if it was in the music papers or something; he'd give them marks out of ten. So we used to communicate like that but I didn't really meet anyone up there that I kind of clicked with or that I thought I could be in a band with. So everything was on hold for a bit and I just kind of drifted."

Mat found himself in a similar limbo. "It was a funny year because it was entirely on hold and nothing really happened and then Brett had enough and decided to move to London for the simple reason he just wanted to be in London. Because I don't believe there's a human being alive who chooses to study Town and Country Planning for any other reason."

Nevertheless, this period produced what is almost definitely the earliest Suede song proper, a ditty called "Just A Girl", inspired by Emily. Brett describes it as, "Quite a well-written, rambling folk song, but a bit of a rip-off of some old thing my dad used to play."

Suede would revisit "Just A Girl" several times during their career, as recently as 1994 when Brett attempted it as an acoustic duet with the newly recruited Richard Oakes, as a possible b-side to "New Generation". A broken string and lack of time put paid to this interesting experiment and the song remains unreleased to this day.

> Just a girl, north of England way
> Came to me one sweet December day
> Is your heart dear as cold as your room?
> I told her several times that I didn't like her tunes...

Brett relocated to London in 1988 to study at University College London, moving into a huge, rambling old house in Wilberforce Road by Finsbury Park with a big group of friends including Mat Osman and Simon Holbrook from Haywards Heath. It was during his first weeks at UCL that he met one of the most important and influential characters in the Suede story.

Justine Frischmann was the daughter of a Jewish Hungarian refugee who, as a child, had lost his entire family in Auschwitz during the Second World War and been sent to a boarding school for refugee orphans. He ended up becoming a brilliant architect, inventing earth-quake-proof foundations and becoming involved in the design of Centrepoint and Canary Wharf, two of London's most famous land-marks. Following in her father's footsteps, Justine was sent to private school and subsequently enrolled at UCL to study architecture.

Queuing for registration one day she spotted a strange creature of indeterminate sex in front of her. "I wasn't sure if he was a boy or a girl because he had earrings in both ears and a bag that his sister had given him that was like a handbag, basically. And I thought he was really cute if he was a boy. And he was, luckily. He smiled at me in a lecture and absolutely stunned me. I just felt like I knew him or something and became completely obsessed with him."

Justine followed Brett around the college for days before finally plucking up the courage to speak to him with the classic chat-up line, "This tea looks a bit weird." Legend has it that she was so nervous Brett thought she had a speech impediment. "When I first met Justine I thought she was a retard. I thought she had something wrong with her mouth. She almost had a lisp and it's a very attractive way that she used to speak, this kind of lilting, lispy way she used to speak. She says she was stuttering 'cause she was nervous."

Justine persuaded Brett to switch courses to architecture so they could spend more time together and soon they were going on college trips to places like Milton Keynes to study the architecture there.

"I made him sandwiches, and it was the beginning of a beautiful relationship." Brett was equally smitten. "I fell for her, like you do. We ended up going out with each other and having three very, very blissful years together; three of the happiest years of my life, actually, I'll be honest. I had a wonderful time with her. She's a special person for me."

Mat Osman vividly recalls his first encounter with Justine. "The first time I met her she was in Brett's bed," he smiles. "I can remember it clear as day, just coming in one day and there's Brett in bed with this gorgeous girl, and the two of them just sitting there beaming, obviously in the very flushes of first love."

Mat took to her straight away. "She was not really like anyone else I'd ever met. I thought she was absolutely great. She was really, really confident. Where I came from there weren't a lot of girls like that. She was the first person I knew who had a really good visual sense. She was doing architecture. She had an amazing sense of design and how things looked and record sleeves and clothes and was totally sure of herself and surefooted about these things, one of the first people I met who actually loved art. She knew a lot of new art and artists and loved it the way people loved music and I wasn't used to that. And I think she's really ambitious, not in a bad way. She always wants something to happen and me and Brett were much more sitting around, smoking dope and talking shit."

Although her mother's side of the family were very musical and Justine owned and had basic mastery of an acoustic guitar, the idea of being in a band had never seriously entered her head. Up until meeting Brett she had contented herself with strumming along to other people's records.

"She had no interest in being in a band whatsoever," confirms Brett. "It's very strange, when I first met her the only records she had were Joni Mitchell and things like Astrid Gilberto and Van Morrison. And I remember telling her, 'We're not going to listen to them.' I used to be really opinionated about my taste in music. Because for me music was like saying, this is my personality."

When Brett eventually and inevitably ended up moving into Justine's flat on Hornton Road off Kensington High Street, he imposed a strict musical fascism which, arguably, laid the foundations for what would later become Elastica. "I remember moving into her flat, bringing all my records and saying, 'Right, we're not listening to these records of yours any more, this is what we're listening to.' And we'd just play the Happy Mondays and stuff from then on. And it's funny now because her musical taste was very much influenced by the kind of records I bought around then. I played her the Fall for the first time, she'd never even heard of them, she'd never heard of Happy Mondays and stuff like that. It was quite educational for her in a sense, but we taught each other lots of things which is what relationships are about I guess."

Justine fell into the fledgling band by accident, when she joined in with one of Brett and Mat's irregular jamming sessions. Brett hadn't even told her he'd been in a band at school. When he did, she insisted on hearing some of his songs. Impressed by what she heard, she encouraged him to take it up again.

"We were still farting around. Even though I knew all I wanted to do was be in a band, I still didn't really do much about it," admits Brett. "Me and Mat would get together and play and write occasionally. I wrote a song called 'Justice', about splitting up with an early girlfriend, which is actually not a bad song for what it is. We were listening to stuff like The Lilac Time, quite light, leftfield pop sort of thing, it was quite like that, lots of major seventh chords, that sort of thing. I remember Justine started singing along, she was listening to us playing one day and I think she just started singing harmonies to 'Justice' or 'Just A Girl', one of those really early songs."

The still unnamed trio started to take things a little more seriously and even got as far as recording a demo of "Justice" in a cheap studio in Brighton. "It was one of these places that's five pounds an hour and me, Mat and Justine literally recorded a track of acoustic guitar, a track of bass, a track of electric guitar, a drum machine and a vocal. It was quite a fresh sounding thing. I was actually quite proud of it at the time, proud enough to play it to people."

They became very close as a unit. Whenever they weren't rehearsing at Mat's place, he would be round at Brett and Justine's, kipping on the sofa. "Whenever there was a bang at the door it would be Mat. I think he was going through a weird period of his life 'cause he'd left university and he hadn't got a job. He was at this transitional point, he didn't have any real relationship."

Brett too was going through a massive upheaval with the loss of his mother to cancer in September 1989. It's easy to surmise that this was the single momentous turning point in Brett's life, though the reality is a lot less clear cut. "It's not really the sort of thing that happens to you and it seems like, 'Right, I've got to get my shit together.' Your mother is one of the most important people in the world to you and you're just utterly fucked up by it. Cancer's a pretty horrific thing and you just see people deteriorate. She was living up in the Lake District with a guy and because of that I saw her every couple of months. She left my dad in '87 or something like that and moved away to the Lake District with this guy. And I didn't see her and obviously she got cancer. And she told me she had cancer and she said she was going to die. And it's a very, very difficult thing to take. You actually don't understand what they're trying to say. It's like, 'What do you mean?' It's a vaguely surreal thing, but horrific. I didn't see her for a while and then next time I saw her she looked…not well. And it's not a very nice thing to see."

Mat Osman remembers Brett being strangely detached from this obvious tragedy. "He didn't talk about it at all, he really didn't talk about it. I look back on it now and wonder if perhaps he wanted to. We've never really been a band that's dealt with our personal lives at all and probably to our detriment later on. Me and Brett had very similar upbringings, very English, and the deal was if you have personal problems then you deal with them. Brett's a fairly strong personality and has always been one of these people who has dealt with his problems on his own. He's not one for chatting about what's going on with his life. I kind of left it to him and Justine to deal with."

From that point, though, Mat noticed a definite shift in his best friend's persona. "He definitely became far more set. How much that was to do with his mum dying, I don't know. But there was definitely a seriousness about what he was doing that there hadn't been before."

It was high time they stopped farting around. One Thursday night in autumn, watching another dismal episode of *Top Of The Pops*, Brett turned to the others and declared: "This is such a lot of fucking bullshit, garbage. We can do so much better than this! This is easy! We need a guitar player. We're gonna advertise for a guitar player. That's what we're gonna do."

The very next day Brett put an advert in the *NME*. It ran in the issue dated October 28, 1989: "Young guitar player needed by London based band. Smiths, Commotions, Bowie, PSBs. No musos. Some things are more important than ability. Call Brett."

Two people responded. One was "a guy who had a guitar". The other was a skinny 19-year-old called Bernard Butler.

"No musos, that was the classic line!" recalled Bernard in a *Guitarist* interview years later. "I mean what was I supposed to do, turn up and just sit in a corner without playing anything? But they'd obviously sat down and carefully chosen this very strange and varied list of influences, and that caught my attention. I knew they were either going to be really weird and just completely rubbish, or they were trying really hard to be different."

Bernard was born on May 1, 1970 in East London to an Irish Catholic family and grew up in Tottenham and Enfield. At four he owned a copy of Brotherhood Of Man's saccharine "Save All Your Kisses For Me" but redeemed himself by buying Blondie's *Parallel Lines* a few years later and graduating to the Jam, New Order and the Smiths. He learned the violin at school but packed it in after the other kids gave him a hard time, picked up a guitar belonging to one of his brothers and never looked back. By the age of 15 he was writing the music for a band he'd started with his brother Phil on vocals (their older brother Stephen wrote the words). The band, named Slowdive (not to be confused with the Creation shoegazers of the same name) and featuring a second set of brothers, Kevin and Eugene O'Sullivan as the rhythm section, got slightly further than Brett and Mat's schoolboy ventures with Geoff. Slowdive actually managed to play a couple of church hall gigs performing covers by the Cure and the Smiths as well as a clutch of Butler-Butler originals before dissolving as the four members left school, in Bernard's case to study history at Queen Mary College in Mile End, London. He'd been looking for a new band to join ever since.

Brett: "I remember him phoning up and saying, 'I've been looking in the music press for years and this is the first advert I've ever wanted to answer because of the bands you mention.' I think especially the Smiths, that was the main one, I don't think he knew so much about Bowie. I know he liked the Pet Shop Boys. It was maybe the wording of the ad 'cause it said 'No Musos'. Most adverts for bands are so po-faced and professional and the whole point of what we were, me Justine and Mat, were three people who had a lot of aspirations but very little actual…we were three dreamers basically. We couldn't put in an advert implying we were some professional band. It had to be quite humble."

Brett originally suggested meeting in a pub down the road to which Bernard replied, "How shall I recognise you, are you going to be wearing a carnation?" They agreed to meet at Mat's flat on Highlever Road W10, which served as band HQ and where Brett had lived for a while before moving in permanently with Justine.

"So Bernard turned up and my first impression was that he was very intense," Brett remembers. "He seemed to be very dedicated, very driven and very serious about what he wanted to do." Bernard barely said a word the whole time and his solemnity immediately earned him the nickname "Laughing Boy" from Justine, but it quickly became apparent that he was incredibly talented. He ran through a few songs on his Epiphone guitar, including a note-perfect rendition of "What Difference Does It Make". According to Mat, this marked the moment Suede was born. "You can't conceive of how bad me and Brett were at the time. There's no way we could have got on stage. And he was great. From the moment Bernard joined we had a great musician. You suddenly feel like you want to force this down people's throats and before that it wasn't really fit for human consumption."

At the same time, it was obvious that there was something the trio could offer him: that this could well be the band he'd always been looking for. "He didn't just listen to our music and say 'this is shit'," says Brett. "There were sides to him that we didn't have and there were sides to us that he didn't have. We were aspirational dreamers and romantics, but Bernard was able to play."

The two parties agreed to give it a go. As he left, Bernard turned to the others and asked, "How old are you lot anyway?"

"Uh, 22," they replied.

"You'd better get a move on then, hadn't you?"

And get a move on they did.

wonderful sometimes

THE NEW PARTNERSHIP PRODUCED immediate results. Bernard began presenting Brett with rigidly mapped out bedroom demos of the chords and guitar parts from which Brett would compose the lyrics and melodies.

"I was technically able to write songs on my own but I was always aware that songs just written by me would be a bit run of the mill," admits Brett. "The blueprint was always the Morrissey-Marr thing. I think me and Bernard were quite in tune in that way."

Bernard was a huge Smiths fan and had been to see what turned out to be their last gig, at Brixton Academy in December 1986. His description of their guitarist says a lot about his own attitude to being in a band: "Johnny Marr did (and does) what he wanted for all the right reasons – always. He is the first contemporary musician where too many others waste their time living the rock excesses of the past and not working. A great guitarist."

The first fruit of the Anderson-Butler collaboration was "Natural Born Servant", a shuffling pop song with breathy vocals, very much of its time. "I guess it was like a baggy thing, influenced by all those bands like the Mondays," says Brett. "It had a loop in the background. We were quite proud of that." Like most of Brett's early output the lyrics were bitter but vague autobiographical explorations of class and poverty. They featured a call and response chorus of "Say what you want with this life," with Justine replying, "You're a natural born servant, this is the time to open your eyes."

Other than strumming along in the background and the occasional backing vocal, Justine would be the first to admit that her musical input was minimal. "I used to read the lyrics and say if they were good and stick my phase pedal on in choruses but apart from that I didn't do a great deal really. There were a lot of chiefs and not enough Indians in that band. So I was quite happy to be an Indian."

The band liked the song enough to demo it at a cheap studio in Stratford along with another new song called "So Liberated" as well as remakes of "Justice" and "Just A Girl". But it was their next demo, and lead track "Wonderful Sometimes" in particular, that marked the first real breakthrough and which would earn them their first recognition.

"They sounded streets ahead of what we'd been doing before, and Brett's lyrics were utterly different," says Mat of the first Anderson-Butler songs. "That was one of the things that happened really quickly. He went from writing "Somebody's Daughter" to "Break The Law", very quickly. That was a song about changing yourself and becoming a different person and not being stuck in small town mindsets. It's a continuing theme, about not being stuck with what you were born [with]. And it was a fascinating process to see someone dramatising their life. The strength of the music made him far more extreme about the things he wrote and far more personal. Again, that might be something to do with his mum, but definitely the lyrics he was writing weren't rock lyrics. They were good because he's got a way with words, and quite funny a lot of the time."

A sprightly tune with Smithsian leanings, "Wonderful Sometimes" did indeed feature some witty lines such as "You couldn't do your hair, you couldn't do your job, you couldn't liven yourself with a cattle prod," and "Do I just love you 'cause you look quite good?".

"We were quite excited about it as a little band," says Brett. "Excited enough to start sending it out to people." First, though, they needed a name.

"I'm really not sure who came up with Suede," says Justine, "I might just be believing the folklore, but I think it was me. We had to find a name because we'd done this demo and we wanted to send it out to *Music Week* and Lamacq and stuff. The first idea for the name was The Perfect, which was just dreadful, and stupid comedy names like Suave & Elegant. I remember everyone saying that they thought the Beautiful South was the best name ever and they were pissed off that it had gone."

As a response to the Beautiful South, Mat suggested the Southern Way, while Bernard put forward the Foundry. "He wanted something that sounded honest – and like the Smiths. Surprise, surprise."

Over the years the reasons given for choosing Suede have been many and varied. It was short, it looked good on posters, it was inspired by a laundromat, it harked back to "Blue Suede Shoes" and Morrissey's recent hit, "Suedehead", it was a truncated version of Suave & Elegant, Brett liked the way the S curved into the U. Whatever, it stuck.

"I think it was me," concurs Justine. "But only because I was the one that was doing the most brainstorming, just to come up with lists of things. I knew I wasn't that useful to them musically so I was trying to be helpful in other ways, whatever way I could be really."

One of these other ways was to haul the bands tapes round the A&R departments of various record company offices. "We used to kind of use Justine a bit, because she was a pretty girl, to get our foot in the door," Brett smiles. "Justine's never been afraid to use her sexuality like that, to get what she wants."

"I was doing my bit, trying to be useful," she says. "I had to do it 'cause I was the token girl, you know. So I'd just sit there all day waiting for Ben Wardle or whoever just to hand them a tape. I was doing what I could, which was kind of limited."

Though no one could ever have guessed it, this innocuous introduction would have repercussions which would affect Suede's world for years to come. Without wishing to get too carried away, it may well have changed the face of popular music for ever. Ben Wardle was a talent scout at East West, at the time a subsidiary of WEA, just off Kensington High Street and near to Justine and Brett's gaff.

"She'd gone down and got a meeting with Ben," remembers Mike Smith, the publishing guru largely responsible for the success of Blur and Elastica who was then at MCA Publishing. "He told me that he'd had a meeting with this really striking-looking girl, didn't discuss the music at all, just went on about this really attractive girl. And that was the first time I knew about Suede, and he was going to get me a tape and the tape didn't materialise." Not even Nostradamus could have predicted the cataclysmic results which would stem from such innocent beginnings.

The newly christened Suede, meanwhile, had worked up enough of a repertoire to begin gigging. Their first public performance took place on March 10, 1990 at the Sausage Machine, a weekly club in the basement of The White Horse in Hampstead. Suede were on first, supporting The Prudes and The Ruby Tuesdays.

"I think there was a mate of ours who was doing the lighting for The

Ruby Tuesdays and we managed to blag it like that," remembers Brett. "It was one of these weird, dreamlike experiences. I remember getting off stage and wondering what happened, almost an opiated state, just nerves, the first time being on stage. I'd just no idea how we'd come across."

Justine was even more nervous. "I couldn't see or speak for the whole gig. I just remember my hands sweating and I was meant to do backing vocals but I couldn't open my mouth so I think that was the first and last time I had a mic in front of me."

Mat was in similar state. "I remember terror and hours of trying to decide what to wear. And we looked fucking awful. The thing that seems odd when I look back at it, when I met Brett at school he had an incredibly distinctive dress sense, he wore suits, and hats, you laugh but proper hats and blazers and things that were utterly out of time. Like a lot of bands we kind of got caught up in the scene. I think on the first gig I probably wore a hooded top with flowers on it, and flares. All I remember thinking was we survived and we didn't get pelted with vegetables."

A couple of floating indie punters were impressed enough to chat to the band, enthusing about their set and asking to be put on to their mailing list. "I remember being quite encouraged by that," says Brett. "Then we just trawled around playing gig after gig, places like the Cube Club at the Bull & Gate and the Rock Garden."

Even more encouraging was the fact that Gary Crowley had started championing the band on his influential *Demo Clash* show on Sunday afternoons on Greater London Radio. "Wonderful Sometimes" won the listeners' phone-in poll several weeks running. Among the most enthusiastic voters was Brett's father. "I remember sitting there, waiting for his song to come up, getting on the phone and phoning up ten times in a row," says Peter Anderson. "They got about seventy per cent of the votes for five weeks until they had to take them off to give somebody else a chance. It wasn't the same sort of band, totally different to what it is now, but it was a good song. I think that was the start into the big time."

"Wonderful Sometimes" soon turned up on a cassette compilation of new bands put out by London's Powerhaus venue. Named *What The World Is Waiting For*, after the flip to the Stone Roses' era defining "Fools Gold", the cassette represents Suede's first official release.

It also caught the attention of *Melody Maker* scribe Mick Mercer, who went to see the fledgling band several times during their semi-residency at the Bull & Gate's Cube Club.

"It was a bit of a shock," confessed Mick in a letter to this author years later. "I'd gone along because their demo was so good." Mick had even sent it on to a friend at EMI, telling him to sign them, but the band he witnessed was a severe disappointment. "Justine lurked at the back with her hairily suave and elegant armpits, Brett looked a complete twat and the rest of them were anonymous. There were some obvious good ideas there, but they were trying so hard to be a cred Happy Mondays band, right down to Anderson's unbelievable Ryder shuffle, which had to be seen to be derided, with attempted cockiness which actually came over as unpleasant."

His review appeared in the issue dated July 21, 1990 and was less than complimentary. "I was told to expect a popped-up version of Stone Roses played by glamour-pusses. Instead, I encounter four would-be presenters for *Blue Peter*." Brett was described, not without a grain of truth, as "A man with seemingly witty lyrics, he lacks confidence enough to project them and tucks many of his better lines under his chin. The expected wah-wah drowns them."

The review ended with a swipe at the band's perceived privileged background. It was well known in indie circles that Brett and Justine shared a comfortable Kensington home, paid for by her father. "It would surely be churlish of me to suggest that 'Break The Law' is their defiant refusal to pay the Poll Tax, because mumsy's already taken out a standing order." When Suede returned to the Cube Club the following week, a showdown was inevitable.

"I'd popped in for a drink and a chat with promoter Chris King before the doors opened. Because Chris was short staffed I helped out by doing the lights, but after Brett found it necessary to slag me off twice in about ten minutes I gave up and went to the bar. After the gig had finished Justine came over and berated me in a half hearted way."

"We can't afford to pay our poll tax!" she apparently protested.

"Well, maybe," mused Mick. "As her dad's rich enough to buy her a house in Kensington High Street, we'll have to treat it with scepticism. The boys said nothing as they filed out, although one of them gave me the thumbs down sign – the sort of tigerish gesture so rarely seen outside of *Just William* books."

Mick's main gripe seems to have been the band's flagrant bandwagoneering. "Why did the band play baggy music? Only desperate bands do this, hoping to get coverage by fitting in. They normally make this pathetic move after two or three years of getting nowhere. Obviously

Suede had no clear ideas, the original Suede was a con. The Suede that got signed was another case of re-invention. If they were always genuinely into early '70s' Bowie with '80s' Smiths, they'd have been doing it from the start."

Brett's original "Guitarist Wanted" ad proves that Bowie and the Smiths were indeed genuine passions, but in most other ways Mick's criticisms were entirely justified. Suede at this point were a muddied mess of baggy rhythms and too many effects pedals, distracted by the slavish devotion to all things "Madchester". The band would later heap scorn on their early output, Bernard dismissing their songs as "'Lilac Time' b-sides".

Camcorder footage from a gig around the same time at Oxford Poly incriminates the band as an unfocused muddle, kitted out in a mish-mash of tracksuits, Joe Bloggs tops and woolly jumpers. A brief clip was included on Channel 4's *The Word* at the height of Suedemania in 1993, to hoots of derision from the studio audience. The song was a tuneless dirge called "The Labrador In You". "I think we even thought it was shit at the time," laughs Brett.

While titles like "Natural Born Servant" and "The Labrador In You" hint at the bestial S&M imagery that would later become a trademark, Brett distances these early lyrical fumbles from Suede as we know it now. "I don't think I'd developed the sexual side of the writing. I remember wanting to write about my background. Something like 'Natural Born Servant' was very much a comment on the class I was born into. It was a thing about being born as a taxi driver's son and how I was expected to end up as that. I've always felt quite angry about the way class perpetuates itself and felt that my one ambition would be to elevate myself above that. I'm not talking in financial terms or whatever, I didn't want to end up living in a council house in Haywards Heath. I always thought there was more to life and that's probably what the early songs were about."

According to Brett titles like "So Liberated", "Carry Me Marry Me", "Be My God", "Maid In London" and "Deflowered" were more a comment on social – rather than sexual – repression. "And things like 'She's A Layabout' were kind of a celebration of, not really nihilism, 'cause it wasn't destructive, but dolelife that I've written about again, sort of 'This is what I am and I'm really proud of it and I won't make any excuses for it. I'm a layabout, good for nothing and I'm proud of it.' That's what the germ of early songs were about. But they weren't any good!"

An interesting anomaly in the early Suede songbook was the only Osman-Butler composition, a song called "Perpetual". "Mat actually wrote the words to that, which always amuses me. They were a little passionless to be honest. I don't think it was that interesting," grins Brett. "My cartoon image of Mat, we have this joke that he's like 'Emotions Man', this kind of robot. It sounds like I'm slagging him off, he's a lifelong friend and a smashing guy but it's very funny him writing words from my point of view 'cause I think he's always been a little bit scared to express his emotions, certainly publicly. So it's always been an entertaining thought."

Suede's dalliance with baggy may have been ill-advised, but it was certainly understandable. After all, it had turned around the careers of the Soup Dragons, Primal Scream and a hundred jangly also-rans who suddenly discovered that there had always been a dance element to their music. Also riding on its coat tails were four art students from Colchester who rehearsed in the same studios as Suede at The Premises in Hackney Road. The band was called Seymour, but on signing to Food Records their A&R man, Andy Ross, persuaded them to change it to Blur.

On October 18, 1990, the day after Blur released their first single, "She's So High", Suede supported them at the Zap Club in Brighton. They made an immediate impression on Justine, particularly their blond-haired, blue-eyed frontman, Damon Albarn, who she would later describe as the most beautiful boy she'd ever seen in her life. "Musically, I thought Blur were really good, actually. That first time we were supporting them I thought they were really amazing, really energetic. Damon was really rude to me, though."

Justine remembers Andy Ross chatting to Suede in the dressing room after the gig and asking Brett, "What do you want?"

"Everything," Brett replied.

Andy seemed impressed and the Blur singer became immediately threatened. "Don't talk to them," said Damon. "If you try and sign them I'll never speak to you again." It was the beginning of a bitter rivalry which would soon become much, much worse.

The Blur support would be Suede's last gig for several months. The band realised they needed to find a drummer if they were to stand any chance of catching up with contemporaries like this who actually had record deals. It was to be a long and arduous process.

"It became obvious that we needed a drummer partly because the drum machine kept breaking down in the middle of gigs and sounded pretty dreadful," says Justine. It was time for another ad in the music press, in this case *Melody Maker*.

The first applicant was Justin Welch, just turned 18. Originally from Nuneaton, near Coventry, he'd moved to London two years previously having been expelled from school for swearing at a teacher. He was the absolute epitome of the crazy rock sticksman, with a fondness for narcotics that far outweighed the occasional pill or spliff back at Justine's that the others enjoyed.

"I remember meeting Justin and him being the wildest, little insane kid I'd ever met in my life," confirms Brett. "The first night we spent with Justin he did a rehearsal with us, played the drums like Animal out of *The Muppets* and then drove me and Mat home and smashed his fucking car up. We had this huge car crash. He spun his car 360 degrees in the middle of Hackney Road and smashed it into a police van. So the first night we met Justin he was virtually arrested!"

Justine, who was following in her Renault Five, which was used to ferry the band's equipment from A to B, couldn't believe no one was killed. "They just had the most horrific crash. Justin's car was banana shaped!"

Amazingly, they came out unscathed and Justin, now nicknamed "Angel of Death", officially became Suede's first human drummer. Unfortunately, he failed to inform his new band mates that he was also officially the drummer in several other bands. As a result his appearances at The Premises became more and more erratic until, after a few weeks, he stopped turning up altogether.

"Justin's great, a really nice guy," says Brett. "I just don't think he really dug what we were doing and at the time we were still developing. He was in [the band] Spitfire, he was in loads of bands. He did a few rehearsals and he played on some demos. We weren't that good at the time. I think he had other options and if I'd have been him I would have done the same thing."

Justin stayed long enough to record a few tracks with the band at Battery Studios in West London. These included a new version of "Natural Born Servant" (sans Justine's backing vocal), plus early takes of "She's A Layabout", "Art" and more significantly the track which was earmarked as their first single, "Be My God".

"We'd just got to the stage where we thought it was time to start getting stuff out there," explains Brett. "So we signed a dodgy deal with this thing called RML, which was basically just a guy with a couple of grand to throw around which was a mate of Mat's from Haywards Heath."

The track in its original form was an eight-minute hypnotic groove, not a million miles away from Blur's debut, with a gaspy, suffocating chorus of "C'mon, c'mon, c'mon, c'mon, c'mon, c'mon, c'mon, c'mon, have me, grab me".

"I was aware that it wasn't anything special," says Brett with the benefit of hindsight. "I wasn't jumping up and down about it. This was before I'd discovered how to write, definitely. I wasn't kidding myself that it was great. It was okay, it was interesting and it had potential." Nevertheless, it was undoubtedly one of the better numbers in their existing set and would be the last of the Justine-era songs to be ejected.

The entire episode is one which Suede have always tried to wash their hands of. "It's all my fault," concedes Mat Osman, bravely. "It is. It's a guy I know from school, probably through Gareth. His parents were well off and he'd heard some stuff we did and wanted to record a single. And no one else was interested. It's kind of that classic thing you're told not to do, signing with someone who doesn't know anything about the music industry. And he introduced us to some strange characters and we just wanted to make a record. And he offered to pay for it. And it wasn't very good and we didn't want him to bring it out. And we had a row and he just kind of disappeared. I think he realised there wasn't much point." Not for now anyway.

At the end of 1990, the band took a Christmas break during which time Justine went on holiday with her family. When she got back, Brett was in a tizz. Damon Albarn had been trying to get in touch with her. Innocently assuming that Blur might be wanting to offer Suede another support slot, Brett encouraged Justine to call him back. Damon asked if he could meet up with her. Justine wasn't sure. With cruel irony, Brett naively egged her on, knowing that her beguiling charms had done them favours in the past. "Go, go for it, we might get another support!"

Incredible as it may seem, the chain of events leading to this epoch defining scenario is as blatant as a knife with bloody fingerprints on it saying "It was me m'lud".

"I do remember vividly Damon and Justine sitting on the stairs at the back of the venue, chatting afterwards, and didn't think anything of it," says Mike Smith of the Zap Club gig in Brighton. "And then when I got back to London a day or so later, Damon called me up and wanted to know if I had Justine's number. And I didn't, but I called Ben Wardle and he gave it to me and I passed it over to Damon. I knew he was quite taken with Justine."

Ouch! So let's not beat about the bush here. You've got three of the most creative people since the Beatles all desperate to shag each other. One of them tells the other one to metaphorically flash her tits to the local record company. Who then passes her number on to the bloke one rung up the ladder. And the annoyingly talented varlet latches on to another challenge slightly more stimulating than Buckeroo.

"So I met Damon and he was very forceful and in my face and on the first night told me that I was going to have his babies," says Justine. "And it all got a bit complicated for a bit..."

"From then quite quickly Damon and Justine started seeing each other and I used to go to gigs with Damon to go and see Suede," continues Mike Smith, "and I think the first time I saw them properly was at ULU. And I didn't especially like the band. Justine was very low key, head down, hair hanging down over the Rickenbacker, not really doing much. Bernard being pretty demonstrative as a guitar player, throwing an awful lot of shapes. And I remember the first time I saw Brett, thinking he reminded me of Mark E Smith for some reason. And I didn't pick out the melodies – I didn't really see the songs at that point. I couldn't really connect with the band and I pretty much dismissed them in terms of their being a band that you'd want to try and sign. And there was a degree of antagonism as well from Damon in terms of baiting Brett. I think at the time Justine was probably seeing both of them."

Justine claims her relationship with Brett had been on the rocks for a few months. "I'd done six months in an architecture office and it was horrible and he was at home doing the housework and hoovering and stuff. And he said, 'Oh yeah, it's gonna be really great when we leave college. You'll be out working as an architect and I'll be in hoovering and I'll make dinner for you.' And I was like, 'Uh, uh, that ain't gonna happen!'"

Brett remained blissfully unaware of Justine's infidelities for several weeks. "It had a little while of not being totally honest, which obviously I regret," she admits. "But I was young, I was 20 or whatever, that's pretty young. It wasn't like Blur were successful or big or anything. They were like one rung above us on the ladder but I actually thought they were pretty good. Bernard thought they were good too. He used to come to a lot of the gigs. I don't remember if me and Brett went to any

Blur gigs, I don't think we did. But it became pretty obvious quite quickly that he didn't want to hear about Blur. So me and Bernard used to secretly go and watch them."

With most of the band oblivious to the emotional time-bomb ticking away, the search for a drummer continued. They couldn't believe their luck when the next person to respond turned out to be none other than Mike Joyce, formerly of the Smiths.

"It was one of the most incredible things to happen to us," recalls Brett. "We put an ad for a drummer in the paper and Mike Joyce sticks his head around the door. We were all massive Smiths fans so it was like *Jim'll Fix It.*"

Mike had been idly glancing through *Melody Maker* when a "Drummer Wanted" ad, name-checking the Smiths as an influence, caught his eye. "I think there might have been another group in there that I'd worked with, but I thought, how more qualified can you get than actually being in the band itself?

"So I phoned up and this guy answered, one of their early managers that Bernard used to really dislike, I can't remember his name. So anyway, I spoke to this guy and I didn't actually mention it was me. When I told him that I lived in Cheshire he was kind of downhearted."

The rest of the conversation went something like this:

"Well, I'm sorry but I'm afraid we're a London-based band."

"That's not a problem, I've worked with London-based bands before, I can commute. It's only a couple of hours on the train."

"Who have you worked with then?"

"A band called the Smiths. My name's Mike Joyce."

A terrible silence ensued. Finally the voice on the other end piped up, "Okay, we'll send you something up." "He was obviously trying to play it very cool," laughs Mike. "Like you do."

Suede sent Mike the tracks they'd recently recorded with Justin. He was immediately impressed. "I thought it was fantastic, I just knew. Bands do demos all the time and this sounded like a pop group. It was there. People can play in groups for years and years trying to achieve some success and it's pretty obvious that they're never going to make it, ever, no matter what they do, no matter how good the songs are, no matter how great they look, no matter how fantastic the musicianship is, they're just never going to make it. It's the little sort of X-factor that groups have that catapults them above everybody else, even though the songs might not be that great or they might not look that great, they just have that thing. And straight away as soon as I heard that tape, I just thought, this group…" On February 21 Mike packed his kit in the car and set off for Hackney Road. The band still couldn't believe their hero was seriously auditioning to join their group.

"We thought he was taking the piss until he arrived at the door," Bernard told rock genealogist Pete Frame. Together, Mike and the band ran through most of the numbers on the tape, plus two newer songs, both noticeably faster, punchier and shorter than most of their other material. Unsurprisingly, Bernard couldn't resist playing some Smiths riffs between songs.

"I listened to Bernard and it shocked me," says Mike. "It sounded more like Johnny than Johnny did. It was just weird, very weird and the fact that he was quite thin and kind of gangly and he was young and he had the same guitar as Johnny and the same look as Johnny and the same kind of impetuosity and that kind of sneering look, it was fantastic. He played some Smiths riffs and it was terrifying how like Johnny he sounded."

Both parties thoroughly enjoyed the experience. For Suede it was a dream come true. For Mike, after years of playing totally different styles with the likes of Sinead O'Connor and the Buzzcocks, it was a nostalgic return to the sound of the Smiths. Unfortunately, that was also the problem. Mike recognised that the band still had to forge their own identity. They were still fans rather than having fans themselves.

"When they said, 'D'you wanna join the band?' I said, 'Well, I do, but I don't,' because it sounded so much like the Smiths," explains Mike. "In a nutshell they had a singer that sounded like Morrissey. I mean, the fact that he sung falsetto, the only person who can sing falsetto is Morrissey or maybe Klaus Naomi. But with that and this sort of androgynous look and Bernard being a carbon copy of Johnny Marr and Mat sounded just like Andy. And I actually said, 'If I join the band it'll probably do you more harm than good because you'll have the last piece in the jigsaw of the exhumed corpse of the Smiths,' that's what it felt like."

"It just would have been ridiculous, wouldn't it?" Brett agrees now. "A band with no profile suddenly getting him as the drummer. It would have been like 'Mike Joyce featuring Suede', so it wasn't really healthy from anyone's point of view."

While the band can smile about it now, at the time it was terrible. "They didn't understand that argument at all," says Mike. "They kind of looked at me as if to say, 'You're stupid, fuck it, let's just go for it!' I remember thinking that they'd stand a better chance of really hitting them hard without me if they just got some young kid in there."

Mike wasn't quite out of the equation yet, though. "I wanted to help them out as much as I could without actually being in the band, because I felt like their dad. Apart from being genuinely lovely people, I just wanted them to do really well."

The band were still pressing ahead with the idea of "Be My God" as their first single. But while they were reasonably happy with the title track, they weren't sure about the others, particularly "Art", which everyone felt could be much improved upon. "They were talking about getting producers in and people were talking about five grand a track," says Mike. "So I said 'I'll do it for nothing, come on!' I'd never done anything before, but I think they were still a bit wary of the studio environment so I thought I might be able to help them in that respect." As a result, Mike helped the band with several recordings over the next month.

"Bernard and Brett used to come up here quite a few times and we'd hang out in the basement and we'd write some stuff and just hang out and go into Manchester. There was a track called 'Holes' and some others. We did a couple of tracks with Bernard playing fuzz bass with me just putting a drum pattern down on a drum machine. The terrible thing was, though, that Bernard was a bit like Johnny. I'd have this little bit of a drum riff or whatever and Bernard would just come along and say, 'Well what about this?' He had such a definitive idea of what he wanted to hear that I felt I was just kind of getting in his way. It was a bit like that in the studio when I did that work with them, I felt Bernard should have been producing it a lot of the time because he had such definite ideas. I mean, obviously, that's why he branched out on his own and he's doing it himself."

Brett, Bernard and Justine also recorded a new version of "Just A Girl" at a studio called Drone in Manchester. "It was a shitty little demo studio but we did one track and I liked the way it turned out and brought them all back in to hear it," says Mike.

The band weren't too enamoured with the result. "It sounds too clean. We want it to sound a bit more like this." They nipped out to fetch a rehearsal tape from the car outside. "It was just a cacophony," laughs Mike. "And I was saying, 'If you want that I can just close my eyes, turn up every single knob, turn the speakers upside down, put them in a bucket of water and that's what it'll sound like!' Maybe I was trying to clean up the roughness too much. I always thought with the Smiths you could have your singles sounding quite sweet and radio friendly and then when you get in a live situation you just bastardise it and go nuts. So that's how I looked upon it."

For the re-recording of "Art" the band booked themselves into Sussex Studios on March 10. The results weren't entirely satisfactory. "We got cheap studio time and it was an all night session but people were just too tired, shouldn't have been in there, everyone was just flaking out," Mike recalls. "I remember trying to tame Bernard a little bit 'cause he'd want to come in with lead guitar from the first bar. He'd start off with this incredibly complex, incredibly fast lead guitar part so that by the time it got to the first chorus, it couldn't get any higher, it had peaked before the song had actually reached a crescendo. I was trying to explain to him that if you start off with something that's quite groovy and a chunky riff and then when it gets to the middle eight you can let rip. But again I realised that it was like trying to explain to Morrissey what lyric writing is all about."

While the slick new version of "Art" was an undoubted improvement on the scrappy original, Mike's involvement, as he himself had predicted, only emphasised comparisons with the Smiths. With a funked-up rhythm track, it now sounded all but identical to "Barbarism Begins At Home".

"I knew there was a similarity in there," Mike admits. "But there was a similarity in everything they were doing at that time to some Smiths' track. After we parted company I said, 'Keep in touch, send me the stuff, I'll always be here.' I didn't hear for a while and then I got this tape of songs and it sounded definitely un-Smiths. It had changed quite radically. It had got a lot harder and a lot more aggressive. I think rather than putting their ideas forward in quite a meek and mild way, now they were just smashing it in people's faces. I think their confidence just grew massively."

The change in the band's sound can actually be traced back to that first rehearsal with Mike. Of the two new songs tried out, the first, "Going Blond", represented a transitional phase in Brett's songwriting. "I was using a kind of stream-of-consciousness, white rap thing. The lyrics were good but the melodies weren't happening. There was an interesting Surreal head-switched-off thing going on."

The lyrics, which begin, "See that animal, get some heavy metal," are the first to have the inimitable Suede stamp. Although the song was never officially released by Suede, Justine would later pinch the words and more than a hint of the tune for Elastica's "See That Animal".

The second number was even more crucial and is probably the pivotal track in Suede's history. The musical bones of the song came from one of Bernard's earliest forays with Slowdive. The lyrics and melody were still to be fleshed out properly by Brett save for the chorus, an unmistakable falsetto shriek of "Animal lover!".

"I remember thinking it was a big jump," confirms Brett. "I remember being quite proud of it, it was quite powerful. All these songs had been fumbling about and this was definitely setting an agenda. It was quite a dark, powerful, sexual, slightly paranoid song and I started to want to write with that kind of persona and started to develop that persona which led to 'The Drowners' and stuff like that."

The impetus was of course Justine, whose affair with Damon was becoming less and less discreet. The popular story is that "Animal Lover" was allegedly a reference to her returning to Brett's bed late at night, with fresh fingernail scratches down her back.

Although Justine was still officially going out with Brett at this point, even the neutral Mike Joyce couldn't fail to notice the sexual tension in the camp. "I just thought, 'What the hell is she doing in the band? What's the point?'" he says. "You can't have a guitarist like Bernard and have a second guitar. That's ridiculous. And of course she's quite strong in her opinions about things, which is good, especially in such a male-dominated environment as the music industry. I thought it was really cool of her to be not taking any shit. But you just can't have second guitar when you've got a guitarist like Bernard and you can't have second vocalist when you've got a vocalist like Brett, so it's like redundant. She was a passenger because of the sexual politics that was going down between them all at the time. It was just an ego thing for either Bernard or Brett depending on what was happening at the time."

Justine confirms that it wasn't just Brett who was affected by her dalliances. "There was definitely a sense that I was their bird, all of them. I spent my time with all of them. I was variously sister, mother, girlfriend, manager, whatever to the lot of them. When I was pretty close to Bernard I was pretty close to him. I wasn't sleeping with him but I was pretty sisterly to him. I was talking to him about his family and probably having conversations with him that the others hadn't had. He'd never had a girlfriend. I certainly don't think he was in love with me. When I made the move from their bird to kind of Blur's bird they were all fucked off with me in the end, they were all a bit tribal about it and macho about it. I could understand Brett doing it but I couldn't really understand the others doing it. They all got a bit territorial."

While the impending drama unfolded, the mundane quest for a drummer continued. "It seemed to be like this procession of drummers that weren't really excited by what we were doing," says Brett. "There was a friend of Bernard's brother and I actually can't remember his name, he did some rehearsals with us, not any gigs. It seemed to be this constant story that we'd get a drummer and they'd play with us for a while and then sort of make excuses and want to go off, almost like someone who doesn't fancy you. 'How are you fixed for Saturday?' 'Um, I can't make it that night!' So we were being jilted by all these drummers."

It seemed that Suede were going nowhere fast. "The gigs were all terrible," admits Mat Osman. "We had no presence whatsoever. We were scared. We had a drum machine that would always break. I remember not particularly enjoying them and just feeling gratified that we had enough friends to fill the place. But the trouble is that only works for the first five and then everyone's like, 'I've had enough. I'm not gonna see him again and pay three quid!'"

Nevertheless, the band were about to undergo a metamorphosis that would see a seismic shift in their fortunes. Within a few short months they would be almost unrecognisable.

AFTER MONTHS OF EXHAUSTING the traditional routes, Suede eventually found their drummer by accident when a 25-year-old punk from Stratford overheard their tape in the office of one of their managers. At the time the band had an unusual management set up, with three different university union entertainment managers looking after them, as Brett explains: "We were being managed by, among others, Ricky Gervais at the time and these two other guys, one called Norm and one called Nadir. Nadir knew Bernard from Queen Mary College and that's how we met him."

The irony of the name wasn't lost on Justine. "Nadir's an Indian name and it means the opposite of zenith. Nadir means literally the bottom and it kind of sums up that period of time really. No offence to Nadir 'cause he's a lovely guy, but it wasn't the right thing for us at that time."

Ricky – later to find fame as creator and star of *The Office* – and Norm both worked in the "Ents" office at University of London Union. "I heard a demo and it had two tracks on it, 'Wonderful Sometimes', which I thought was really great, and 'Natural Born Servant', which I thought was not so good. It was a little bit dirgey, I thought Brett was singing a little bit below his range," remembers Ricky. "It was sent to me at ULU and then Nadir Contractor, who was Ents manager at Queen Mary's said 'Have you listened to that Suede demo?' and I went, 'No, is it any good?' and he went 'It's really good'. And he came and played it to me and said, 'I want to manage them, will you manage them with me?' because I knew A&R and I'd tried and failed myself so I think he thought I knew more about the music industry than I did. And the other guy who was at ULU, Norm, said we'll manage them together. To be quite honest, I'm sure Norm won't mind me saying that Nadir did most of the footwork. I think he was keener about working in the music industry than anyone I'd ever met. And we had a meeting, the three of us, and they said, 'Yeah you can manage us.'"

Also working at ULU was Simon Gilbert. "He was the manager of the ticket shop so we worked with him," explains Ricky. "He loved music, he was always playing stuff too loudly in the ticket shop."

Simon first heard Suede by chance when Norm was listening to their demo in his office. "He was playing this tape and I said, 'Who's this?'" recalls Simon. "And he said, 'It's a band I manage.' I asked if I could audition 'cause they didn't have a drummer and he said, 'Don't be stupid, you don't wear flares and you haven't got a fringe!' He actually meant it, 'No, you can't have an audition!'"

Simon had been playing in bands since he was 14. Like legions of others, Brett Anderson among them, the catalyst had been punk rock, and the Sex Pistols in particular.

"When I heard *Never Mind The Bollocks* I nearly fucking wet myself," grins Simon. "It was like when people reckon they see Jesus. I cut off my hair, I suddenly became a different person. Up until then nobody spoke to me and as soon as I became a punk all the girls loved me and all the blokes thought I was really cool. I was the first person in the whole town that cut his hair. I remember walking down the road with all these chains on and this policeman stopped me. 'Have you got a dog? Where is it? Why have you got those chains on?' He just couldn't understand it. I walked round the corner and Toyah Wilcox was doing a film and I thought, 'Thank God! I've been saved, there's another punk in Stratford!'"

Shakespeare's birthplace was even further removed than Haywards Heath from London which, as the home of punk, seemed almost impossibly romantic to the young Simon.

"All I used to dream about was London. I used to walk over this bridge and it had this round sign. I used to imagine it was an Underground sign and I was going to get the tube into the city. We took a day trip and went straight down the Kings Road. We got there at six in the morning and everything was closed so we went to Safeway and nicked a pint of milk. We probably had enough money but we just thought, that's what punks do. We went to Seditionaries and Jordan was there and Vivienne Westwood. I said, 'Where's Malcolm?' and she said, 'He's in the European court trying to get a film about sex with children to be approved!'"

Simon's first band was Dead To The World, fronted by a girl called Kathi Jeary. They made their worldwide debut at Wilmcote Village Hall near Stratford when Simon was 15 and even got a track, "Action Man", on one of Crass Records' legendary *Bullshit Detector* compilations in 1984, making it the earliest entry in Suede's discography. Since then he'd been through a string of bands including Plastic Blood, the Hop, Flack Off, Sirens of Seventh Avenue, the Abstracts, the Probes and the Shade, some in London, some back home depending on his financial circumstances at the time.

"I was just pissing about, just earning enough money to move back to London," says Simon. "I thought I'd give it one last chance and if I didn't make it this time I'd give it up and start my own cleaning business. I'd actually started doing it. It was called 'The Cleaning Company'. It was a piss-easy way of making money, getting all these contracts for cleaning and getting someone to do it for £5 an hour while I was getting paid £10 an hour for sitting on my arse – brilliant scheme. Obviously, I didn't really want to do that, but I'd been in so many bands I thought, 'If it doesn't happen this time I'm going to give up.' And it did happen, thank God!"

Suede was to be his lucky thirteenth band. First, though, he had to circumvent his boss's refusal to let him apply for the job. "There was something about Suede that wasn't your run-of-the-mill band. There was a complete edge to it that I related to. I found out that Nadir was co-managing them at QMC. So I asked him and he said yes."

A rehearsal was duly arranged at The Premises on March 21. "I thought I'd done badly after playing 'Be My God' with a different beat," recalls Simon. "And Brett didn't speak to me on the first occasion!"

The band liked what they heard, though, and agreed to let him join on a trial basis, as Brett fondly remembers: "Simon came along and he was actually technically in the band for about six months and he still thought he was on a trial period! I remember him asking me if he's actually in the band and me suddenly realising that we'd never told him that he officially was, which was really sweet. But that's typical Simon. He was and always is an absolute gentleman, a lovely, warm man."

After just four rehearsals, the new line-up's first gig took place on April 30, 1991, at Covent Garden's Rock Garden, a nasty but important venue where the Smiths had made their London debut nine years previously.

Simon's recruitment had an immediate and significant effect on the band. Many of Suede's early drum machine-driven efforts were already on their way out and Simon's hatred of all things twee hastened the process. "Art" was never to be played again and other songs were for the chop at his insistence. All traces of Suede's unfortunate baggy period would soon be erased.

"'Maid In London' was awful. I really hated it," says Simon. "I was determined. I did not want to play this song. It was really hideous. It had this beat like the Stone Roses' 'I Am The Resurrection'. I just hated it. I phoned Brett up and said, 'Can we not play it?' So we didn't. So we were down to about four songs."

Fortunately, Bernard and Brett were entering an incredibly prolific period of songwriting. Blatantly influenced by Simon's punk leanings, "Painted People", "The Drowners" and "Moving" all sprang from this period. "I think he had enough kind of glam in him stylistically to advance Suede in that direction," agrees Justine. "If you ask me how that happened, I think Simon was a big part of that. I think one of the first things he played was the beat to 'The Drowners'. I think that was like the new song when he arrived and he just got it straight away and came up with that beat, and it was like 'Yup'. I mean that beat is just something that Justin would never do in a million years and it's something that you would never do on a drum machine in a million years either."

A live drummer also gave the band the opportunity to jam properly for the first time. "I was playing around with another song by Generation X and Bernard just started to play along to it," recalls Simon. "And that's how 'Dolly' evolved. I think 'He's Dead' reared its head quite early on as well and at one stage there was Brett doing one verse then Justine doing the other, swapping round. She did the occasional backing vocal on stuff like 'Going Blond'. That was a great track, I loved that but it sort of fizzled out."

In tandem with Simon's arrival, there was a more personal reason for the angst and drama inherent in the new material. Justine's relationship with Damon Albarn was no longer an open secret and, in May, as Blur crashed into the top ten with their second single, "There's No Other Way", Brett moved out of the house to make way for his nemesis.

"It was a lot to do with me and Justine splitting up," agrees Brett. "That was the catalyst that turned Suede from whatever into a band that could write and play. It was my personal agony at splitting up with Justine and the sense that I had huge emotional stuff to deal with in my head because of it and it just came out on the page and it was also a real desire to get off my arse and get my shit together."

Not for the first time it seems that Brett expressed his intense feelings through music rather than any kind of dialogue with his peers. "It was really odd. It was one of those things that again we didn't talk about much," agrees Mat. "It wasn't till much later that I realised Brett wasn't really cool with it. They always presented the fact that they'd gone as far as they could and it wasn't working, but I wasn't aware at the time quite how fucked off he was. And there was a strange period when Justine would invite us along to Blur things, I remember going to an album launch or something and it just being a bit strange. I couldn't really work out what was going on."

As if the emotional pain wasn't horrific enough, Brett was also plunged into severe financial hardship after three comparatively comfortable years at Justine's flat, which even Simon describes as "Well swanky!" He moved into a tiny, one-bedroom flat at Moorhouse Road in Notting Hill with his best friend, Alan Fisher, an unlikely ex-public schoolboy from Haywards Heath, and a terrapin called Cliffy who Alan accidentally boiled to death after leaving the poor creature in the bath with the hot tap running. Both Alan and the flat itself would have a huge influence on Brett as he plunged himself into a hedonistic lifestyle that would last the best part of a decade.

"Brett had lost his mother and I broke up with him and it was a very messy break up. It kind of had to happen but it was difficult and traumatic," says Justine. "I helped him to find that flat with Alan. It was a brilliant little flat and it was right in the middle of that whole Powis Square area and it had that whole bohemian fuck-up Notting Hill vibe to it. And Alan was always really into taking drugs and I think Brett wanted to drown his sorrows with whatever was around and it just got a little bit more out of hand than it had been. We'd been doing Es but we never did coke or anything. We smoked a bit of weed but it wasn't a druggy scene, it was quite a creative scene and we were at college studying. But I think after we broke up he really threw himself into that lifestyle and tried to block out the demons in that way."

"He's a very private man when it comes to his love and his life but being mates with him you can actually see what he's going through. I could see that he needed help," says Alan. "He needed a mate to be around him. At one point Brett told me that the band was the most important thing to him and that helped him get over Justine when she left."

Brett and Alan became obsessed with Nicholas Roeg's cult classic, *Performance*, starring Mick Jagger. "Me and Alan watched that video till it wore out," confirms Brett. "Our flat in Moorhouse Road had that opium den, hippy vibe. The constant procession of oddball characters was also in keeping with the film."

Coincidentally (or not), the film was shot at Powis Square, Notting Hill, literally spitting distance from Moorhouse Road. Alan paints a vivid picture of their lifestyle at the time:

"We weren't really going out to parties and stuff, we weren't very sociable, we didn't have that many friends. We were just sitting at home, with these wooden floorboards, bohemian curtains and candles and beads and flowers. It was the most beautiful place in the world, it was something out of a Bowie film, like *The Man Who Fell To Earth*. It was an absolutely gorgeous flat.

"We had a kind of gangster living upstairs, called Kevin, who became a really, really good friend of Brett and I. We never actually left the flat. If we'd had a cigarette machine in the flat, we'd never have left the front door for a couple of years. It was just walk up one flight of steps and knock on the door. He was absolutely hardcore. Brett would sit around playing the guitar and we had some really beautiful friends, like this hippy couple who would float in and out. We'd just sit there taking copious amounts of Es."

Remarkably, these circumstances, far from destroying the band as might be expected, actually brought its core elements closer together. "It was a weird period because we'd split up and because of that me and Bernard got closer as well because I didn't have Justine any more as a friend," says Brett. "Alan has always been a great friend and was there for me and Bernard was there for me as well, he was there for me as a friend. In the early days me and Bernard were good friends and it's something that people might not know now. There was a weird period where she was still in the band. I was writing songs like 'Pantomime Horse', which wasn't directly about her, but it was a celebration of my own tragedy. It was definitely kicked off by the fact that I was fucking depressed and stuff like 'He's Dead'...I couldn't have written them if I was happy, they were the product of an unhappy mind."

Justine couldn't fail to notice the new direction the lyrics were taking. "It was pretty obvious. It was pretty grim actually," she sighs. "You know, standing there in rehearsal. We'd be doing 'Pantomime Horse' and he'd be like [sings] 'I'll be gone by the end of the year'. I don't know if that lyric actually ended up in the song, or you know, 'Did you ever go round the bend?' He was pretty fragile for a while and it just wasn't good. I think everybody was pretty worried about him. I felt terrible about what had happened. But I knew we would have broken up whether or not I'd met Damon. We hadn't fallen out of love, but it had run its course. We were so close and spent all our time together and it just got too much. Lyrically, Brett was pretty honest and it got more and more difficult to listen to. I was really proud of him making brilliant lyrics out of it and I wouldn't have expected any less but it was not great to hear it. It was sad and difficult."

"'I would die for the stars she said,' that was a reference to Justine choosing Damon over Brett because he was famous and stuff," adds Alan. "The lyrics are pretty self-explanatory."

The watershed song for Brett was "The Drowners", which would become the band's first single a year later. With a pounding tom-tom intro echoing Adam And The Ants' finest moments, a dangerously sleazy guitar riff and an octave-vaulting chorus that seemed to be the third instalment of a trilogy starting with "Somewhere Over The Rainbow" and "Starman", not to mention some playfully perverse lyrics, it represented a quantum leap in the band's creativity.

"It was kind of like suddenly finding a key to a door that had been locked," enthuses Brett. "It was really quite a spiritual experience, suddenly realising that my life was going to change."

It wasn't just the band who recognised that they'd hit upon something special. "I remember he came in one day and played me a tape of 'The Drowners' and I thought, 'Oh my God, you're going to be the new David Bowie!'" says Alan Fisher. "It really was that good. I was that convinced. I actually had total belief in him from that moment. And since then I've been so passionate about them. You know, Brett would tell you there's been three things in my life, which are Suede, Man United and cocaine. And I think Suede probably comes first and that's nothing to do with him being a mate. If I hadn't liked the music it would have been quite difficult living with him over these years. We had the same taste in music before we met. I grew up with punk and David Bowie – *Hunky Dory* was my favourite album of all time – and that's before we knew each other."

After this breakthrough there was no looking back. Brett and Bernard became almost addicted to their craft. After a year in the baggy cul-de-sac, Suede were firmly setting an agenda, brandishing a rare intelligence and passion that was the antithesis of the music around them. "We didn't throw anything away, it was all quality stuff," says Brett. "Once

I'd found this key that opened the room called 'writing a song', I couldn't stay out of the room. It was great. I remember we wrote 'Moving' and 'Pantomime Horse' on the same day, it was insane!"

Justine has a more sober assessment of Suede's progress. "When the band started it was baggy central, Stone Roses and Manchester was the big thing and two years later that had pretty much been and gone and the band started feeling its way and getting its own thing going. It was a two year period from 'Wonderful Sometimes' to 'The Drowners'. I think they just got more and more confident. A song like 'Pantomime Horse' is a very confident song in terms of writing, across the board, the arrangement and the chords and the lyrics. Something like that a band has to be writing together a while to do."

No longer would Brett be accused of "tucking his best lines under his chin", as Mick Mercer had put it. From now on the lyrics and melodies would be brash, up front and in your face. "One of the musical principles that I was writing around, writing the melodies on the first album was that I wanted them to be so strong that they could be sung by one person and still come across, rather than be intricate and clever," explains Brett. "If you listen to the album there's not one harmony vocal on it, it's all melody. That was the principle. There are actually octave backing vocals on things like 'Metal Mickey' and 'The Drowners', but it's the same notes."

The rest of the world still had a lot of catching up to do, however, and despite the obvious strength of the new material, the gigs remained miserable, poorly attended affairs. Simon's second appearance with the band was at The Venue in New Cross. "We played to one person, my cousin," he remembers. "There were other people at the bar, but they weren't watching at all. Everybody hated us and there was my cousin clapping. But I was still convinced that it was the right band to be in. Absolutely."

For the next gig in June, at ULU – unremarkable aside from the fact that Mat was consigned to a barstool throughout thanks to a broken guitar strap – Simon invited an old friend from Stratford, Duncan McBain. His solitary comment proved prophetic: "Great band there, but you really ought to get rid of the girl!"

After the gig, the band and their friends went back to Simon's flat in Stepney, which he shared with his old friend Kathi Jeary from Dead To The World, to chill out and get stoned. As they were about to leave, Alan turned to Simon and asked, "Who do you live here with then?"

"Oh, Kathi," said Simon, "a friend of mine from school."

"What, is she your girlfriend?"

Simon started to blush, "No, just a friend."

"What, you're not gay or something?" grinned Alan.

Simon took the plunge. "I said 'Yes!' I actually liked the band so much I wanted to tell them. I wanted to tell these people the sort of person I was and what I really was. But after I told them I remember my heart sinking and I was thinking, 'Why did I tell them? I'm not going to be in the band any more!' I remember Bernard sitting in the chair, visibly shocked, Brett didn't hear and Alan was embarrassed and everyone left really quietly. And I thought, 'Oh my God, that's it, they'll phone me up tomorrow.' And they did. Brett phoned me up and said, 'You know what you said last night, you weren't joking were you?' And I said, 'No, I wasn't,' and he goes, 'That's fantastic. Don't worry about it, don't think there's going to be any problem.' So this band made me come out really."

Although Simon had been worried about the band's reaction, at the back of his mind he'd suspected they would be more than comfortable with his confession due to the blatantly ambiguous nature of Brett's recent lyrics. "There was definitely something about 'The Drowners'," he admits. "Because he was singing about a bloke. I wouldn't have come out if it wasn't for Suede and a hell of a lot of the fans I've met have come out because of Suede. I wouldn't have come out because of Andy Bell or Jimmy Somerville. That would have kept me well in the closet!"

Sure enough, far from being dismayed, the band, and Brett in particular, were actually rather chuffed. "They thought it was quite cool," agrees Alan. "I know Brett was like, 'Oh cool, we've got a gay drummer.' Anything goes, sort of thing, anything that makes you stand out a little bit."

Suede would later be accused of flirting with gay imagery to sell records, an accusation which still rankles Simon. "What we wanted to portray was that it doesn't matter if you're fucking two-headed bisexual whores," he explains. "Anyone's welcome in our camp. Here's a band that's opening the door that says you don't have to wear a leotard and mince around, here's an opportunity, fucking take it. And don't dismiss it. It really frustrated me that people didn't get it."

And whatever the rest of the band's personal preferences were, they certainly weren't strangers to the gay scene. "Lots of our friends were gay," confirms Alan. "And I've got a twin brother who's gay, so I was very comfortable around gay people full stop. I was probably more comfortable than Simon was in a funny sort of way. I remember when it all took off we went to Amsterdam with the band. Brett and I and my brother and Simon stayed on. We took Simon to a few gay bars and stuff and coaxed him and talked about men and stuff to make him feel comfortable. I got on really well with Simon. I always give him a kiss whenever I'm with him and we'll talk about gay things like felching. I always seem to be introducing him to gay terminology!"

Simon was to experience another near epiphany at Suede's next engagement, at a Cambridge University Ball on June 19. "That one was fucking brilliant, I remember it very clearly," grins Simon. "We got it through a friend of Justine's and we got paid a ridiculous amount of money, like 500 quid! I thought, fucking hell that's brilliant, first proper gig. And when we got down there it was a real Cambridge ball, ball gowns and everything and we played to two people, nutty-looking student professors and they were dancing madly in this tent. The Manic Street Preachers were playing in the other tent and between each song you could hear them, getting loads of applause."

There was another reason for the night being so memorable. As well as being the first gig of substance, it was also a gig of some substances: "We all dropped E before going on stage and it was the first time I'd ever had E," confesses Simon. "I was going, 'Oh, shall I just take a bit?' and Mat was like, 'Go on, take the whole lot!'"

As the band reached the climax of their 20-minute set, a song called "The Bike Tragedy", which would soon be re-titled "To The Birds", the drugs started to kick in. "We were starting coming up and the combination of taking E for the first time and playing in this great band that you love was just…wooah!"

But while Simon was having the time of his life, Justine was becoming more and more disillusioned by their apparent lack of progress. "We kept having little excitements," she says. "You know, suddenly something would happen, like Mike Joyce answering the advert, or Gary Crowley picking up on 'Wonderful Sometimes', or there'd be a rumour that someone from a record company was coming down. You have hopes for it but you also know that there's a hundred thousand gigging bands in London at any one point and so the odds aren't really in your favour. It always felt like one step forward and two steps back. I just felt that we couldn't get a break. By the time I left the set was basically the first album. It wasn't particularly my cup of tea but I knew it was quality. I could see it was a good band. I just felt like something had to give."

The first indication that their luck might be about to change was a gig at The Falcon – a 100-capacity venue in the backroom of a Camden pub – on August 2. John Mulvey from the *NME* was in the audience and he was impressed, if not by what he saw, then at least by what he heard by this "Hotly-tipped London 5-piece" and their "Gaudy dramas with grubby guitars". Perceptively he singled out "Moving", "The Drowners", "To The Birds" and in particular "Pantomime Horse" for effusive praise – the latter's obvious debt to "That Joke Isn't Funny Anymore" seen as a positive bonus – while noting that one or two others, particularly "Going Blond", needed to be relegated to the dustbin of pop history.

The glowing review was such a godsend that Brett can scarcely believe Justine was still part of the group at the time. "While she was in the band there was such a cloud. Nothing good was happening around that time. And I remember that first review, for a band struggling around it's like winning the lottery, seeing a positive thing in a music paper that you spend most of your life reading cover to cover, it was really exciting."

In fact, she would be around for a good few weeks yet. "I was still in the band. I remember Damon was on the cover of *Melody Maker* and we got that first review in the *NME* the same week."

Also present at The Falcon was wilfully debauched singer-songwriter Momus, infamous for titles like "Tender Pervert" and "The Homosexual". He recalled his encounter with the band in a recent online interview. "Suede came knocking on my door ten years ago trying to get on Creation Records. I met them when Justine was still in the band. I was trying to date her. She was so attractive, but that never happened. She's from a very rich family. I was at a party for the Jesus and Mary Chain and she was waiting to talk to me. I was wondering, 'Who is this girl waiting to talk to me for hours?'"

Justine's latest suitor even went as far as filming the show. "He kept zooming in on my tits!" laughs Justine. "I remember him saying, 'Mat looks like Bobby Gillespie, the drummer looks like Billy Idol, the guitar player looks like John Craven, miles away on the other side of the stage, and then there's you, what the fuck are you doing in this?'"

The video reveals a band very close to Suede that would become a household name. Save for a few (un)subtleties, such as Brett bellowing "He's Dead" through a megaphone, the music is all but identical to the versions that would eventually be committed to vinyl. Visually, however, the band are still far removed from the pin-ups they would eventually become and it's hard to stifle a giggle at Brett's painfully self-conscious dancing. Image was apparently something the band paid little attention to. "We did discuss it," counters Justine. "But I think the thing that me and Brett were going through was we liked the idea of being totally non-anything. We were quite into the idea of just having grey T-shirts and not really trying to be anything and just letting the music speak for itself or whatever. Brett could have worn a bin bag and still looked good. He just had a real style about him."

According to Justine, the pair bonded strongly over the way things looked. "Brett was always really visual and I'm quite a visual person and a lot of the imagery on the first albums was stuff that me and Brett had been into. You know, the stuff on the first few singles. We were always collecting our photography books and things that we thought might be useful with the artwork."

Justine was also put in charge of the band's T-shirts. "That was another little job I had. We used to do them ourselves. The first T-shirt we had was really simple. It was 'Suede' with the two Es the same colour, then all the other letters a different colour. I'd heard this thing that to remember words, people that can spell well remember words visually, they don't spell them out loud. And the best way to teach someone how to spell is to put every letter in a different colour so that you remember it visually, rather than using a logo or whatever."

In the wake of the *NME* review, RML were understandably keen to move ahead with the release of the proposed "Be My God"/"Art" single and duly began pressing 12-inch white labels. The *NME*'s news section announced that "The groovy capital-based five-piece's debut Mike Joyce produced EP is scheduled for release this summer". The band, however, had other ideas, as Justine explains: "We actually got 'Art' and all that shit printed up. I think Nadir was still at the helm at that point. I can't even remember who the deal was meant to be with or anything. For some reason we decided we hated it by the time it came to be pressed up. We'd already done much better stuff by that time and we'd moved on and didn't want it to come out. I think someone pressed 500 of them up and we hated it and I wrote 'Fuck, fuck and double fuck' all over mine. I think we dumped about 100 into a skip and then a few years later I saw one going for 70 quid, which was pretty heart-breaking."

The RML debacle no doubt hastened the band's decision to switch management. "The gigs were getting better and Brett and Mat said, 'We've got to get rid of Ricky,'" Simon remembers. "And I thought, 'Oh, God. I'm working for him!' But he came in and went, 'Well, it's business innit? No hard feelings.'"

"It was funny really because I'd been in bands and had failed miserably," reflects Ricky. "I think I was even in an awful joke band while I was at ULU called Son Of Bleeper, the name's bad enough. And Suede actually supported us. We'd put them on anywhere."

Mat remembers Son Of Bleeper all too well. "They just represented everything that was bad about music," he laughs. "What I'm really hoping is that it's going to turn out in 20 years' time that it was a spoof. If it was then it was the driest humour of all time. Norm, who was their drummer, always reminded me of Fletcher in *Porridge* but with headphones to drum, and Ricky looked like a fat David Bowie singing 'Here Comes Johnny' about this guy playing the blues and making his guitar talk!"

"I think I made the right decision to follow comedy," grins Ricky. "Because of course when I met Suede I was a rock star and they were an improv comedy group. I can't remember correctly but I think I was only involved for a few months, and then obviously they immediately moved on to much greater things and got real managers. So I think we each made the right decisions. I know for a fact that they were trying to get into comedy. Mat was a comedy juggler, Brett was a clown and Simon did comedy improv on a Saturday night. He was very much the Tony Slattery of the group. That's not true. It's all not true. And they'd better be nice about me or I'll sue!"

Happily things turned out nice for both parties. *The Office* is a tour bus favourite while Ricky chose "Animal Nitrate" to soundtrack his latest stand-up video, *Animals*.

"I've got a demo that they've probably forgotten about," reveals Ricky. "It's got stuff like 'She's Too Tall' and other tracks that are probably even more embarrassing than 'Here Comes Johnny'. No, I think all their songs were pretty good. 'Animal Nitrate' is one of my favourites, I love 'Stay Together' and I know that's right on the cusp of Bernard leaving.

"I still don't know quite what happened but I can almost imagine it. He was just a very serious young man, Bernard. I think he was very intense and wanted to do a bit of a Morrissey–Marr. And he was a great guitarist."

The band met their new manager through their old drummer, Justin Welch, now a full-time member of the then up-and-coming Spitfire who, ironically, had just landed the main support slot on Blur's *Leisure* tour. Despite having left Suede in the lurch, Justin was still a close friend of his old band-mates, not least Mat who he shared a flat with for several years. Spitfire were managed by Jon Eydmann, an A&R man at Fire Records who instantly took a shine to Suede.

"The music to me sounded like the Buzzcocks or something like that, with David Essex singing," remembers Jon. "I grew up with David Essex and thought he was excellent and obviously loved the Buzzcocks so it was like a match made in heaven."

Jon immediately began securing support slots for Suede with hot new bands. "I was definitely aware that we were supporting real bands and I think that was down to Jon," agrees Simon. "I was still working at ULU selling tickets for the Frank And Walters and it was a real big thing. 'Oh great, there's an established band!'"

For one member of Suede, though, it was the end of the road. With Blur now stars of *Smash Hits* and *Top Of The Pops*, Justine was spending more time with them than with the band she was supposed to be in. On one infamous occasion she turned up late for rehearsal having spent the day on the set of the video for Blur's third single, "Bang", a song Bernard would later describe as "The worst song of all time".

"I think it probably was close to one of the worst songs of all time," shrugs Justine. "Just because it's pretty glib and it's pap. I mean 'She's So High' is actually pretty great. And I think after it 'Bang' is pretty horrible. So I chose a good video to be in!"

The final straw came at a gig supporting psychedelic rockers Doctor Phibes And The House Of Wax Equations at ULU on October 30, 1991. According to Justin Welch in an interview with *Record Collector*, Bernard broke a string midway through the set and curtly despatched Justine out to the car to fetch a spare one. "Bernard couldn't get his guitar in tune and it was a real mess live. Justine was fed up playing with her amp turned right down and with Bernard's tantrums or whatever."

Whether that story is true or not, this was the end of the line. "And she left," says Brett. "We played this terrible, shambolic gig at ULU. We were utterly awful, but it was actually the first night we ever played 'Metal Mickey' live. We'd just written 'Metal Mickey'. I remember being in the car with her after that gig and her saying that was it, she didn't want to be in the band any more. I think she didn't really believe in Suede. I'm not really convinced that she knew how good we were. I think she thought we were a little bit inept and would never really get our shit together. I think she was aware that there were occasional parts of the Suede thing that were great and it wasn't till she actually left, to be fair to her, that we did manage to completely focus everything and become Suede and that probably couldn't have happened if she'd still been in the band."

Justine disagrees. "I definitely believed in it. I believed in Brett and I thought he was really gifted and I thought they deserved to get somewhere. We'd get the *NME* every week and in it there'd be another shit band being praised. In the end it was just really weird. I just couldn't see why nothing was happening. I was just like, 'I'm getting out of this 'cause I just can't stand it any more!'"

"I don't think she could handle having an ex-boyfriend in the band, being depressed and writing shit about her," says Brett. "I think there was a side to Suede that she didn't like, definitely. She hated songs like 'Pantomime Horse', she hated things like 'To The Birds', and the ones that were obviously tragic and depressed. She really liked 'Metal Mickey', she loved 'He's Dead', she thought that was brilliant. She loved the guitar line to that, she still plays it quite a lot on the guitar, which is quite strange."

Justine's love of all things short and punky would later form the blueprint for Elastica. "I always really liked 'Going Blond' [later to be reworked as Elastica's "See That Animal"] and I liked 'Moving' as well because they were a bit faster and they didn't have huge guitar solos," she says. "The last demo I was involved with was 'The Drowners', 'Moving', 'He's Dead' and one other. And 'Metal Mickey' was cool. That was the new song when I left because Brett was still singing 'She's so high!' in the chorus...so 'nuff said."

It's easy to speculate that "She's so high" was a reference to Blur's debut single of the same name, but Brett strongly denies any connection. "I'm fucking sick of Justine implying that Suede were in any way influenced by Chas and Dave," he seethes. "I have always thought their songs were crap and certainly wouldn't steal any of their meaningless lyrics."

To this day, Brett visibly rankles at the very mention of either Blur or their singer, almost always referring to them as "Chas and Dave" the East End pub-rock duo who against all logic scored a number of hits in the '80s with Cockney singalongs like "Snooker Loopy".

"Years later, I tried to get Brett and Damon to put it all behind them," reveals Justine. "Only a few years ago, I finally got them in a room together. And they shook hands and neither of them could speak. I think Brett was really afraid of losing his demons, he needed to hate Damon. I can't ever say the word 'Damon' in front of him, or 'Blur'. I do find it childish. It's the kind of behaviour you expect from the cast of *Romeo and Juliet*. It's kind of sweet that they're all that wound up and passionate about it, but it's a bit daft really."

This vaudeville feud no doubt hastened Justine's departure from Suede, but there were artistic squabbles too. "There was definitely a side to what we were doing that she wasn't digging at all," Brett confirms. "It was splitting into two types of writing. There was this punky sort of thing, driven, more sexual thing and then there was the sadder thing that we developed later on. It was personal problems but it was also musical difference, the age-old adage."

"I was fed up standing at the back, looking like a useless twat when I knew I wasn't," she summed up in the *NME* two years later. "I thought it would be better to be Pete Best rather than Linda McCartney."

With the band's rapid rise to fame in the Spring of '92, they were understandably eager to underplay Justine's role and contemporary accounts suggest that she left as early as 1990 or certainly soon after Simon's arrival. The traditional version, recounted in many overviews, official and unofficial, would have us believe that after a few disastrous gigs, Suede ditched their rhythm guitarist, reinvented themselves and spent years rewriting their entire songbook. A nice story but, sadly, a fiction. Suede were a five-piece until the very eve of their meteoric rise. Less than four months after Justine's last gig the band had a record deal and a few weeks later were hailed as "The Best New Band In Britain". And, significantly, she played on the majority of the demos that gained the band such accolades in the first place.

Although groups conveniently forgetting about ex-members is nothing new (Pete Best in the Beatles, Wally Nightingale in the Pistols, James Maker in the Smiths), what has fascinated followers of the Suede soap opera is that in this case it was the band themselves, and one member in particular, who seemed to keep dredging up the subject in interviews. As early as March 1993, when Elastica barely existed, had yet to play a gig and were unheard of outside Camden watering holes, Bernard declared: "There was one other person in Suede who was ejected swiftly when it turned out she was having nothing but a negative effect."

What is true is that Justine's romantic entanglements – together with the fact that her very presence created an obvious barrier between the delicate Anderson-Butler axis – meant that her departure brought a welcome lift of tension and emotional baggage which could very well have crippled the band on the brink of success.

"It was a strange contradiction," ponders Brett. "The fact that the breakdown of my relationship with her was definitely responsible for Suede actually becoming Suede. If I'd still been happy there's just no way I'd have been able to write with the same aggression and energy that later became our style. But it also took her to leave to get us together as a band."

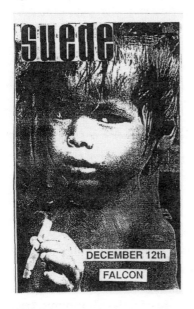

DECEMBER 12th

FALCON

The music had long been in place. Something less tangible now lifted it to a higher plane: a sense of chemistry, of equilibrium which, for the time being at least, united four individuals as an entity far greater than the sum of its parts.

"I think Bernard completely came out of his shell after Justine left," says Mat. "They were really different people in so many ways. Justine was very clued up and had that kind of confident social worldly wiseness that you get from being taken seriously all your life and Bernard was kind of the opposite. He was a lovely bloke, I lived with him for six months and he's a lovely personality. But he's kind of prickly. He's quite defensive and can be hard to get on with. And they were very, very different. I don't think they understood each other at all. And I think Brett in personality and in background was far closer to Bernard than he was to Justine. He's got his foot in both camps. He's got this arty, worldly wise sense to him but he's also got this working class council house side to him. At the end of the day he was more like Bernard than he was Justine.

And three people can't run a band, it's hard enough with two people. And when Justine left there was a focus."

Suede were free to reap the rewards of two years' hard slog.

The band re-grouped the following week for their first rehearsal as a four-piece, at that stage still unsure as to whether they'd need to replace their rhythm guitarist or not. "I remember thinking, 'Oh shit, what's it gonna sound like?'" Brett needn't have worried. "It sounded fucking great! Musically, it didn't really suit the band to have Bernard as a lead guitarist and Justine as a rhythm guitarist behind him, I don't think it technically worked. Bernard's guitar style is intricate and melodic and crafted and Justine was chugging away a bit heavy handed. But that's just because there was a mis-match of styles, I mean what she went on and did with Elastica was absolutely brilliant, I was so proud of her. And it was all about the simplicity which was her style."

The new line-up made their live debut on December 4 at the Underworld in Camden, supporting the Bridewell Taxis. Justine was in the audience. "Suddenly they were all wearing shirts and it was just four boys on stage and it was so much cleaner-looking and clearer. They really blew me away. I was like, 'Shit! This actually sounds amazing. Fuck! What have I done?'" she laughs. "Well, no, it wasn't really like that because it had definitely got to a point where I was sick of the politics and I was sick of the stress of the politics. Chemistry-wise it was hard going. Mat was always absolutely brilliant company, fantastic company. Simon was cool, but Bernard was always tricky. I mean I was very, very fond of him. I really was and when I left the band I was his friend. But there was always a lot of trouble between him and Brett and I don't think it was Brett's fault. I mean, Brett's quite a stable, logical, easy-going person but for whatever reason it got more and more difficult. And it occurred to me that we hadn't even got anywhere and it was already difficult, and if we got anywhere it was only going to get worse."

Justine's prediction would prove all too true, but for the time being at least the band were working together in almost perfect harmony. "We were really united as a band at this point," confirms Brett. "I remember that being the happiest time for the first version of Suede. Between Justine leaving and releasing the first album was absolutely brilliant. We were writing stuff so good that I felt as though no one could touch us. I felt we'd discovered a style of writing which was unique and was incredibly exciting and I felt justified in doing because I thought it was really saying something. Every single song we wrote, we were obsessed with rehearsing and writing and we loved what we were doing and I remember the songs just flowing and flowing."

By this time there was no doubt in Brett's mind that success was just around the corner. Peter Anderson remembers his son's absolute conviction. "I think the thing that was most incredible was the fact that he just phoned up one day after he'd left UCL and said, 'I'm going to go on the dole, write good songs and make it big in the pop world." And this was while he was scrubbing toilets and doing voluntary work, before it all started to take off. And I always said, 'If that's what you want to do, I don't care what you do as long as it makes you happy." And he just had such so much self-belief that he did exactly what he said he was going to do. That's the amazing thing."

It was while doing voluntary work at a local community centre in Highgate that Brett's empathy with the daily drama of the ordinary British housewife was fostered. "There were all these housewives that used to trundle in with their handicapped kids, and their mascara would be running because they'd spent the whole morning crying, and the only escape they had was to get a load of Valium down them. It wasn't more glamorous or exciting than my lifestyle, but it was certainly incredibly intense." Inspired, Brett wrote the lyrics to "Sleeping Pills" in one sitting, during his lunchbreak at Waterlow Park.

Combined with some of Bernard's most breathtakingly audacious music so far, "Sleeping Pills" suggested a whole new direction for the band. "It wasn't the first ballad we'd written, but it was the first really beautiful piece of music," says Brett. "I wanted to address real issues rather than just talking about meaningless rock rubbish. Even allegedly normal people feel the depths of depression or the extremes of happiness. I've always been a big fan of Mike Leigh, who explores all that kind of stuff. And how bleak are some of the things he does?"

Brett and Alan watched Leigh's *High Hopes* almost as much as *Performance*. "I think the undercurrent of sadness and beauty directly influenced the style of writing I was developing at the time. For me, our initial vision of what became called Britpop was like a Mike Leigh film. Bands like Chas and Dave and all that lot turned it into a *Carry On* film."

Another landmark song arrived around the same time and came about in an unusual way. "We had a rehearsal planned and for some reason Mat and Simon couldn't make it and we couldn't cancel it," recalls Brett. "So me and Bernard went along and we just went into this room and we wrote 'My Insatiable One'. We wrote it in about an hour and I remember there was me, Bernard and a mate of his, I think his name was Paul, I remember him being there. And me and Bernard just wrote this song and it was like, 'Wow, that was good!' And it was completely written. It was one of those songs that occasionally just kind of writes itself, it was one of those inspiring moments where the song didn't exist an hour ago and all of a sudden it exists. For me one of the most rewarding things about writing is that beautiful feeling that you've created something that didn't exist an hour ago. And writing isn't always as spiritual as that. Writing can be a fucking perspirating pain in the bollocks, but occasionally it is like that."

"My Insatiable One", originally titled "High Wire", would shortly become one of Suede's most celebrated and controversial songs. With lines like, "Oh, he is gone, and he was my inflatable one," it was understandably interpreted by many as a gay love song, complete with blow-up sex dolls. "People assume that when I'm writing about a man, it's from my own point of view, and it's not always true," countered Brett at the time. "The song was seen as this huge homoerotic anthem – completely misconstrued. Even the lyrics were misquoted. It was supposed to be much more a song about sadness. It was written from someone else's point of view." That someone else was Justine Frischmann, as Brett now admits. "It was a song about me through her eyes."

After one more gig at The Falcon on December 12, 1991 drew to a close with Suede being championed from an unlikely source. The *NME*'s Christmas issue included Damon Albarn's tips for 1992: "Pulp, Smashing Pumpkins...and Suede."

ON JANUARY 3, 1992, Suede appeared at the *NME*'s "On For 92" night at The Venue in New Cross, alongside three other hotly tipped newcomers: Midway Still; Fabulous; and Adorable. Among the throng of music industry liggers was Saul Galpern, a former A&R man who had been instrumental in signing Simply Red. He was now in the process of starting his own label. He had an office, bags of enthusiasm and a name – Nude Records – but precious little else.

"I really didn't think that I would start the label and two months later I would see a band and it would change my life," reflects Saul. "I thought, 'It's gonna be a fucking struggle, it'll be two years before I get anywhere.'"

Saul had been tipped off by a contact at the Moonlight Club where the band had played back in October and had even gone as far as calling up to ask for a copy of their latest demo. "To be honest with you it didn't really affect me," says Saul. "I think there was so much going on in my head that I hadn't really focused on the music. It's not gonna be great is it? You just don't expect it to be great. And I never listened to it again."

Ricky Gervais claims he actually posted the tape to Saul. "I think it's because I'm sort of known now that it crops up from various sources that I managed Suede or I looked after Suede and I think both of those terms are way too grandiose for what I did," says Ricky. "It started off that way but I did so little, Nadir did all the work and I think Norm paid for the demo. I did one thing, this is my claim to fame, I actually sent the demo to Saul at Nude. So I was instrumental, but that was the postal service that got them signed really!"

Despite being nonplussed by the tape, Saul decided to check them out at The Venue. "I got there early and there was loads of A&R. Everybody was there, a lot of people at the bar. I think Suede were first on or second on. I just remember seeing them and thinking, 'Fucking hell! Jesus Christ!' I just couldn't believe it. I was totally blown away by it. I thought, 'They must all be watching this, they must all be seeing what I'm seeing!'"

Gone were the nondescript grey T-shirts and embarrassed shuffling replaced by '70s shirts, spangly tops and a confidence that was staggering. "They were so out of flavour with everything that was going on at the time," says Saul. "I thought, 'He's a star, he's like Bryan Ferry! I can't believe how good this is!' You know, four or five songs into the set and it's 'Pantomime Horse', it was amazing."

Astonishingly, hardly anyone else seemed to share Saul's enthusiasm. "I think I was lucky. All the A&R posse had been to see them before when Justine was in the band and I think they thought they were crap. So I think this was one of the first gigs without her, which is interesting, and so they were just stuck at the fucking bar, everyone like Alan McGee and Andy Ross were all just waiting to see Adorable and Fabulous. And I'm thinking, 'How the fuck am I gonna get this band?' Maybe I was dreaming it."

After the band finished their eight-song set with "To The Birds", Saul went straight home to look for their demo. He couldn't find it and assumed it must be in his new office on Langham Street. "But then I couldn't find it at the office either. So eventually I went back home and it was there. It was lying on top of the stereo on its own. It was the weirdest thing."

He decided to act fast and phoned the band first thing on Monday morning. "I spoke to Bernard who was kind of cool. I think he lived in Hackney at the time. And I said, 'I saw your band, I thought they were absolutely fantastic.' I think I rang about nine in the morning because I was determined to be the first in. I didn't have funding, I didn't have a label, I thought, 'I've got to get this band!'"

He gave the same spiel to Brett. "The funny thing was I thought the show we did was amazing, the songs we did were great but Saul was the only person that actually committed himself," says Brett. "And that's why we committed ourselves to him later on and had faith in him. He actually phoned me up and told me how much he loved it and I'm a bit of a sucker for flattery sometimes so I thought, 'Okay, why not?' And still the majors were there and looked at us and I'm sure if it had been now we would have got pounced on."

In fact, Saul wasn't the only person who'd spotted the band's potential. A scout from Island Records called Nigel Coxon was also impressed and immediately offered them some demo time at Island's own studios in Chiswick. "Nigel was at the 'On' thing, he was one of the first ones to say 'Come and do some demos for us' basically," remembers Simon. "That's sort of the beginning of when it started to take off, when Island came along."

Also in the audience was Mike Smith, who had now moved to EMI Publishing. "They'd changed quite remarkably from the band I'd seen before," he recalls. "Bernard in particular was getting a much bigger sound from his guitar and was much more impressive. But I suppose I still had the same prejudices that I'd had before. I didn't really connect with Brett's vocal style and I think one of the hardest things about A&R is that you can go and see somebody at an early stage when they're still trying to get their sound together and just dismiss them. And it becomes incredibly difficult once you've done that to revise your opinions. And I think I was always fighting against my prejudices on that front. Plus, it didn't help having Damon's opinions as well!"

As it turned out, Mike signed headliners Adorable instead. "I didn't have anything like the conviction that other people did that Suede was going to take off and I had enormous faith in Adorable. And for one week back in February of '92 it looked like they were gonna be the bigger band!"

On January 22 Suede demoed "Metal Mickey" for the first time, along with new versions of "The Drowners", "Pantomime Horse" and "He's Dead". "They sounded brilliant," says Simon. "I thought, 'Great, we've got a record deal!'"

Island's initial interest would eventually lead to naught and Saul was already plotting to bag the band himself. His first move was to get them a publicist, or to be more accurate, two publicists: John Best and Phill Savidge. "John and I had been at Virgin," explains Phill. "Even though John was brilliant he had had a big row with Virgin, told them all to fuck off. He was essentially sacked, even though he was too good to be sacked. I hung on another six months until I couldn't stand it any longer."

John started his own press company, Best In Press, who immediately landed a major coup by winning the 4AD contract, handling some of the coolest bands around like the Pixies and Cocteau Twins. He was soon joined by Phill and the company was eventually renamed Savage &

Best. As someone who had been sacked by a major himself, Saul considered them to be the perfect people for Suede. He was right.

Phill especially fell head over heels in love with the band the moment he heard them. It's probably fair to say that part of the reason was an empathy with the ambiguous nature of Brett's lyrics. At the time, Phill, with his long hair and huge hooped earrings, had more that a hint of androgyny himself. (The first time I met him, I thought he was a girl.)

"The tape came with a covering letter which talked about Brett's view on the songwriting craft. It was written like a biog of what this song was about and the gender malfunctions within Brett's songs. I was reading it thinking, 'This is really lucid, this person's really got a handle on this band.' Then at the end, when it said 'Lots of love, Brett' I thought, well they would have a handle on it. But it was written as if it was by a fan almost, which sums it up in a way, because Brett is a fan of Suede."

John Best sent his only copy of these demos to Steve Sutherland, then assistant editor at *Melody Maker*. He fell for them instantly and offered the band a "Sidelines" piece, a short section introducing various new bands. The band duly trooped down to a studio in Sly Street on January 30 for a photo-shoot with Tom Sheehan and an interview with Steve. It would prove to be a portentous occasion, though no one realised the significance at the time.

The band finally met up with Saul Galpern the following week at Bernard's place. "Typical band, the singer turns up late," remembers Saul. "I knew Brett was a star the moment he turned up late. It's fucking perfect. I remember there were pictures of the Smiths all over the wall and the Stone Roses and stuff like that and they just seemed all happy and like a band. The chemistry just felt like a band and they were all cool and quite casual. I did the whole passionate thing."

"Saul wanted to put a couple of singles out and he was the only person who actually offered us anything at that time," remembers Simon. "Then the next day Jon Eydmann sorted out some publishing from Polygram, which was great 'cause we were able to buy equipment and stuff like that which we needed. And from then on we kept on having these meetings with Saul. It was getting very frustrating 'cause we were never getting to sign anything, it was all up in the air, all to-ing and fro-ing."

Saul was determined to get a deal in place before the rest of the music business caught up. "All I remember after that was trying to get it together, get a lawyer and Bernard wanted to use his brother and I said,

'No, you need a music business lawyer.' So we used his brother for the first two singles only. I felt I didn't want to force them into a dodgy record contract thing, at the end of the day if it's working, it's working, and they'll want to carry on."

Suede finally signed a two-single deal with Nude Records on February 17, 1992, for the princely sum of £3,132. It was Saul's genuine enthusiasm that won the band. "He was just really into the music," confirms Simon. "He was on his own and he was going to start up this record company because of us. I think we had this punk ethos built in, you know, don't trust the big bastards, stick with a small label. And then all the big record companies started getting in touch with us, MCA, Warner… Island made us an offer to sign us after the deal with Nude had been done. I think we said to them, 'We can't sign, we've just signed to Saul!'"

Mat Osman admits that a large part of the decision was down to the fact than no one else seemed interested. "To be honest we were getting pretty panicked," he says. "We did that 'On' gig and people like Alan McGee were there and Adorable got signed and I just couldn't see it. Saul was the first person who was talking to us about Roxy Music and Kate Bush and got the songs. And he had some history. We knew he'd signed the Fall, which he probably doesn't know to the day was his hugest saving grace. And the other thing is he told us he'd been sacked by a load of record companies!"

"It was essential that we didn't get signed too early," Brett reflects. "It was essential that we did have to struggle and did have to spend two years playing toilets and did all that hard work, because that's the only way that bands get good. It's just one of those nasty things that you have to do to come out the other end."

Suede's first show after signing with Nude was a return to The Falcon on February 28. "That was bizarre," says Simon. "We soundchecked in the afternoon as we normally did and it was all horrible and dingy. And we came back to play about seven o'clock and it was absolutely fucking heaving with people. We were like, 'What are all these people doing here?' and somebody says, 'Morrissey's here, Morrissey's here!' And in he walked. I just remember seeing Morrissey at the bar. I couldn't believe it."

Brett remembers the gig well. "People like Morrissey turned up and Suggs was there and Kirsty McColl. It was like this celebrity hang out and I thought, 'What are they here for?' But there were a whole lot of people who'd heard about Suede as an underground thing and I'm not

TO THE BIRDS **SUEDE**

really sure if that can happen any more. These were the days when you were still able to build up a following without some major record company pouncing on you and destroying it. I know it was only ten years ago but it felt like a purer time."

Checking out the band for the first time was Malcolm Dunbar, then head of A&R at East West. "I remember going to the gig at The Falcon and being completely blown away. They were one of the best bands I'd ever seen. I thought Brett was one of the most natural performers and I thought Bernard was probably one of the best new guitarists I'd ever seen. I couldn't believe he'd never heard of Mick Ronson, or listened to a Bowie record, it's just not what he was into."

The show itself was an absolute riot. "It was fucking rammed solid," says Simon. "It was really weird, from playing to no one to that. That was the turning point. After that we never played to eight people again. It was very strange."

Things were about to become even stranger. "All of my friends, people like Alan, and all of the people that were close to the band were getting really excited," says Brett. "We were discussing the possibility of the band taking off, that was the dream," confirms Alan Fisher. "We'd go for a walk, put our fake fur coats on and guzzle beer. We'd sit there and say, 'I can feel it, can you feel it? There's something really happening here!' It's quite a strange thing to relate to somebody now, now that it's happened it seems obvious. And it was obvious that he had talent and could write songs. But it's a strange feeling to suddenly realise that this is someone who's actually capable of making a mark on the history of music. There was no doubt in his mind, he knew he had something. It wasn't just Brett going, 'Do you believe in me?' He didn't ask for any confirmation. It was just a matter of reiterating that I could see what he was thinking. It was quite a strange relationship in that way. Obviously, most of his songs around that early time were about Justine and the pain he was going through and then there was an almost new drug indulgence thing coming in, things like 'Animal Nitrate'. When your life's fuelled with drugs and taking drugs to have sex, you can see parts of yourself in the songs."

Malcolm Dunbar was equally smitten and although he'd been pipped to the post by Saul's two-single deal, was determined to sign them long term to East West. He met the band on March 13 at the Marquee where they were supporting Catherine Wheel and Radiohead.

"I met them at lunchtime and they were soundchecking," remembers

Malcolm. "I agreed with them that we should do some demos, no strings attached. The funny thing is that when they'd gone in and made their first record, I still thought that the songs they'd done that day captured the band a lot more excitingly. They've got an energy and a passion that's just absolutely fantastic. I think Bernard mixed it in the end with the engineer that owned the studio. Bernard struck me as the one that was most interested in the studio. Even at that early stage he was there all hours. He was definitely the one that loved to be in the studio. But I thought the results were great, got even more excited about the band, tried to sign them even more."

The band took the opportunity to record "Sleeping Pills" and "Dolly" for the first time, two songs that were both variously considered as potential singles. "I remember them saying, we'll do 'Sleeping Pills' and I was like, 'I haven't heard that, go on then,'" remembers Jon Eydmann. "And it was obviously absolutely amazing and Malcolm was on the phone being Malcolm and promising the world, quite literally."

"It was just one of these bands that captured everybody's imagination," continues Malcolm. "There were a lot of real music fans and East West hadn't been going that long therefore it didn't have that many credible bands and so for Suede to come into the office when everybody was talking about them was a real coup. So they got a lot of attention and there was a good vibe in the office. They came in two or three times and talked and blagged records and I think they really enjoyed it."

They certainly did. "When we were getting chased by record companies we were absolutely skint, we had no money," says Mat Osman. "We lived off record companies. We used to go through the cupboards and then straight down to Notting Hill record and tape exchange. I remember getting a Bruce Springsteen live box set and thinking, 'Fucking hell, that's got to be worth thirty quid,' and getting down to record and tape exchange, and seeing three new copies that had just got there, and realising I'd have to be a little bit quicker in future!"

That same month, Suede recorded their debut single at First Protocol Studios. One of the first people to hear it was their old adversary, Damon Albarn. "Damon said something really small to Bernard at some Blur aftershow," remembers Justine. "He said he thought 'The Drowners' should be remixed, he didn't like the mix of 'The Drowners'. And Bernard stormed out and never spoke to me again. I carried on going to their gigs and I was really excited for them. I really wanted them to do well. I still felt like they were family even though I'd moved tribes, which was something that I think they all had problems with."

At the beginning of April they recorded four tracks for the Mark Goodier show on Radio 1. "That was really good. The version of 'Moving' was much better than the album," says Simon. "By this time everyone was talking about Suede, although it still wasn't in the press yet."

It soon would be. Toward the end of the month, Simon went down to Tottenham Court Road to buy the new issue of *Melody Maker*, which was supposed to include the "Sidelines" article they'd done with Steve Sutherland. He couldn't believe his eyes when he saw his own face staring up at him from the front page. "I got to the stand 'Where's *Melody Maker*? There it is… Oh my God!' I just saw this picture of me. 'Is that me?' It was a complete surprise, a complete shock." Alongside the band photo was the legend, "Suede: The Best New Band In Britain".

Jon Eydmann was equally gobsmacked. "I remember standing at some tube station waiting for them, because we needed to go and see some people for a meeting. It had come through from Saul and John Best that we were going to have this little feature. So I bought the *Melody Maker* and I didn't look at it. I opened it up and started looking for the feature and went, 'Fucking hell, that's good!' and then closed it again and nearly had a heart attack. It was like, 'Oh my god, oh my god!' I didn't know what to say. And then they turned up and Brett was always pretty cool and didn't really say very much. Bernard looked like he was gonna shit himself. No one really knew it was going to happen."

If anything, the article inside was even more incredible, boldly declaring: "Suede are only the most audacious, androgynous, mysterious, sexy, ironic, absurd, perverse, glamorous, hilarious, honest, cocky, melodramatic, mesmerising band you're ever likely to fall in love with."

"He had a lot of bollocks to do that," says Simon. "Especially then. I mean, you can do that nowadays and nobody bats an eyelid. Steve Sutherland, incredibly genuine bloke."

While music press hyperbole is now commonplace and "Best New Bands In Britain" appear to arrive every fortnight, it's worth remembering that at the time this was extremely rare and Suede were in fact the first band to make the *Maker* cover without even having released one note of music. Brett would continually stress that the cover was as much a bane as a blessing. Yet in retrospect it seems clear that for once the press were spot on.

"The 'Best New Band In Britain' thing should be Suede's trade mark because everybody gets it now and Suede were the first," says Saul

Galpern. He'd been tipped off the night before when he bumped into Steve Sutherland checking out another band at the Bull & Gate. "What? They're on the cover? Oh, my god! Fuck, they're going to sign to EMI now… The moment that appeared, it just went ballistic."

Life would never be sane again. The day after the *Melody Maker* cover, "The Drowners" received its first play on Radio 1. "We were rehearsing at The Premises and we knew it was going to be on at some time," remembers Simon. "So we rehearsed a couple of songs and I said, 'Oh shit, put the radio on!' So we ran downstairs, got a radio, brought it back upstairs, turned it on and it just went, 'And now Suede…' as soon as we put the radio on. And that happened with 'Metal Mickey' as well. So yesterday I had the front cover, today we're on Radio 1. Things happened every day. We did the video for 'The Drowners' two days later."

Suede's first gig since being cover stars took place at the Africa Centre in Covent Garden on April 28. In a neat twist, the very last two tickets Simon sold were for that gig. He packed in his job at ULU the next day. Mat, who'd been doing sub-titling work at the BBC, would soon follow suit while Bernard dropped out of university that same week, just before he was due to take his exams. He showed his tutor *Melody Maker* and said, "This is the first big thing that's ever happened to me. I'm not going to pass my exams." Bernard recounted the tale to *Vox* a couple of years later: "This guy I'd been lying to about my essays said, 'Good luck. Fifteen years ago a young man called Bruce Dickinson came to my office and told me he had to go on tour with his band Iron Maiden. He didn't do too badly.'"

"I remember the queue at the Africa Centre was ridiculous," says Saul Galpern. "There was record companies galore and publishing companies galore. I remember Jarvis trying to get in. That was an insane gig. Before you know it, everyone had come to see it."

"It felt like the Pistols at the 100 Club," grins Simon. "We got a brilliant review, every review was brilliant, every gig was brilliant, it just never stopped."

"I think that was the one where Saul got locked out and ended up having to crawl in through a window," laughs Malcolm Dunbar. "That was just crazy. By the time they did the Africa Centre there wasn't a label that wasn't talking to them."

The gig had come about after Jon Eydmann had been contacted by promoter John Curd. "For some strange reason he rang me up and asked me to go for a meeting with him and his mate John Smith, which was weird because they basically said they wanted to manage the band!" In the end they agreed to do some gigs together. Jon wanted to do something unusual, so they settled on the Africa Centre. "It was funny because John Curd's a big old geezer and he wasn't taking no shit and if you do a gig there it has to be a multicultural night, so we had to go and find some black guy to go on first and he went and found a busker! And then someone turned up who wasn't on the guest list. It was Chris Wright, the bloke that used to own Chrysalis. This guy drives up in a Rolls Royce or whatever in the middle of the road, with a driver, gets out, walks over the road, says his name. And John Curd goes, 'You're not on the guest list, you're not getting in. And the guy goes, 'But I am...' And John goes, 'I don't give a fuck who you are, mate. You're not on the guest list, fuck off. You're not getting in, there ain't any tickets.'"

"The Drowners" was finally released on May 11, 1992. With almost tedious inevitability it was awarded Single Of The Week in both music papers. "Start learning the words," advised *Melody Maker*'s Jim Arundel. "You're going to need them."

But not everyone was so enamoured with Suede's apparent omnipotence. While Suede were being touted as musical saviours, their old chums Blur saw their finest single to date, the ferocious "Popscene", peak at a lowly (for them) 32. No matter that "The Drowners" actually only got to 49, Damon was already plotting his revenge.

"I remember Damon picking on Brett in the press for no reason and I thought it was really mean because ultimately I'd left Brett for him," says Justine. "So Damon had no reason having a go at Brett at all and he started it. But Damon's the kind of person that will have a go at anyone. It's friendship through animosity with Damon, that's the way he works. I don't remember Brett making comments, but I certainly remember Damon making comments, as soon as Suede started to do anything he was putting the boot in."

Neither party was entirely innocent, however. "It was funny because it was so fucked up. It was just 'boys will be boys' with them," continues Justine. "They were all just so un-cool about it, they really were. They were all so stupid about it. They went through phases of being friends and then hating each other and Bernard loved Damon and hated Damon, it was just ridiculous really."

The press adulation certainly raised the stakes, as Brett would be the first to agree. "A lot of other bands were quite bitter. There were a lot of cynical people at the gigs, but there's something really exciting about facing an audience who've been told you're the 'Best New Band In Britain', with their arms folded, going, 'Come on then, impress us.'"

This was particularly true outside London, where Suede were still very much an unknown quantity and the locals were understandably wary of these seemingly over-hyped London ponces. During the band's first foray north of the border, they played a now legendary gig at Ricos in Greenock, a notoriously rough port on the west coast of Scotland, which as with most of Britain's once-proud industrial cities had been ravaged by the worst excesses of Thatcherism. The majority of the threadbare audience stood at the bar, saying nothing, save for one enormous, intimidating punk with a huge mohican. Throughout Suede's set he stood right in front of the band screaming obscenities, of which the most memorable was, "You effete, southern wankers!"

Relieving themselves in the gents afterwards, Mat and Bernard were alarmed to see the mohicaned heckler burst in. "Have youse seen Suede?" he demanded, eyes glaring. Mat and Bernard glanced at each other nervously then, affecting their best Scottish accents, replied, "Och, we don't know. We're no' from London!"

The promoter who had organised the gig lived in the neighbouring town of Gourock, which if anything was even more depressing than Greenock, and had arranged for the band to stay in a cheap hotel there. "There's tons of ghost cranes that don't work any more from the dockyards that are all rusty and fucked," describes Jon Eydmann. "But they have a tourist information centre that is like a giant yellow kettle, like an old kettle that you hold over a stove. So that was quite exciting for a start."

Nothing, however, could prepare them for the surreal scenario awaiting them at the hotel, resembling as it did a scene by Hieronymus Bosch. "We got back to this hotel and it was full of people shagging on the stairs and puking," recalls Jon incredulously. "And it was like just what they do. And they thought we were weird, we were weird southern poofters for going, 'What the fuck?'"

Tripping over the fornicating couples to get to his room, Bernard was bemused to discover it was already occupied. "The amusing thing is that it would have to happen to Bernard," laughs Jon. "It couldn't have happened to Simon or Mat. It would have to happen to Bernard that he tried to get into his room, and he couldn't get in there because people were shagging in his bed! And when we complained, the people that owned the hotel – who sit behind a wire cage – said, 'Don't worry about it, they're regulars!' So Charlie [Charlton, future manager] went and kicked the door down. They left. They went out of the window I seem to remember."

Suede finished their Scottish jaunt with a gig in Edinburgh supporting the Fall. Before the show, Jon Eydmann met up with Malcolm Dunbar, who was still intent on signing the band to East West. "Malcolm was brilliant. He took me out and we just walked round Edinburgh," recalls Jon. "We went to the castle, we went to the pub and he said to me, 'You do realise that every A&R person is going to be here tonight?' And I said, 'Don't be stupid, we're in Scotland, it'll be empty.' And I got back to the venue and he wasn't wrong. It was just a queue of A&R people. I was so pissed by the end of the night, cause they just kept buying me drinks!"

"We walked into the venue and one of the A&R guys was actually selling T-shirts in the venue over the counter to other A&R people," adds Malcolm. "And that's true. Every record label turned up at that point."

After the show the band drove back to London overnight as they were due to fly to New York the next day, courtesy of Sony America who were also courting the band.

"I can remember Charlie loading me into the van, on top of Mat's bass amp," says Jon. "And I slept on top of Mat's bass amp all the way back to London. We came home and I probably had an hour at home. We went to the airport, we flew to New York, we walked into the hotel and the person that had been selling the T-shirts walked out of the lift, and had beaten us there! We all tried to hide behind the same pole in the hotel, we ran away from him and hid. Mat was like, 'I can't fucking believe the bloke's done this!' And everybody else was pissed off that he'd flown back from Scotland and then flown from London to New York and been told by his boss to follow them everywhere and he'd taken it quite literally. So that was pretty nuts."

It was while in New York that the band received the single's midweek chart position. For a hip new band like Suede, the majority of sales take place in the first few days after release, so the midweek placed them well inside the Top 40. "I'd never been so excited," recalls Saul Galpern, who'd travelled to America with Jon and the band.

It was also in America that they got to see the finished edit of the video. "They Fedexed the video over and Brett watched it at least nine times, over and over again," remembers Jon. "I just have this image of him sitting on a bed cross-legged, with this big portion of chips and a big portion of tomato sauce going 'Again! Again!'"

The band have since heaped scorn upon their videos via the commentary section on their *Lost In TV* DVD retrospective. "It's one of these wrong assumptions that musicians can make good actors," says Brett. "Or actually want to be in their videos," adds Mat. But as Saul Galpern recalls, their initial reaction to their video debut was very different. "They thought it was fantastic, of course they did!"

"I remember at the time thinking it's a little bit tatty. I guess it was good in a way because it had quite a lot of personality. Because we were a bit tatty," concedes Brett. "We had our own style but it was a tatty style. And the video reflected that and it was expressive and cheeky in the same way as the band was. So I guess it was successful in that way but I don't really think it's a high point in video making."

The promo was directed by Lindy Heymann on a shoestring budget of £1,200. "We met her through Saul," explains Brett. "She was really into all the visual references, she was really into the Veruschka thing [artist and cover star of "The Drowners", body-painted to look like a man]. She seemed to connect with the slightly bizarre, twisted world that I was getting into, vaguely sexual art and stuff like that. She was cool. And she made this video for £1,200 and you just couldn't do that any more. She got a lot of favours from people, virtually everyone did it for free. I remember a lot of the crew actually coming up to me and saying, 'We really like the song, we think it's great.' And they were actually doing it because they liked the song, which was brilliant. I expect quite a lot of them were doing it for experience as well but there was quite a nice sense that people were doing it because the music was cool. Maybe they thought the music had something to say."

The video received its first screening on May 23 on the Saturday morning *Chart Show*. Perhaps the greatest music programme of all time, the *Chart Show* eschewed tedious interviews, irritating presenters and inferior live bastardisations of your favourite songs in favour of a format that displayed genius in its simplicity: wall to wall videos of the latest releases and all the chart hits, including, significantly, the best of the then thriving independent chart. For all the praise and attention heaped on them by the London-centric media, this was probably Suede's first introduction to a wider public. And if you'll pardon the personal indulgence, it was the moment that changed my life for ever. I literally fell out of bed watching them and bought the 12-inch the same day. My first impression was that they sounded exactly like Adam And The Ants and had at least one cracking bird in the band. So I was half right.

By this time Suede had embarked on their first major tour, as support to Kingmaker. Hard as it may be to believe now, Kingmaker were one of the hottest bands in the country, though their main claim to fame was that they sold more T-shirts than records, which perhaps sums up the quality of their music.

"We did supports with Kingmaker and just blew them off stage every night," remembers Saul Galpern. "There just wasn't anybody else around, they were on their own, they really were. Until Oasis and the whole Blur thing."

Immediately after the Kingmaker tour, Suede embarked on their first proper headline jaunt, kicking off with a show at the Underworld in Camden. This marked the debut of the Suede "family".

"What happened is we stole everything from Spitfire," laughs Mat. "When we started getting some attention and, more importantly, some fans, we didn't know anyone, we didn't have crew, and Justin was playing with Spitfire. We went to see them at the Underworld and he introduced us to Charlie and Pete Sissons and Matty Wall and we nicked them. These were the first people we'd met who carried things and sold T-shirts."

Charlie Charlton, who would ultimately become Suede's permanent manager, had been working with Jon for some time and helped out at many a Suede gig. He had actually encountered them much earlier, at the Bull & Gate in 1990 as guitarist with Motorcycle Boy, who Suede supported on more than one occasion. "I don't think I even realised they were the same band," he reflects. "All I remember is everyone fancying Justine."

As the gigs got bigger, Charlie brought his mates, Pete and Matty, to lend a hand. Matty would eventually go on to tour manage Elastica, but Pete, who would soon be promoted to guitar technician, works for Suede to this day.

"Jon passed on a couple of Suede's crappy little gigs to Charlie, so he did a few and I did the first one at the Underworld, which was around the same time as 'The Drowners' came out. I was selling T-shirts but we all did a bit of driving and backline, everybody mucking in," says Pete. "Every gig was absolutely rammed," he adds, "frighteningly so. I was selling T-shirts in the back corner of somewhere like Bath Moles with a capacity of 150 and of course the promoter would try and ram it as full as possible and I was just pinned to the wall with shirts all around me. That was happening everywhere, it was exciting."

Brett remembers the tour fondly. "We did the toilet tour of the UK, the Princess Charlotte in Leicester and Bath Moles Club and stuff like that and Southampton Joiners Arms. And I just remember it being a riot," he says. "You know, when there's a sudden change in the temperature and all the flying ants come out; it's like they've almost passed a message to each other. And all these Suede fans suddenly emerged from the concrete like flying ants. The intensity came to some weird physical boiling point and they all just came out and went mad. All these people that had been kind of hiding in the shadows just decided to let themselves go. From then on the gigs did tend to be absolutely hysterical. Generally, they were mad, mad affairs."

For the band it was a total vindication of everything they had worked for over the past two and a half years. "When you first start when you're in a band, you play to this big, empty crescent shape. People just stand at the back, so you've always got this huge gap at the front of stage. And all of a sudden we had this mosh pit down the front, loving it," remembers Brett. "And there was something really exciting about that because we had literally released one single. There were a couple of gigs that were insane before we'd released any records and it was based on people getting into it just because they'd heard about it and they'd come along and we actually started to build up a bit of a following. I'm not sure if the machinery of the way the modern business works so you get that phenomenon any more, where people start following a band around before they have any records out."

Obviously, the press adulation had a lot to do with the gigs being constant sell-outs, but Brett denies that the fan hysteria was simply due to the music papers raving about them. "People would come to check us out and they'd be quite confrontational gigs and that made it quite exciting as well because we'd always have something to prove," he says. "It's like football when Man United play someone, the teams always raise their game 'cause there's always a lot to prove. I've got really good memories of those times. It was a really good laugh. It was a nice time to be doing it. I remember it being a great summer and an insane, surreal world. I was taking a lot of E, that was the drug I was doing at the time. I hadn't started to get into cocaine really."

"It was electric seeing all these kids," adds Alan Fisher. "It was just amazing, just watching these Suede fans and the emotion of the audience. It's like going to a wedding, you've got tears in your eyes, it's just unexplainable. Seeing your mates on stage and hearing their songs. Four hours before the gig starts I'd take a few Es and stuff so I was ready to peak just as the set starts. I was filming the concerts as well. It's only now I can really appreciate it, best days of myself. In the early days it's so exciting, I mean it's still great now, but when you've got that young blood in you and you're taking drugs for the first time it's absolutely so exciting. You feel like you're rock'n'roll, it's fucking great. I actually really miss those days."

Malcolm Dunbar remembers the first signs of pressure beginning to show around that time. "After the gig in Leicester, Brett just wanted to get home that night. So I gave Brett and Kevin Patrick a lift home from Leicester. Kevin, I think, was working for one of our labels in America and we even talked about doing some kind of joint deal. Brett left his cassettes in my car, two brilliant cassettes, Kate Bush and Bowie's *Aladdin Sane*. The attention at that point was probably starting to get to them and I think he just wanted a night off back in London."

Kevin Patrick, former A&R Vice-President for Island Records in the States, had become head of the new Medicine label, a new WEA-affiliated imprint. He fell in love with the band instantly. "They sounded so purely English," he told *Billboard*. "I grew up in the '60s loving English groups like the Kinks and The Creation, then David Bowie and T-Rex in the '70s, then the Smiths in the '80s. There is absolutely a solid line to Suede in the '90s. I've waited my whole life for a band like this." Happily, Kevin would eventually go on to become Suede's A&R man at Columbia in the US.

Meanwhile, life at Moorhouse Road carried on as normal, albeit a very strange version of normality. "I don't think the lifestyle changed at all actually," says Alan Fisher. "Except Brett had to go on tour. But you don't remember all the days, when you're taking drugs for days and it's four days with no sleep, maybe a kip in the morning. That's when we had that guy living upstairs. It was non stop, it was actually non stop."

Jon Eydmann remembers the madness reaching new levels of insanity during the band's first visit to Ireland, which he describes as "Bonkers from start to finish". At the Dublin show, U2 turned up to watch the new pretenders to their rock throne. The pressure was noticeably starting to affect Bernard. "There was definitely The Edge and I think it probably was Adam Clayton," recalls Jon. "And obviously The Edge wanted to talk to Bernard about guitars and Bernard didn't want to talk to The Edge. So I'm like, 'Fucking hell, sorry he doesn't want to talk to you!' It was a bit embarrassing actually, having to explain to The Edge that Bernard didn't want to talk to him."

The band crossed the border to Belfast overnight by which time Bernard had acquired a large, furry toy rabbit from somewhere. "He wouldn't leave it alone and carried it everywhere. It was a big furry rabbit that he was cuddling and sitting around holding it all day," recalls Jon, incredulously. "And he just went off with this rabbit claiming he was going to look for some carrots!"

The gig itself, in a tiny venue, was absolute mayhem. "It was amazing, people were bouncing about all over the place," confirms Jon. "And in 'The Drowners' there was a particular section where, because it was all moving, and everything on the stage was moving, Bernard's effects unit fell off and there was no guitar. And Charlie got it back on just as the song kicked back in after the middle eight. And everyone was like 'Hooray!' Obviously doesn't sound as good as if you were there, but it was brilliant. So everyone was completely on a high apart from one person who was insistent that he was still a human being and had to leave the venue through the front door, which was very difficult because there was tons and tons of people there who obviously wanted to rip his clothes off!"

The original plan had been to exit via the back door and drive back to the hotel as quickly as possible before the baying crowd tore them to pieces. "But obviously this didn't happen because we couldn't leave without Bernard. So we had to get the rest of the band in the van, out the back, down the road, and someone had to drive the van along very slowly with the door open while me and Charlie put a circle round Bernard, walked him through the building, out the front door, and then chased down the fucking road to jump in the van."

The chaos didn't end there, though, as they had to go through exactly the same process at the other end. "The idea was that we'd get back to the hotel before all these people turned up but we couldn't because of this shenanigans," says Jon. "So when we got there we had to get them all out of the van again, and there were all these people around the van – they wouldn't let them go in. And when they did get in the hotel, there was these two tanks turned up, pointing towards the hotel! It was really odd. It was like royalty or something, you know, on the balcony and all these kids downstairs shouting, 'We want Suede! We want Suede!' And they wouldn't go away for ages. And I think they actually did try and play a song, on a piano or something, but I don't think anybody could really hear it. It was hilarious, it was just total stupidity, a brilliant day."

Suede had clearly hit a nerve, tapping into an alien nation of alienation. For the first time since the Smiths, here was a band that truly mattered to people, and particularly people who had never had a voice before.

"Obviously the lyrics had a lot to do with it, but it was a crowd of people who were isolated," says Mat, "be it either actually geographically, they were the only person who loved music in their area, or they were just lunatics. You had this strange sense that this was a crowd of individuals, a gang of outsiders. I know so many people who met at Suede gigs, people who're still together now who met at Suede gigs. And there was something really insurrectionary about it. I think we were quite aware that we were outsiders trying to push as far as we could in."

Suede genuinely introduced a sense of belonging to a whole army of people who, much like the band themselves, had never really fitted in. "It was weird with Suede because we didn't really have any roots," Mat continues. "We're all from different suburban shit holes and it was really strange to find out this gang was there, it just wasn't from the same place. It was this vague scattering of freaks, equidistant from each other around Britain."

Here was a band that could change lives.

high rising

"THE DROWNERS" TOUR ENDED with a show at London's Camden Palace where Morrissey was once again in the audience. In much the same way as the Smiths had covered James's first single, or he had worn a Primitives T-shirt, or recorded Bradford's "Skin Storm" as a solo artist, Morrissey was on a mission to champion his favourite new band by learning the words to "My Insatiable One".

"I didn't actually see him but apparently he had a notebook and was scribbling down the lyrics," says Brett. "I remember I was in Portobello Market one day, and there was this guy selling bootleg tapes and he said, 'Oh, there's Morrissey doing one of your songs in this gig in Switzerland. And he gave it to me and I took it home and it was quite a bizarre moment, one of those really surreal moments like a bizarre dream, listening to Morrissey and his backing band doing a version of 'My Insatiable One'! He missed out all the swear words and there wasn't the thing about the inflatable one, it was a slightly sanitised version. But, yeah, it was good."

Brett would return the compliment by nominating the Smiths' re-issued "This Charming Man" as "Single Of The Decade" soon after, although the mutual appreciation society would shortly take a nose-dive.

Malcolm Dunbar remembers the Camden Palace gig well. "It was an absolute joke. There were all these labels who'd flown over from America there," he says. "I remember Tom Zutack being there from Geffen. I remember Kevin Patrick. After the gig we went to the kebab shop in Camden with the band, we got absolutely smashed and pissed and Brett and Bernard were arguing outside the kebab shop. There was a tension even at that early stage that you thought, would it last? And unfortunately it didn't. I think they were different types of characters. Brett obviously likes the limelight, obviously being a frontman has a specific temperament. And Bernard always struck me as being quite homely."

Jon Eydmann's phone was by this time ringing non stop, as their lawyer, Kaz Gill, received seemingly endless offers from record companies. "Kaz would ring me up and go, 'There's another one!' And we'd wheedle through the ones that were definite no-nos and then possibly go and see the might-bes," says Jon. "And we went to America again, courtesy of Geffen, which was Tom Zutack who signed Mötley Crüe and Guns n' Roses. So that was quite weird really, 'cause you wouldn't have thought he'd be the right person to do the band."

This latest trip to the States was another surreal experience. Tom Zutack travelled in first class, while Jon and the band sat at the rear of the plane in economy. "We didn't see him the whole flight. And then he jumped straight in his Morse-type Jag and we were left with these two girls that looked after us," says Jon. "And we went to the hotel and then went into Geffen and met him and he was a bit of a strange man, really. He just assumed that because he'd done all this that we were definitely, definitely gonna sign to Geffen."

Although the Geffen deal was very attractive (Saul Galpern describes it as "insane"), the band still had plenty of other offers to consider, including one from Kevin Patrick who took them out sightseeing during their day off. At the end of the day they had a few drinks in Brett's room along with their two chaperones from Geffen. "It was a nothing kind of evening and we just got drunk and talked rubbish," says Jon. "The girls left and we all went to our separate rooms and went to sleep."

Jon was more than a little disturbed to be awoken in the middle of the night and find himself rolling from side to side on the bed. The phone rang and Susan, one of the Geffen girls, explained that there was a minor earthquake but that the hotel was built on roller-foundations for that very reason, so there was no need to worry. Jon immediately agreed to call all the band members to make sure they were okay. The moment he put the phone down, however, it rang. It was Bernard, who was understandably shaken.

"What's happening?"

"I explained the situation to him," says Jon, "and he told me that I was his manager and if I cared about him, I should make it stop!"

On their final day in LA, Suede were invited to Tom Zutack's cliff-top mansion in Malibu where he obviously aimed to win them over with his flash lifestyle and all the latest technology, which included an enormous widescreen TV and one of the very first DVD players. "You know how bemused Mat gets," laughs Jon. "He was extra bemused, his eyebrows were almost off the top of his head. We sat down in this house watching a Kate Bush DVD and stuff and he obviously had a pool and all this kind of thing. And there was me, the band, that's five, him and these two girls. So there was eight of us. And he ordered, like, 18 pizzas."

Not quite knowing what to do with himself, Jon announced he was going outside for a swim while Brett and Mat climbed into a hammock and the two Geffen girls stood either side and rocked them backward and forward.

"So they were just smoking this joint between themselves while these two girls gently rocked them," smiles Jon. "And I'm thinking, 'This is the most bizarre thing in my whole life!' So I got out of the pool and went and sat in the hot tub, which he had bubbling away. And the sliding door of the house opens up and he walks out. He's quite a big man. So I'm sitting in this hot tub, and it's coming up to my neck. And I thought to myself, 'He's got his shorts on, if he comes in this fucking hot tub with me, I'm gonna drown!' But he didn't. He just sat next to me and went, 'So you've seen how we do business in LA, are we doing a deal?'. And I just said, 'I don't think so, but we've had a nice holiday!', which is not necessarily what he wanted to hear."

This latest adventure marked the point where the band came to suspect that Jon was perhaps not the ideal manager for a band who seemed well on their way to becoming international superstars.

"Tom Blu-tak was trying to be all business-like and going, 'Hey, Jon, any questions about the company?'" remembers Simon Gilbert. "And Jon just went, 'Nope.' And he just carried on swimming and I just thought, 'Hmm, time for you to go.'"

Back in Blighty, with "The Drowners" riding high at number one in the *NME* Independent Charts, Suede had a welcome few days off. Mat spent the last weekend in June at Glastonbury with his flatmate, Justin Welch, where they bumped into that other ex-Suede member, Justine Frischmann (footage of both Justine and Mat backstage at the festival can be spotted on Blur's video documentary, *Starshaped*). Inspired by Suede's recent success, she and Justin decided to form a band and soon began jamming at The Premises with Damon on bass. "When they actually got somewhere it made me feel a lot better about everything because I just thought, there is light at the end of the tunnel," says Justine. "At the end of the day if you persevere for long enough you do get somewhere if you're any good. And I think that was one of the reasons I felt encouraged to go back into it." According to legend, Brett suggested "Dad" as a possible name for the new group, but after considering Spastica and others, they settled on Elastica.

Perhaps more than anything, Suede's greatest achievement is the fact that they quite literally changed the face of music for ever. And while doubters may argue that many of the bands they inspired and influenced would have happened anyway, in Elastica there is bullet-proof evidence of a band that could simply have not existed otherwise. Quite apart from the fact that they had two ex-members of Suede in the band, the two were inextricably linked. Mike Smith cites them as the reason he stayed in a music industry he was becoming increasingly disillusioned with, especially once it became apparent that he'd made a huge *faux pas* in choosing Adorable over Suede.

"Elastica were everything I'd gotten into the music industry to work with," says Mike. "I was so excited. And that committed me to staying in the music business. And it worked out better than anyone could have expected. It was interesting because John Best was heavily involved. And John was very much known as Suede's publicist above all else, and he seemed to have a slightly Svengali role. And I think Brett as well had quite an important influence. There was suddenly a good scene going on, especially in Camden where you had Justin living with Mat and their flat was a place where a lot of people were hanging out."

"Everyone used to crash round our house," confirms Mat, "used to do a load of drugs, play a load of records, go out some more. It was quite an innocent, pleasurable time. I loved it. I don't know what that says about me as a human being, but I've absolutely no problem with a couple of years of mindless adulation. It was a new way of a band like us appearing, just absolute mass coverage. I really enjoyed it. The band and Justin and friends of ours would come out, people like Alan. And we went out every night, went to see bands, went to clubs and lived in poverty because we didn't have any money still. It was great. It was really, really exciting."

Meanwhile, Damon and his pals were about to find themselves on the same bill as Suede for the first time since their Zap Club *tête-à-tête* almost two years previously. This time, however, things would be very different.

The show at the Town & Country Club was billed "Gimme Shelter", a benefit organised by the *NME*. "Suede were on quite early. Three And A Half Minutes were on first, then Suede, then Mega City Four and then Blur," recalls Jon Eydmann. "Blur were really pissed and didn't really seem like they knew what they were doing. I don't think at the time anyone thought much about it other than thinking Suede were amazing and had blown Blur off stage, because Blur were already in the position where people had started slagging them off. People were like, 'They're that bunch of drunkards that hang around The Good Mixer with the bloke from Food.'"

Already bruised by the inexplicable commercial failure of "Popscene", it seemed that Blur were now being battered by all sides. A substantial amount of money had gone missing from the band's coffers ("I don't think it was Mike Collins, their manager, being a crook. It was just down to him being inept," believes Mike Smith), their record company was rejecting their latest material, and on returning from a gruelling US tour with their tails between their legs, they now found their arch rivals all over the music papers.

"I was very aware of the implicit rivalry because at that point Jane Oliver, Justine Frischmann's best friend, was working for Savage & Best. And she was going out with Graham Coxon, so she was very thick with Blur," explains Phill Savidge. "Blur were on tour at the time and Jane was kind of like, 'Bloody Suede, what is this?', because Suede were always the band that were never gonna succeed when Blur were succeeding. And I kept going on about Suede so much that they were gonna be massive and she was like, 'Don't be ridiculous', but all this time she was actually in the office just watching them become enormous. Suede became big in that period while Blur were on tour in America. I always thought Jane was the original inspiration for *Tank Girl* 'cause she lives with Jamie Hewitt (later, of course, to mastermind Gorillaz with Damon) and they've got three children together and he wrote *Tank Girl* when he did *Deadline* (an unlikely but brilliant cross between *2000AD* and *Select*). That's why Blur were always in *Deadline* and Suede were never in *Deadline*. That was the only bloody paper we could never get in!"

With all this in mind it was perhaps inevitable that the evening would be a disaster for Blur, though in retrospect it represents a defining moment in the history of Britpop. Mike Smith remembers the occasion all too vividly, having taken a new girlfriend along to try to impress her. "The gig was messy, but Blur did play a lot of messy gigs. They played drunk in those days, it wasn't a complete shock that Blur do a show drunk. I'd seen shows where Alex had fallen off the stage he'd been so pissed. I think it was more the fact that they put on a bit of a tired performance. I think they were just a little bit exhausted. They'd done quite a lot of work in America and it wasn't paying off. And they were beginning to lose the momentum that they'd built up in '91. So it was a band that had slipped into a decline, whereas Suede were absolutely the band of the moment, they had completely got the *zeitgeist* right and were wholly in the ascendancy. And they shone that night. Brett was incredibly dynamic and exciting. Blur were clearly outclassed. I don't think I quite realised it at the time, it was only when the girl I was with was looking at me confused saying, 'Why have you brought me to this show? Suede are clearly a much better band.' And I was going, 'No, no, no, you don't understand!' But she was certainly right that evening."

Blur were clearly aware of how disastrous their performance had been. So much so that when ex-Teardrop Explodes turned Food MD Dave Balfe stormed backstage to give them a verbal kicking, all four members of the band had already scarpered.

"It was a really important moment for Blur because for them it was, 'Shit, how do we take it forward?'" reflects Mike Smith. "The real need to reinvent themselves became apparent and I think that gig probably did them an enormous amount of good."

For Suede, meanwhile, the only way was up. They made their debut festival appearance at Reading during the August bank holiday weekend. It was the first chance for the idly curious to see what all the fuss was about. "They were either headlining the *Melody Maker* tent, or second from the end. That was when only a select few people had seen Suede," recalls Phill Savidge. "The London media had seen Suede, but Reading was the big showcase for most people. The tent was absolutely rammed. I was off my head. It was the first time they played 'Animal Nitrate', which was amazing."

The song, which was the band's first composition since "Sleeping Pills", had its lyrical origins in that first *Melody Maker* cover story when Brett had declared: "My fantasy has always been to have a song about some bizarre sexual experience in the Top 10."

Whether the lyric was written before or after that quote, Brett can't quite recall, but the sentiment had been a lifelong ambition. "I had this sort of belief that if you have this position of power in pop music, you should use it. You shouldn't just use it to maintain your career and keep releasing bland rubbish. I'd always thought that you should occasionally just use it to really rub people up the wrong way. I've always had this love of songs that I've found out are kind of sinister after they've been a huge hit, almost these songs that are like this evil little person that's been let in through the back door. Songs like 'Man With The Child In His Eyes', which is supposed to be about masturbation and stuff like that, which housewives were singing. I loved the idea that this slightly evil thing had got under people's skins after having been invited in. I guess 'Animal Nitrate' was obviously a bit evil. You obviously wouldn't let him through the front door, d'you know what I mean?"

Bernard's original demo had gone under the working title of "Dixon", not, as some might assume, after their original accountant, Frank Dixon, but as tacit acknowledgement of the main riff's debt to the theme from *Dixon Of Dock Green*. Despite the song's obvious commercial appeal, the band had originally never considered it to be single material, as Jon Eydmann recalls. "I wouldn't want to take credit for something I didn't do but they played it to me on a four-track and they said, 'What do you think of that? We think it's a b-side.' And I would have said, 'Don't be fucking stupid, that's brilliant!' I don't know if they were joking or if they meant it. I wouldn't want to say I was the one who thought it should be a single, because everyone thought it should be a single. It was an amazing song, best thing they'd done to date. It was great."

At that point, though, the band's intention had always been to release "Sleeping Pills" as the third single, following the tried and tested ballad-for-single-three formula. "I think I was starting to get a bit pretentious and I probably thought 'Sleeping Pills' was much more sophisticated," concedes Brett. "I thought the lyrics to 'Sleeping Pills' were my favourite lyrics at the time. Maybe I thought 'Animal Nitrate' was a bit throw-away."

Before that, though, the band had to record single number two. "Metal Mickey" had always been the prime candidate. Bernard had come up with the main theme on the tube one day and has mentioned "The Shoop Shoop Song" as its musical inspiration, though the guitar solo at least owes a lot more to the Kinks' "You Really Got Me". In the studio, however, "Metal Mickey" would be the first Suede track to undergo a major rearrangement, courtesy of producer Ed Buller. Rather than abruptly ending after a single chorus as the band played it live, Ed suggested an extended fade-out incorporating that most un-Suede of musical devices, the key change.

"We were sort of getting into creating a formula a little bit," admits Brett. "With 'The Drowners' we had that really exciting, swoony outro and we kind of wanted to do the same thing with 'Metal Mickey'. So we wrote a coda part where it changes key. And to be honest I think it would have been better to keep the metal brutality of the song, to play on its punkiness. 'The Drowners' and 'Metal Mickey' were very different songs and I think it would have suited having a harder feel to 'Metal Mickey'. It is what it is, it's a jumping-up-and-down song."

Ed Buller had been the band's producer since the first single and would be their closest musical collaborator for years to come. Saul Galpern knew him from his time at Island. "I've always really liked Ed as a person," says Brett, "he struck me as someone who had a great enthusiasm for music and a great enthusiasm for Suede. We hit it off and it worked out for a while. And I like the way he worked and in the early days Bernard liked the way Ed worked. I think as Bernard got more technically aware, because he always had a fine ear, he very soon saw flaws in what Ed was doing. But I think songs like 'The Drowners', I quite like the production on that, it's got a very strong Suede identity. I think songs like 'My Insatiable One' sound great, still. But it wasn't till we got to 'Metal Mickey' that the production thing started to fuck up a bit."

Other than its nod to the pill-gobbling robot from the godawful early '80s children's sitcom of the same name, the title has always been a matter of conjecture. At the time the band coyly sniggered about it being "The nickname of someone we know", leading many to surmise it was yet another reference to Justine Frischmann, or possibly her Doc Marten-wearing sidekick, Jane Oliver, who allegedly once worked in a butcher's shop. The hypothesis is reinforced by the original chorus line running "She's so high," rather than "She sells meat," but it's an allusion that Brett hotly contests. "No, 'Metal Mickey' was not about Jane. It was about Daisy Chainsaw and the early '90s indie-punk scene, specifically Katie Jane Garside, who blew me away."

Whatever, "Metal Mickey" was Suede's first pop single, and first *bona fide* hit, entering the charts at number 17 and earning the band their first *Top Of The Pops* appearance. It was the kind of epoch defining performance that recalled similar gender-bending "What the fuck was that?" debuts by David Bowie and Boy George, respectively twenty and ten years previously. Backed by an enormous Suede logo, the band looked and acted like they owned the show, Brett's arse-slapping antics leading the bemused presenter to splutter, "Interesting use of the microphone there!"

"We got really drunk before we did it, because Polygram sent us loads of Jack Daniel's," remembers Simon Gilbert. "And I couldn't understand afterwards why everyone was saying, 'Wow, did you see Suede on *Top Of The Pops*? Outrageous!' All my mum's friend's thought Brett was a woman."

Suede's *Top Of The Pops* appearance was also significant in that they were the first band ever to appear on the show without a record deal, an accolade often erroneously attributed to Glasgow candy-popsters, Bis. With the release of "Metal Mickey", Suede had fulfilled their initial two-single deal with Nude the week before and were now open to offers.

By this time, though, Saul Galpern's Nude, who had hooked up a unique deal with Sony – making them a tiny independent label with major muscle backing – was the only serious contender. "Deep down I kind of knew they were gonna sign eventually," says Saul. "Suede were the first band to do *Top Of The Pops* without a deal and I think they actually agreed to do it while we were re-recording 'Metal Mickey'. I remember being in a room in the studio and they said yes and it was such a relief."

Jon Eydmann agrees that it was Saul's enthusiasm and the band's reciprocal loyalty to him that won the deal and that there was never any sense of selling out to a major label. "I don't think anyone saw it as signing to Sony. He had the deal with Sony so we did sign to Sony, but it didn't really feel like that because we didn't really deal with them. We only ever really dealt with Saul. It was totally down to loyalty to Saul that we signed to Nude-stroke-Sony. The only other person that was

Blandine, Sandra and Brett Anderson on holiday, circa 1970. "Blandine unfortunately got named by my dad. Luckily I got named by my mum."

Peter and Sandra Anderson's wedding day, 14th July 1962. "You went round to Brett's house and his mum was painting and riding around on a tricycle and his dad was doing archery and conducting classical music in the living room."

Brett the sportsman (back row, second from left). "He was very good at cross country running and football. He got chosen for the cross country team and would go into these competitions and he'd nearly always be first."

Brett and Mat in Geoff, 1986. "We played literally one gig in our whole history which wasn't even the four members of the band. Mat couldn't be bothered to turn up."

Gareth Perry and Brett in Geoff, 1986. "There were some good songs but Gareth never really came from the same school as me and Mat. It was just the fact that we were all interested in music."

Lust at first sight: Brett and Justine, 1988. "We ended up going out and having three blissful years together, three of the happiest years of my life."

Mat and Justine contemplate the future. "The first time I met her she was in Brett's bed. I thought she was absolutely great. She wanted something to happen when me and Brett were just smoking dope and talking shit."

Simon, Justine, Brett and Bernard at the Borderline, 1991. "I didn't especially like the band. Justine was very low key, head down, not really doing much. And the first time I saw Brett, he reminded me of Mark E. Smith."

One of the last gigs with Justine, late 1991. "I was fed up standing at the back, looking like a useless twat when I knew I wasn't."

Damon, Bernard and Justine at the *Leisure* album launch, September 1991. "They went through phases of being friends and then hating each other and Bernard loved Damon and hated Damon, it was just ridiculous really."

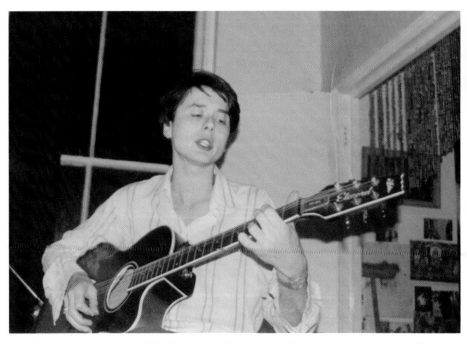

Brett in Moorhouse Road, late 1991. "I remember he played me *The Drowners* and I thought, 'Oh my God – you're going to be the new David Bowie!'"

NME On night at The Venue, New Cross, 3rd January 1992. "I just couldn't believe it. I was totally blown away. I thought, 'They must all be watching this, they must all be seeing what I'm seeing!'"

The Venue, 3rd January 1992. "He's a star, he's like Bryan Ferry! I can't believe how good this is!"

Simon Gilbert with early manager Jon Eydmann and his son Sam. "I had to tell him he was fired which was fairly horrible. It was a big thing. It wasn't just Jon. We knew his girlfriend well, and his kid. And I'm really glad he doesn't bear us any ill will, because I probably would."

Nude supremo Saul Galpern with Brett backstage. "Saul was the first person who was talking to us about Roxy Music and Kate Bush and got the songs. And the other thing we liked is he told us he'd been sacked by a load of record companies!"

Suedemania, May 1992. "You know, when there's a sudden change in the temperature and all the flying ants come out, all these Suede fans suddenly emerged from the concrete like flying ants. The intensity came to some weird physical boiling point and they all came out and went mad."

"We did supports with Kingmaker and just blew them off stage every night."

Brett at Moorhouse Road, Notting Hill, where most of the lyrics for the first album were written. "It was the most beautiful place in the world, it was like something out of *The Man Who Fell To Earth*."

Bernard in Amsterdam, April 1993. "The rest of the band were getting fucked up and partying and being a rock'n'roll band and Bernard wasn't. He was going to his bedroom and playing his guitar."

Bernard, Simon and Mat with Japanese ticket sales awards, July 1993. "My overriding memory is sitting in the dressing room listening to these little Japanese girls sat in the car park singing *Animal Nitrate*, like a chorus of three year olds. Definitely melted Bernard and Brett's hearts."

Simon meets his public, July 1993. "It was real crazy, big time madness. But great fun!"

seriously in with a chance was Malcolm, because we all got on with him really well."

"One of the reasons we couldn't sign the band was that in those days the independent chart was really important," reflects Malcolm Dunbar. "In those days to be in the independent chart in a band's early stages was incredibly important. And I agreed with that. I think I offered them an album deal right away and my big problem was no matter how hard I tried, Warners were very inflexible about independent distribution. I couldn't convince the powers that be to give the band independent distribution on early releases. And so no matter how much I tried they insisted."

"Metal Mickey" also won the band their first *NME* cover, proof if any were needed that Suede were now far more than simply an invention of the rival *Melody Maker* (who in less than six months had already given them two front covers and two cover inserts). The shoot took place at photographer Steve Double's studio in Aldgate East and the cover proclaimed "The Godlike Genius Of Suede" with Brett peering through a crucifix.

"Bernard had a problem with the cross because Bernard's Catholic," remembers Phill Savidge. "I don't know if he was claiming it was blasphemous. It's obviously not. It's an image. It's a shape. A cross is a shape and I think it suited the purposes of the piece. So it was just Brett who was on the cover of the *NME*, which Bernard wasn't very happy about but Bernard had refused to be photographed through the cross. And I know that magazines home in on the singer because of the attention span of the audience. It's just too fickle to make it work in any other way. Maybe that was the first seed of doubt in Bernard's mind that it wasn't really working with him being in Suede, because so many journalists were writing about lyrics, and were saying what a great guitarist Bernard was, but not in so much depth."

As Phill points out, though, if people were more interested in reading about chords and guitar riffs than lyrics and the opinions of androgynous frontmen then guitar magazines would outsell *NME* every week. "Amazing lick! E, D, does that work?" jokes Phill. "At that point Bernard became a bit unsettled by the press because he thought, 'Why should I bother because you're just going to write about Brett?' And I can understand that but it's simply the nature of the medium. I mean I've got a feeling that Morrissey and Johnny Marr didn't get on but Johnny walked more because he wasn't perceived to be the voice of the Smiths and John

Squire walked because he wasn't seen to be the voice of the Stone Roses and that Bernard walked because he wasn't the voice of Suede. But then again, they didn't sing, they were literally not the voice. So it's understandable, but I think that's why bands break down."

Tellingly, all three of the guitarists mentioned, not one of whom had ever expressed any desire to be a frontman in their early years, went on to launch their own solo singing careers, none of them with anything like the success or acclaim of their initial songwriting partnerships.

Jon Eydmann remembers the pressure definitely starting to affect Bernard around this time. "He ran round [to] my house in his underpants and I wasn't in, and it was my fault. What can you say?" he sighs. "I'd even that up by saying that he used to babysit my kid. It's not that he's a nasty man or I don't trust him. I think he's probably a really nice bloke. But he did do some very strange things and I'm sure it was down to the fact that he couldn't handle the pressure that he was under, but couldn't think of a way to actually deal with it. And obviously other things were happening. We were all probably taking far too many drugs to be perfectly honest. Has anyone ever said that?"

Brett recalls a similar tale, presumably the same incident. "I think Bernard's always been highly strung, I remember some story about Bernard having a panic attack, and Mat and Bernard used to live in Camden, they used to live a few streets away from each other, and what I seem to remember is Bernard arriving on his doorstep in just his boxer shorts. And basically he'd had a panic attack. I can't remember what it was about. I think me and Bernard are quite similar kinds of people, we're both quite nervy people, we both kind of live off our nerves. I would admit it myself, I'm highly strung, I'm not Mister Laidback at all, but that's how I get things done."

Brett himself was also beginning to feel the negative effects of fame for the first time. "We did the SW1 Club around then, and I remember starting to develop hypochondria," he admits. "I remember every single important show I was waking up with a psychosomatic disorder, which was like a sore throat on the day of a gig and sort of thinking I had flu or stuff like this. I know how people's brains work, it's just having so much pressure. It's a way of dealing with it. I'm sure Neil [Codling] could tell you all about that!"

The SW1 Club was another show arranged with John Curd and, as with the Africa Centre, it was total insanity. "There were far too many people there and there didn't seem to be any stage security," recalls Jon

Eydmann. "I remember me and Charlie doing it, which was quite odd. I remember at the time thinking, 'I wish this wasn't happening,' because there were people crawling all over the stage and me trying to get them off. I'm obviously not the biggest person in the world and I'm not really designed to be stage security. And Mat was shouting, 'Turn my [effects] pedal on!' because he couldn't get to it 'cause there was people everywhere. It was pretty chaotic, but it was a great gig, it was brilliant."

"The pressure was definitely getting to me a little bit around that time," Brett continues. "I remember constantly sitting there half an hour before the show with hot lemon, coughing and things like this, then getting on stage and everything would be fine, a load of old fluff like a phantom pregnancy or something. And I remember at the SW1 Club being ill again. I'd constantly be going to throat doctors and things like this, so there was a lot of pressure. I remember the 100 Club gig being like that, not being that good, that was when there was probably more media than fans at the gigs and there was a lot of people scribbling and I couldn't quite create the chemistry. It was okay, it wasn't amazing."

Another unexpected result of the band's rise to *Top Of The Pops* status was that Mat's old friends from RML came out of the woodwork, threatening to sue for £60,000 or reissue the aborted "Be My God" single. An out-of-court settlement meant that RML were not allowed to release the band's early recordings, but neither were the band, effectively burying the tracks for good, although many of them have resurfaced on various bootlegs over the years.

And, of course, there were the drugs. The band's gargantuan habits, and Brett's in particular, were now rapidly spiralling out of control. "A bit of money turns everybody on to coke," says manager Charlie Charlton. "Once you start and no one's telling you to stop, you don't."

As far as Brett was concerned, there was no dividing line between these excesses and the band's – or at least his own – creativity. For the time being at least, the drugs did work. "I've always seen drugs as quite useful towards songwriting," he told the music press at the time. "I'm quite a user in lots of ways, because I consider nothing more important in my life than songwriting. If I get into any situation, I see it as an opportunity to use to expand my songwriting."

It was a dangerous philosophy, but one which his best friend, Alan Fisher, seemed all too keen to subscribe to. "There were a couple of times we'd done six Es too many," recalls Alan cheerily. "One night we had about 100 Es and they were a bit dodgy and I polished the lot off.

I think Brett had two. I went to hospital the next day and I thought I was going to die. But it didn't bother me at all. I actually thought, 'Brett's gonna get a really good song out of this!' Honestly, it sounds really childish now and silly but my favourite Bowie song is the 'Bewlay Brothers', which is about his half-brother and, you know how that song's so sad, I had this fantasy that Brett would write something similar to that and it would be about our friendship. I thought it was quite beautiful, it would be a beautiful way to die, for one of his songs. At the time all I lived for was his music. I was actually living a life to create fodder for his lyrics."

While this might sound like reckless lunacy, one of the finest songs of the period was inspired by a similar incident. The band had been rehearsing a number called "Stonesy" for some time as an instrumental. Yet despite its obvious potential, the lyrics and vocal melody had remained tantalisingly just out of Brett's reach. "I couldn't find 'the note'," he says. "And I remember I had this little writing room in a studio called The Strongroom out in East London, and just getting it one day and writing 'So Young'. It was sort of written about this experience. My girlfriend at the time, Anick...collapsed once when we were doing E and it was sort of about that. It was kind of reflecting that experience, being on the knife-edge of youth. 'Why not? Let's do it!'"

Brett had met his latest flame in a pub called the Duke Of Cornwall in Notting Hill a few months previously when she was only 16 and still at school. They went back to Brett's place in Moorhouse Road and predictably got off their faces. But when Brett awoke the next morning, she had disappeared. "I didn't know where she'd gone and she'd vaguely told me that she was at school somewhere round here. So I literally went round every school in the area trying to find her. I literally was banging on all these school doors saying, 'D'you know this girl called Anick, she's quite small and she's Indian?' And I eventually found her. I found her school, which is down in Kensington High Street, about three days later."

The *carpe diem* sentiment of "So Young" was blatantly expressed in its alternative title, "Chase The Dragon", by which it would be known until the eve of the first album's release.

Before recording their debut long-player, Suede had been invited to record a track for an *NME* charity album themed around cover versions of number one singles. Covers, along with encores, were something that Suede had never considered before, but after rejecting the Specials'

"Ghost Town" and "Silver Lady" by David Soul, the band plumped for a radical reworking of the Pretenders' "Brass In Pocket".

"I really liked what Suede did to the song, having never liked the original," Chrissie Hynde told the *NME*. "Our version didn't rock. To me, it sounded like weak disco." The Pretenders frontwoman was being particularly generous considering that Suede's attempt was easily the limpest thing they had recorded so far, teetering as it did on the brink of self-parody. Recorded for tuppence in a Southall studio, a clumsy apology was issued claiming that a demo had accidentally been sent to the final cut rather than the proper version. In fact, there was no demo. The band saved face with two vastly superior performances of the song around the same time, one at the first of what would become legendary fanclub-only gigs (in this case a return to their very first stage in the bowels of the White Horse) and the other on Channel 4's yoof-flagship, *The Word*.

Charlie Charlton remembers the album sessions at Master Rock Studios in Kilburn being particularly traumatic. "The band would go out and do all these gigs, which were really celebratory affairs, then we'd come back to London and Brett would just carry on partying, doing that thing, once you've been that high on stage, how do you follow it up? And he'd come into the studio and Ed was just like, 'Well, he's off his face, he's been up for two days. I can't do this!'"

Nevertheless, Suede's creativity showed no sign of ebbing. If anything, Brett and Bernard's songs were becoming increasingly audacious. The band's entourage certainly seemed to think so. Charlie was awe-struck the first time he heard "The Next Life", a stark ballad comprised of Bernard's first serious piano part and a soaring falsetto from Brett that echoed the best bits of "She's Leaving Home" by the Beatles. "I think it was in Leicester, in a slopey-floored dressing room with a crappy old piano in it," he remembers. "Saul had just pitched up from London and Bernard went, 'Oi, have a listen to this!' Brett, I'm sure he didn't lie across the piano like Marlene Dietrich, but he did lean against it, or sat on it or something. And Brett just stared at the ceiling singing it and we were all like, 'Fuck! That's amazing!'"

Even now, Brett looks back on this period as a creative high. "I felt as if everything we were writing at that time was like, 'Wow, listen to this one!' We were in 'The Zone', as they say," he smiles. "I think the reason these songs were so good was that I was using truth as something creative, instead of maybe in the very early days I was kind of vaguely trying to hint at something. I went, right, I'm just going to write about things that have literally happened, that have moved me or affected me and use those to power the songs. That's my advice to anyone who wants to write songs, to actually just talk about the truth. I think if what you're saying is powerful enough, then the song will be powerful. It will automatically have a stamp of authority."

Sure enough, all the latter-day lyrics for the first album were directly influenced by extremely personal and emotional experiences in Brett's life. "The Next Life" was a lament to his lost mother, "So Young" was about Anick's overdose, while "Breakdown" dealt with his schoolfriend Simon Holbrook's slide into extreme depression.

Perhaps the most literal of all, however, was "She's Not Dead", a true story of the joint suicide of Brett's Aunt Jean and her clandestine lover. The song was even called "Jean's Not Dead" for a while. "I was pretty young at the time. She had this lover and he was black and Haywards Heath is a small town and in the early '80s I guess it was very taboo," Brett explains. "And basically they committed joint suicide together. They drove a car into a garage and just turned the exhaust on and killed themselves. The only person that knew what that was about was me and my sister, they're the only two people in the world that knows what that song's about. But because it's about something truthful I think there's a sense of the detail, things like the ankle chain and stuff like that, is the kind of detail that can only come from truth, that can't be conjured up."

Although the band hadn't appeared live since the SW1 Club gig in October, their public profile was by now bigger than ever. In December Brett graced the cover of the *NME*'s Christmas issue, dolled up in a pastiche of Sid Vicious doing "My Way" (his idea, incidentally). With petulant sneer and pistol in hand, the image managed to hark backwards, to the lyrics and artwork of "The Drowners", and forwards simultaneously, throwing down the gauntlet to anyone foolhardy enough to challenge Suede in '93.

Suede, or rather Brett, also hogged the cover of *Melody Maker* for the third time that year, in an awkward embrace with shaven-headed Lesley Rankine of Silverfish. The accompanying article, "The Maker's Sex Special", produced the most notorious quote of Brett's entire career: "I see myself as a bisexual man who's never had a homosexual experience..." It's an epithet that has dogged him ever since, largely by journalists eager to expose Suede as fakes. Most, however, conveniently ignore the explanatory suffix: "...that's the way I approach my song writing". Even at the time he was forced to explain himself further. "If you're asking am I insincere to pose as a sodomite because I haven't had someone's cock up my arse, then no I'm not. The sexuality you express is not limited to the things you've already experienced. I mean, if you're a virgin does that make you asexual? Well, no, it doesn't."

An interview with *The Sunday Times* a year later is perhaps more telling: "I don't regret the bisexual quote. It certainly got us noticed. I was interviewed so much last year, I started to make things up."

the big time

THE YEAR 1992 HAD BEEN A REMARKABLE one for Suede, seeing them leap from the dole queue to indie superstardom. In "Metal Mickey" they'd had a genuine hit single and a cursory glance at the end of year music polls made one wonder if there were actually any other bands out there worth bothering about at all. Although there was a whole host of class acts like Pulp, Radiohead, Elastica and, of course, the revenge-plotting Blur waiting in the wings, it would take Suede's battering ram to open the doors for this new generation. For the time being the alternative scene was still dominated by under-achievers like Ned's Atomic Dustbin, Carter The Unstoppable Sex Machine, the Senseless Things and other bands whose names said it all.

Not only were Suede voted the best new band and "The Drowners" the best single (with "Metal Mickey" not far behind) twice over, they scored high in virtually every other category going from favourite fashion item – frilly shirts, of course – to phrase of the year for "You're taking me ovaaah!"

Despite (or more likely because of) the flak he'd received for certain comments in recent months, Brett, when asked by the *NME* what the last thing he'd had to eat was, couldn't resist answering, "Cock."

The new year brought further reasons to be cheerful with yet another scoop courtesy of Savage & Best. In an unintentional pastiche of *Vanity Fair*'s Demi Moore "Pregnant Belly" cover, Brett, in gut-revealing leather jacket and best come-hither look, was to be found sprawled across the front cover of respectable rock monthly *Q*, which asked "Can you stomach Suede?" There was an unwritten rule at the time that *Q* did not put artists on the cover unless they'd had at least one album, and preferably a decade's worth, under their belts. Suede smashed that rule and the article drew attention to this unique situation by running an exhaustive and comprehensive discography of the group's output thus far: two singles, six tracks in total. It also revealed that the next release was to be "Animal Nitrate" and a song called "Samba".

Suede, however, were clearly not your average *Q* reader's typical band, and the issue turned out to be one of the poorest selling ever of the magazine. But as Phill Savidge points out, the decision to put them on the cover was more a political statement of intent than for any commercial reason. "Danny Kelly had just left the *NME* and become the editor of *Q* and had 'Revealed, the band for 93' and 'That discography in full', which was two singles! And he did that as a kind of 'Goodbye *NME*, hello *Q*'. And that this band was about to be taken over by monthly papers so *NME* and *Melody Maker* had to be on their toes if they wanted to reclaim them. It was a very nascent period in the press. Everyone was quite naive and just trying things at the time. I think it just went a bit crazy really."

With Britain seemingly at their feet, it was with some confidence that Suede crossed the Channel for their first engagement of the year, and their first ever performance outside the British Isles, on January 28. Their destination was Paris for a live radio show with Bernard Lenoir, often described as the French John Peel, a euphemism to describe the only French DJ with anything approaching decent taste. Lenoir's show, *The Black Session*, is hugely influential and massively important to British bands trying to make an impression in France. Unfortunately, Suede were not quite ready for the fact that nobody outside Britain gave a monkey's who these four lanky streaks of piss from England were. They'd swiftly grown accustomed to Beatles-at-the-Cavern type hysteria and instead were confronted by a seated studio audience in neat rows, clapping politely. "Get into it!" demanded Bernard. The Parisians were largely unimpressed and the band's studied arrogance, which had served them so well back home, merely distanced them further from the audience. Only the few diehards who'd made the cross-Channel trip noticed a new song, masquerading under the title "Chase The Dragon", slipped into the middle of the set.

"We hadn't really got used to the whole thing of playing live and it not being an insane riot," admits Brett, "and at a time when every time you stepped on stage it was a complete a riot, it was a bit sterile, it wasn't very good."

The next evening's show, a "proper" gig at the Olympic in Nantes, with Sheffield hopefuls Pulp supporting, was a smoother affair. The audience, if not jumping around, was at least standing up and receptive enough for Brett to shout, "This is a lot more fun than that boring session we did the other night!"

Jon Eydmann remembers the French trip for very different reasons. "They tried to get aggressive in France, they tried to have a rock'n'roll party. And the extent of it was crushing crisps into my carpet. That was as rock'n'roll as Suede ever got I think, crushing crisps. I think we actually got thrown out for being rude to someone who was very famous in France. They asked us to leave the next day."

Bruised but not beaten, Suede returned home to the comforting news that *Select* had already declared "Animal Nitrate" Single Of The Year, several weeks before its scheduled release date. Things were back to normal.

"'Animal Nitrate' was the best single so far," Phill Savidge believes. "At this point I was starting to play the game more and I brought Andrew Collins into the office from *Select*. I said, 'I don't want it in the singles pages, it's too good. This is just a phenomenal single, it shouldn't be connected with anything else.' I played it to him twice and he went away and wrote a whole page, in a monthly magazine! And it must have made the *NME* and *Melody Maker* think, 'Fuck, it's almost out of our domain now.' I also remember rather pompously I Sellotaped a tape of 'Animal Nitrate' to a velvet cushion and biked it to John Mulvey at the *NME* with a note saying 'Another great disappointment!' or something cheeky like that. And it worked. 'Animal Nitrate' went mental."

The single was previewed to the nation in grand style at the Brit Awards ceremony in the posh surrounds of Alexandra Palace. "Fuck me, do I remember the Brits," grins Jon Eydmann. "That was a pretty daunting experience to say the least. Everyone was really nervous and we got given a big old Winnebago thing, which we sat in all day. I think they de-stressed themselves by changing their clothes a lot and Brett recurringly asking me to get him a hair dryer. I went to the production office and they were having Cher problems because she would only take her water in small bottles and they'd bought big ones. So the bloke-from-Suede's hair dryer was not the major concern."

In a perversely appropriate twist, the MC for the evening was *Rocky Horror* creator Richard O'Brien, who announced, "Please welcome the already legendary Suede!" before the band gate-crashed the party.

"Looking back at it, it was fucking awful," recalls Charlie Charlton. "The second I gave Bernard his guitar it went out of tune, I think he banged it or something. So the whole song was out of tune. We had this guy called Levi doing sound for us. He'd never done sound for us before. The sound was fucking appalling. I think Brett sensed it was all going off and went, 'Fuck it! I'm going for it!' And then they went out on stage and there was just this sea of penguin suits..."

Looking like street urchins next to the dickie-bowed audience, with Brett playing the Artful Dodger after a raid on a lingerie shop, the band ripped through the song as if expecting to be pulled off the stage at any moment, which wasn't altogether unlikely. The spectacle of a young buck flagellating himself with a microphone while screeching "what does it take to turn you on now you're over 21?" was not your typical Brits fodder and Suede stood out like a fart at a funeral. At home, the young Brian Molko took notes.

"Everyone was like, 'What the fuck is this?'" continues Charlie. "The sound in the room was awful, the playing was horrific, and it was brilliant. It would be great to see something like that on the Brits now where the entire room goes...'duh?' It was just incredible."

"I think one of the reasons that 'Animal Nitrate' crossed over was that we had broken out of the pages of the *NME* into real people's living rooms," reflects Brett. "We felt like snotty little kids that had gate-crashed this big glitzy party and I felt great about it. I didn't feel intimidated. I thought all these people were a bunch of prats, these fucking stupid showbiz idiots like Cher. I felt even more justified about what we were doing. I felt we were making real music about real things and doing it with guts and passion and I felt these people were just a bunch of fakes. And so we went on stage and just ripped it up. It was really bad musically. It didn't sound good. But it was attitude."

"The performance was amazing," enthuses Jon Eydmann. "And obviously all credit to Bernard for taking his coat off and then playing the song, putting his guitar down and not leaving the stage till he'd put his coat on again. I mean that was hilarious, absolutely brilliant. I know it was a mess, but it was amazing to think they'd gone and done that in such a short period of time."

The aftershow party was a suitably celebratory affair. "We all got backstage and the Es came out, and everyone just got completely fucked up," remembers Charlie. "There was a funfair there and everyone just had a riotous time in the venue, pissing off the people in the penguin suits. It was like performing in front of your parents. I'd never seen anything like it before."

Neither had Saul Galpern's mother, who phoned up her son to offer words of sympathy for what had surely been the end of his promising new band's career. "She phoned up and said, 'Oh, Saul, I'm so sorry! I've just seen Suede on the Brits, are you okay?'" he laughs. "That was the greatest moment at that time."

Perhaps the most shocking aspect of the band's performance was Brett's get-up. His penchant for wearing increasingly effeminate second-hand blouses had already been arousing and outraging audiences, but this lacy number took the proverbial spunky biscuit. "He had a super-gay three-quarter shirt," remembers Charlie. "Every gig would be a different top because they'd just get trashed during the show. And they all wore the same crappy shoes, those moccasins that fell apart."

"I think I was just starting to realise that I was really enjoying pissing people off," Brett muses. "I dunno where all the femininity came from. I think it sort of distorted and it inevitably became the sort of thing that people took the piss out of me for. And even now people still think of Suede and often think, 'Oh, they're that camp band.' And that's my own fault because I probably pushed it a bit too far."

Sure enough, Suede soon found themselves parodied on the then enormously popular *Newman & Baddiel In Pieces* TV show. In a frighteningly accurate pastiche, David Baddiel minced around yelping, "Woops, duckie, what a gay day!" reinforcing the band's prevalent public image.

"We ended up having *Spitting Image* taking the piss and stuff, which didn't really happen to our kind of band at the time," adds Mat Osman. "And there was a sense that suddenly there was one bit of Suede that we couldn't control, which was the image of it."

It's difficult to feel a huge amount of sympathy for the band's protestations that accusations of flirting with androgynous imagery were exaggerated, if not completely unfounded. After all, here was a man sporting girl's blouses and a girl's haircut, spouting comments like "sometimes I feel like a woman" and singing about violent gay sex while battering his microphone-cum-phallus against his buttocks, before announcing that the last thing he had in his mouth was cock.

"It did go too far," admits Brett. "But there was something I quite liked about it, the ridiculousness. I didn't feel it was feminine in a soft way. It was quite aggressive. It was almost sexually feminine, that was the idea. Probably a lot of people thought I looked like an old granny that had fallen into a dressing up box at the time. And I think I did push it too far. I remember we did a thing on *The Tube* and I saw a video of it and I actually looked like I was in drag. But whatever, you've got to break a few eggs to make an omelette."

"Animal Nitrate" was finally released on February 22 and crashed straight into the Top Ten. "It went in at seven and then it stayed at seven, because of the Brits," says Saul Galpern. "So it was a proper hit. And in those days for an indie band to do that was unheard of."

Despite the huge amount of momentum the press had given the band, the single's enormous success still took Brett by surprise. "I was amazed. You know it's about violence and abuse and sex and drugs. It's actually quite a hardcore song. And the fact that it's got a nice little melody and it's radio friendly was highly successful in that sense. It actually crossed over. It went in at number seven and the next week it stayed at number seven. The kind of band Suede is, our fanbase buys our record and it goes in high and then it drops, blah, blah, blah, and that's the pattern it's been. And that record obviously crossed over to another audience, which was great."

But as has been mentioned before, the song was very nearly never a single at all. "When we wrote 'Sleeping Pills' we thought 'Wow, this is fucking great!' We were really proud of the song, we thought, 'This has got to be the third single!'" says Brett. "We wrote 'Animal Nitrate' and Saul said, 'No, we've got to have this as the third single.' And we trusted his judgement and I think he was right."

Alongside frantic live favourite and long lost classic "Painted People", the single was backed with a brand new ballad, until recently known by its working title "Samba" but now christened "The Big Time", an obvious allusion to the perils of fame. "That was probably the first thing that we'd written that hinted at that orchestration," says Brett. "Even though 'Sleeping Pills' actually was orchestrated, we wrote it as a guitar song, and we played it like we did live and the orchestration was just padding. Whereas 'Big Time' had that almost show tune,

Scott Walker thing to it. I was really excited by it, getting the flugelhorn in I thought, 'Wow, that's really cool!' No one else was doing stuff like that at the time. Bands like us didn't get brass players in, or if they did they were playing some corny riff. Bands in our category weren't making music that sophisticated. I thought it was a good tune, I liked the lyrics as well."

The single was accompanied by the first of several promos directed by Pedro Romhanyi. The film brought with it further gender-bending controversy. Scenes involving a fat lady in a bikini and someone kissing a man with a pig's head were cut from various screenings, though to this day no one seems to be quite sure why. The censors would have no doubt been even more perturbed had they known that the band's furious performances were fuelled by vast amounts of cocaine. "The first couple of takes were done and they just weren't very good," explains Charlie Charlton. "Just no one was into it. Someone, possibly Pedro, suggested getting in the mood. So they had a few lines and the takes after that were nuts. And that's the video."

By this time cocaine – the ultimate symbol of rock star decadence – had overtaken ecstasy as Suede's drug of choice. Simon Gilbert had tried it for the first time during the recording sessions for "Metal Mickey" on July 16. From that date his diaries for the next couple of years are increasingly punctuated with the none-too-cryptic code of a small "c" in a little circle. He was determined to make the most of his new-found celebrity status. "I thought it was completely overrated," he admits. "But it's one of the things you do. You're a popstar so therefore you have to take cocaine. It was more an element of that than enjoyment."

In February he moved out of the flat in Stepney into a new place in Gloucester Road. "I thought, 'I'm getting money now, I'm going to move to the poshest part of London,' so I moved to Knightsbridge, which was amazing," he recalls. "This was 180 quid a week, which at the time was fucking shit-loads of money. It was beautiful, it was fucking palatial. Every night they had the horse guards with the cannon trotting by and it was like, 'Fucking hell, this is posh!' Perfect place to do cocaine, which I consequently started doing regularly the day I moved in."

Expanding the increasingly blurred lines of sexuality in Suede's universe, Simon chose the promotional campaign around the latest single to confess his own sexual preferences to the rest of the world. "Simon actually came out in our offices in Greenland Street to the *NME*, to John Mulvey," remembers Phill Savidge. "We were doing individual interviews and he kept saying, 'Will it be allright?' and I said, 'Yes, just do it.' I locked the office door while Simon did his interview and everyone else went and played on the roof."

In a neat twist of Brett's most infamous utterance, Simon declared, "I'm a bisexual man who's never had a heterosexual experience. That's a bit of a statement, innit?" It certainly was, instantly endearing him to a legion of sexually unconfident fans who were beginning to suspect that their hero Brett perhaps hadn't ever tried it that way after all. "At the end of the day it doesn't matter whether Brett's gay or not," Simon sagely observed. "He sings universally – it could be about a gay man, it could be about a woman, it could be anything. What Brett says is so much more positive than saying I'm gay, I'm straight, there's a dividing line and I'm on this side and you're on that side. Fuck the line! I might get a shag now!"

Unfortunately, not all the band's press obligations ran quite so smoothly. Phill remembers a photo-shoot for *The Face* quickly descending into high farce. "There'd been some mis-communication between the photographer and the editors and he thought he was photographing four models dressed as Ziggy Stardust clones," laughs Phill. "Bernard got the vibe that something was wrong, that this guy didn't know who Suede were. It was a six-page piece and it was being cancelled every five minutes. It was total chaos, everybody was trying to score drugs. Some guy came to the studio, some 17-year-old pimp in a suit. We gave him some money for drugs but he disappeared. Someone else was shagging in the bedroom, two guys were shagging, right next to where we were supposed to be doing the photo-shoot. It was a very camp and gay photo session. The drugs did arrive at some point. And they'd brought these Ziggy Stardust clothes. I remember putting on a pair of high heels and going 'Look, these shoes are great aren't they? You can wear these couldn't you?' to Bernard, just thinking at least if we get some pictures then we'll still get six pages. But not a successful move in a way!"

It was hardly surprising then that Bernard soon refused to do interviews altogether, other than with guitar magazines and those specifically relating to his craft. But he wasn't the only one to suffer ignominies at the hands of the music press. After an interview with Amy Raphael for the accompanying *Face* article, Brett became embroiled in a very public spat with his erstwhile hero. "He claimed to have met Morrissey and thought he was a bit of an idiot," recalls Phill. "And the article was published and Morrissey's press officer, Murray Chalmers, said that Morrissey didn't ever remember meeting Brett and we had to write a one-page letter of retraction."

The resultant hoo-ha was dubbed "Suedegate" by the press. "What I was referring to was when I met him as a fan when I was a kid or whatever and I'd gone up to him and he'd been funny with me," explains Brett. "And it got out of control and came back that I'd never met him. And I started saying that *The Face* were talking bullshit, that I'd never said this. It was fucking handbags at dawn. And it ended up with me implying that people who buy *The Face* don't actually read it, so they got sniffy and threatened to sue me or something. And then Morrissey said that thing about Mr Kipling's crumbs, which was very funny. It was very amusing, actually, made me chuckle." Morrissey's latest epigram ended with the stinging rebuke, "He'll never forgive God for not making him Angie Bowie."

Perhaps even more controversial, and certainly of far greater import, was Suede's first appearance on the front cover of *Select*, under the banner "Yanks Go Home!" Without his knowledge, Brett's image was superimposed on to a Union Jack, with Suede cast as nothing less than the pioneers of a new wave of British guitar music. If the Suede-Blur clash at the Gimme Shelter debacle was its immaculate conception, then *Select* was now playing the role of midwife to a phenomenon that would be soon be known universally as Britpop.

"The five bands in the article were Suede, Pulp, the Auteurs, St Etienne and Denim – and we represented three of them. That was Britain," says Phill Savidge. "And there was even a diagram of *Dad's Army*, so that was when it all came together. It might sound xenophobic, but I felt like the indie Biggles at the time. This was a statement by a monthly magazine saying, 'Well, actually, we are doing great music here.' And it was bound to happen at some point. Because you can't go on forever buying American music. They don't come here every day. So you need your own bands."

Although Suede would soon protest that they wanted no part in any kind of anti-American consortium, they hadn't been entirely innocent. Early interviews had them typecast as the quintessential British band. "We're not painstakingly English," Mat had quipped. "We don't refer to Morris Minors...although we do mention Worthing."

Brett himself had further opined, "I still don't understand why English bands persist in Americanising themselves. I don't understand why American music has to be so military and aggressive. Look at Henry Rollins; he's like a sergeant major or something."

Select's rationale was entirely pragmatic. Sister magazine *Q* had already had her fingers burnt by taking the risk of giving Suede their own cover. And even though the band were now about to release the most highly anticipated album of the decade, there was still concern over whether Suede warranted a front cover of their own.

"Even though Brett didn't want to be part of a movement, it needed to be manipulated to move to another level, to make sure that they could carry a cover. So that was the way *Select* covered it," says Phill. "The worst thing they did was put a Union Jack on the front because it just got everyone's back up, but you say that and look what happened. It meant that there was three years of people looking at British music again. So it might have made a lot of people bankrupt and it might have made some shit music towards the end, but it meant there was an agenda, and that people really had to compete with each other. And I think that's good."

The article certainly didn't hamper the careers of Savage & Best's other acts, particularly Pulp, who had recently supported Suede in France and with whom there were obvious parallels. "When we took on Pulp they'd been going for 14 years. People said, why have you taken on Pulp?" Phill continues. "And it was because everyone in our office was seeing Pulp and they were just starting to write amazing songs. But we couldn't get Pulp written about in a monthly. We could get them live reviews but to move to a feature in a monthly paper, the only way we could do it was to put them in this bracket. They needed to be part of a movement because why on earth would anyone write about Pulp otherwise? So it served Pulp's purposes even more than Suede, even though Suede were on the cover."

From that point on *Select* effectively became the Britpop bible, with a clear manifesto bolstered by a cheeky irreverence that caught perfectly the mood of the nation. "*Select* was just out there, much more than *Q* could ever be," says Phill. "*Q* was obviously writing about Bruce Springsteen and *Select* could do what it wanted. And the first thing they could do was say, 'This is our music.' So they did. And it was so Suede orientated that they parodied *Loaded* as *Bloke* magazine with a bloated Brett with a pint glass. And we had a competition to guess the weight of the Suede press cuttings. They had a two-page spread with a photo of the Suede press file! How post-modern is that?"

With anticipation now at boiling point, it was perhaps inevitable that

Suede's debut long-platter finally arrived with a vague whiff of disappointment. Half seriously considered titles of *Half Dog*, *Animal Lover* and *I Think You Stink* had been rejected in favour of plain old *Suede*. The album hit the shops on March 29, 1993 in a sleeve which over-egged the "Ooh, aren't we controversial?" pudding. Half-inched from a book of lesbian photography called *Stolen Glances*, it depicted two androgynous figures caught in a steamy clinch. Were they girls? Were they boys? Did anyone care? It's a pity the entirety of the shot had been cropped to miss out the true controversial component: the girls were wheelchair bound.

As for the contents, the generously apportioned swoonsome ballads fared best, but, singles aside, Suede's punkier edge – a crucial part of their live appeal – was poorly represented. "Obviously, 'Animal Nitrate' sounded great and other bits sounded great, but I just thought it sounded wrong, it sounded woolly, it didn't capture the energy they had live," agrees Jon Eydmann.

"Moving" in particular came in for some serious flak. "The album might have been better if 'Big Time' was on there instead of 'Moving' 'cause 'Moving' for me is just crap," Brett concurs. "It never sounds as good on that album as it did live. There's hardly anything of the energy, it's over-produced, it's all a bit FX, it's a bit grim."

The sudden changes of pace which had been an obvious part of the song's charm were now drenched in a quagmire of reverb and flange. "Can someone please tell me why they decided to do that to 'Moving'?" pleads Jon. "I actually think they did it because I liked it so much. That might be me being paranoid. I always thought it could have been a single and I don't think they ever thought it was. I had a massive argument with them about that. I just said, 'It sounds fucking stupid!', which is obviously not the right way to talk to Bernard. And it wasn't long after that that I did actually say to him, 'You probably need to see a psychiatrist,' which wasn't the right thing to say to Bernard either, which is probably why we fell out."

Perhaps understandably, the reviews tended to be of a cautiously positive nature, as opposed to the drooling sycophancy that had been in danger of becoming the norm. Keith Cameron's review in the *NME* was perhaps the most considered. "Maybe Suede are as relieved as anybody that this record is finally here, at last, with the chance to get it out of their system, to put behind them all the stuff and nonsense of the past 12 months and to move on to whatever the future holds. It's there that these most artful of dodgers will have to prove their mettle."

Unsurprisingly, the album's biggest fan was a Mr Brett Anderson. "When we finished the album I felt really euphoric. I thought it was a classic, a great, great record," he told the press later that year. "And then we got the British reviews for it, and a lot of people had obviously decided that they were going to slag us off. So I don't really think it got the acclaim it deserved. I mean the *NME* reviewed it and gave it seven, and I didn't think it deserved that at all."

"I do remember seven out of 10 and I remember him not being too happy," winces Phill Savidge. "But he's not been happy with a lot of them! I certainly didn't think it was a disappointment in the same way that the Smiths' first album was a disappointment. 'Breakdown' I thought was amazing. In hindsight there's a couple of things I can't stomach any more like 'Moving', but it's worth the entrance price alone just for 'Sleeping Pills' and 'Pantomime Horse' really."

But whatever the press thought, the public knew what they liked and the album shot straight to the top of the charts, the fastest-selling debut since Frankie Goes To Hollywood's *Welcome To The Pleasure Dome* almost ten years before. At one point it was outselling its nearest rival by four to one and it instantly qualified for a gold disc on advance orders alone.

"When we were told it was number one I was overjoyed," says Brett. "We were on tour. We were in Leeds I think. I remember being told and I went to Simon's room to see what he was doing and he was wringing out his smalls over the bath. It was funny, Simon Widow Twankey. At that time I didn't know anything about figures or mid-weeks. I didn't know the difference between a million and a hundred thousand. I really didn't. I'd sort of lost my brain for mathematics. There were a lot of things I had about not destroying my creative muse. One of them was not learning to drive and the other was forgetting about mathematics! So I didn't care about numbers. But I was genuinely surprised and pleased."

While everyone else was celebrating, the album release signalled the end of Jon Eydmann's tenure as the band's manager. "I remember the album coming out and me going to Manchester or somewhere and everyone being okay apart from Bernard," he recalls. "I didn't really understand why he was in a bad mood but it was definitely directed against me. I never did get to the root of that one. Something to do with me not congratulating him on a number one album, I think. I know there was some problem with something that I hadn't done. I went on holiday to Greece with my girlfriend and then came back and wasn't there very long."

As variously driver, roadie, soundman and ultimately tour manager, Charlie Charlton had probably spent more time with them than anyone else throughout the craziness of the previous year. "Mat called and said come over to Simon's in Gloucester Road," he remembers. "I walked in and the band was there with Saul. I thought Brett had been busted. They asked me how I thought it was going and I said pretty good. They asked me how I thought Jon was doing and I said I thought he was coping very well."

The band obviously disagreed. They had already decided that Charlie was to replace Jon, who at just 22 was a good few years younger than most of the band members themselves. "I do remember Saul being particularly cagey, when they were doing the video for 'So Young' and I couldn't understand what was going on," continues Jon. "And then Mat turned up and that was pretty unpleasant really."

"We didn't think he could handle a big band to be honest," explains Mat. "We'd gone to America and

met some labels and he just got drunk all the time. He's very sweet and he loves a laugh but he'd just treat it like a holiday, which I think we all felt was our job. I had to tell him he was fired, which was fairly horrible. Bernard wanted to do it, that's why I did it. Because you really don't want to be sacked by someone who's happy to do it! It was a big thing. It wasn't just Jon; Fiona his girlfriend we knew well, and his kid. There was nothing vaguely professional or business-like about Suede. Jon was out with us every night, his girlfriend was out with us every night. He had a basement office you could fit a chair in. So it wasn't like sacking some big corporation, it was a guy we knew. And I'm really glad he doesn't bear us any ill will, because I probably would."

It was a messy end to their relationship and Jon eventually took Suede to court for wrongful dismissal. "No one could actually say why they got rid of me. So I won, and got paid for it. I never got a gold disc, though."

Happily Jon remains philosophical about the whole experience. "It was bonkers, we weren't very old. It was a bit odd to go through all that and then not see any of them. But it was great, I wouldn't change any of it."

With Charlie at the helm, the band embarked on their first European tour. "The first gig was Finland, which was okay, and the second gig was Stockholm, which was absolutely brilliant," remembers Brett. "I met a Swedish girl called Pernilla and she came to a gig in Barcelona and we had a couple of days off in Barcelona where I was hanging out with her. And I remember meeting Bernard in the hotel or something and he was in a really bad mood. And I said, 'Oh, how's it been going?' He says, 'I've been working, what have you been doing?' And I was like, 'Oh, I've been enjoying myself,' and I got the sense that I was maybe enjoying myself too much. I know what he'd been working on, he'd been working on 'Still Life'. I think we were sort of writing it for the first album, and we didn't know how the fuck we'd arrange it, we hadn't even thought of orchestras and stuff like that. So I got the sense that he was seeing me in a certain way, demonising me maybe, which developed into the whole split between us."

Brett recalls Bernard becoming increasingly agitated with the immediate effects of his increasing celebrity status around this time. "There were a couple of moments I remember with fans where he seemed to get kind of aggressive towards them. It's difficult to try and explain, but he'd get pissed off with the whole thing of being famous, whereas it seemed that me, Mat and Simon were really enjoying it and lapping it up, it was still fun. And Bernard started to show signs that it was pissing him off a bit and people were intruding into his life in one way or the other. And this was even before shows. We'd be walking to a gig and there'd be fans coming up to us and it was kind of weird 'cause everyone was really excited about the show. It wasn't like he was walking around on a Sunday afternoon with his girlfriend or anything like that."

Back in Britain preparations were under way for Suede's biggest London shows to date with two nights at Brixton Academy at the end of May. These were hastily arranged replacements for the previous month's Kilburn National debacle when the show had to be abandoned on the day due to council licensing problems. The shows were to be filmed for posterity by video director Wiz, for a longform video release called *Love & Poison*.

"The cracks were definitely beginning to show then," reveals Charlie Charlton. "Wiz is a lovely, lovely guy, but he had a definite idea of what the band was about, it was a kind of glammy thing. It was perhaps playing on some of the elements that the media had picked up on that the band were starting to feel uncomfortable with and Bernard was definitely uncomfortable with."

"Wiz wanted to believe that something was going on that actually wasn't," Bernard told the *NME*. "He had this image in his head of this mythical rock band that he always wanted to be in – he's a failed indie guitarist or something – and I think he wanted us to reflect that, following this character from her bedsit to the concert where she'd stand in front of her idols. And she was meant to wear a Union Jack vest, and that's something that has nothing to do with me. So we had to put our foot down quite seriously. Wiz wanted us to be this idolised band that people are obsessed about. A lot of people are, I know, but a lot of people like jumping up and down and singing 'What does it take to turn you on?' That's the truth of the matter."

There was, however, a far more serious reason for Bernard's discomfort. His father had just been diagnosed with terminal cancer. "Three weeks before everything had been fine, there hadn't been any problems," recalls Charlie. "And then his dad had said he'd had a bad chest and had been taken into hospital and we didn't think anything of it. And then suddenly his dad had cancer and it was really, really serious. There was no warning, no preamble. There was no emotional communication between Bernard and his family. He was definitely dealing with this bombshell on his own, in the middle of all this madness that was going on around the band and these video people, who are definitely not the most perceptive... And it just wasn't a pleasant situation. Wiz would want the band to do certain things during the soundchecks so he could film it and Bernard would storm off to the dressing room, up three flights of stairs, with his guitar round his neck, stamping his foot. I came in with Wiz and the producer. And we went, 'Come on Bernard, can we just do this?' And he just went, 'I don't want to do this. My dad's dying. I don't want to be here. I'm not doing this!' And then he walked out."

Despite these appalling circumstances, the shows were among the finest of Suede's career so far. *Love & Poison* too was a beautiful artefact, capturing a band at the peak of its powers. There were some memorable images including footage of the band projected against two copulating naked bodies, and five fans pissing the word "SUEDE" against the back of the venue. (One for the trivia buffs: *Melody Maker* journalist Robin Bresnark pissed the middle E.)

Suzanne Bull, who played the part of Angel – the idolatry fan in the film – also starred on the cover of the band's latest single, sitting astride a stone stag, the first time the band had actually shot the sleeve themselves. "All of the early sleeves were simply pictures I found which some graphic designer put the word 'Suede' on and claimed the fucking credit," Brett points out.

With a beautiful rippling piano part courtesy of Ed Buller, "So Young" was arguably the best Suede single so far, certainly the most sophisticated. But it was lifted from a massive selling album, which Suede fans already owned, and so it stalled at 22, still respectable for a so-called indie band in 1993, but nevertheless signalling a noticeable shift in momentum. "It was a real step forward in songwriting terms," reflects Mat Osman. "I think it's a better single than 'Animal Nitrate' but it kind of got lost." This was a shame because although the CD and 12-inch extra track "Dolly" was a throwaway rocker that had been ditched from the set before they'd even been signed, the main b-side, "High Rising", was another breakthrough. A more experimental side to the band was exposed, with Bernard playing harmonium and mellotron in addition to guitar and piano, matched by a beautifully lackadaisical vocal from Brett. As the single slid out of the charts, Charlie called a crisis meeting to discuss Bernard's situation and the band's imminent American tour.

"Charlie told us and we said, 'Fine, we'll cancel the tour,'" remembers Mat Osman. "And he said, 'No, Bernard wants to do it,' which in retrospect was a stupid, stupid thing to do. But we didn't know any better. I look back on it now and it was a really silly thing to do. We shouldn't have done it because the contrasts with Bernard got very wide then. Between his life back home and his family, to be suddenly flown into this tour and doing coke and there's girls everywhere, it's just a fairly light-hearted do. And I don't think he could really handle other people doing that when he was so down. We never should have done it."

The next morning the band crossed the Atlantic for their first tour of the United States. It was to be the beginning of the end.

this hollywood life

AFTER THE MOUNTING TENSIONS of recent weeks it was actually something of a relief to get out of the country. "The first couple of days there were fantastic," remembers Charlie. "We flew into Washington and everyone got through immigration apart from me. I was the one that got pulled. I mean, you've got a bunch of perfumed ponces coming off the plane, dressed in blouses, and they all walk straight through and I'm the one that gets pulled!"

Once Charlie had eventually disentangled himself from customs, the band played their first US date at Washington DC's 9.30 Club. Like most of the tour – a showcase type affair, designed to test the water before their "proper" tour in September – the 350-capacity venue was completely sold out thanks to the blitz of publicity that preceded the band's arrival. The reaction was every bit as hysterical as any British gig and Bernard nearly lost his trousers during the mêlée.

The rest of the tour was largely successful save for a poorly attended show in Boston and a minor catastrophe in Toronto when some of the band's equipment was stolen, sadly not for the last time. In Los Angeles Suede made their US television debut on Jay Leno's *Tonight* show with a slightly raggedy version of "Metal Mickey", which was already picking up plays as a promo-only release on college radio.

Simon Gilbert was having the time of his life, acting out the rock-'n'roll dream to the full. "The coke you get in America is a lot different from the stuff you get in England, it was really strong, real cocaine," he remembers. "And this is a three-day party of no sleep. I went into the tour manager's hotel room and all the papers for the tour, all the accounts and everything, money, cash, everything was just laid out on the floor in a mess. And he was sitting in front of this huge pile of cocaine and Evan Dando was in the corner going, 'Uuuurghh!' It was real crazy. Big time madness, but great fun!"

"LA was fantastic," agrees Charlie. "That's possibly where we had crystal meth for the first time and Brett put a bag on his head saying, 'Bring me a small child!' and Bernard went, 'You're a paedophile!' I'm pretty sure that's when that happened."

This is one of the most legendary stories in the annals of Suede mythology. Accounts differ, but the most popular version is that, after deflowering a young virgin, Brett leapt on a table and demanded, "Now bring me a nine year old!"

"It was just a silly joke, you know," protests Brett. "Just some stupid thing you say when you're off your tits. It turned into some ridiculous thing. It was just a joke."

Brett was certainly fuelled to the max. "Was it crystal meth or crack? It might have been when we did crack for the first time," ponders Charlie. "We were at some bar in LA, sat round the table. Brett got taken out the back by some Suede fan who said, 'D'you wanna try this?', gave him a glass phial, had a bang on it, got a headache, didn't think anything of it, came back in, got on the table, put a brown paper bag on his head and said, 'Bring me the head of a nine year old,' or something like that."

Whatever the truth of the matter, Bernard was conspicuously unimpressed by his colleagues' increasingly wayward behaviour and during the soundcheck for the LA show, he disappeared altogether. "He fucked off during the soundcheck, no one knew where he'd gone," Charlie remembers. "I found him walking down the street and I was running backwards in front of him going, 'Bernard, what are you going to do? Bernard where are you going? You're in Downtown Hollywood. If you go this way you're gonna get shot!'"

Bernard eventually returned and the gig itself was another resounding success, but for the rest of the tour, the two parties barely spoke.

"I remember thinking this is utterly ridiculous," says Mat. "People were throwing themselves at us. Everyone wanted to see us, everyone wanted to hear the songs and I was just thinking, 'If you're not happy with this then something is wrong, because this is as good as it's gets.' Obviously, aside from his personal problems at the time, if being with the rest of the band in a situation as good as this is painful to you, then you should go, because this is as good as it gets in a band. You're over in the States for the first time, everyone wants you, everyone's pushing at you, everyone's out to make sure you have a good time – people are employed to make sure you have a good time. It was crazy."

"Yes, it did start to go wrong with Bernard, very wrong," admits Brett. "I think a load of it was everyone else was probably taking too many drugs and meeting too many girls and enjoying ourselves. And Bernard was in love with his girlfriend, Elisa, and obviously he didn't want to be unfaithful to her and everyone else was just enjoying themselves and I think he felt very isolated by that."

The widening chasm was exacerbated ten-fold by his father's illness, which the rest of the band seemed to have put to the back of their minds, if not forgotten about all together.

"That's part of the problem, no one accepted any responsibility or did anything human," agrees Charlie. "There was no 'I'm really sorry for what you're going through'. There was just this blind tunnel vision. 'We're doing what we're doing and if you can't do it, then fuck you.' That's part of the problem. No one talked to anyone. We were guys in our early 20s and generally you don't know how to articulate those kind of feelings. What do you say? 'I'm really sorry about this.' Fucking hell, it's your dad! You can't imagine what that feels like. Whereas Brett, who'd been through the same thing with his mum, just got on with it. There was never any moment where the two of them sat down and Brett went, 'I'm really sorry about what's happened. I've been there.' There was none of that. They were just two polar opposites and that's kind of what the magic was."

As if to compound their current difficulties the band returned to the UK only to find their staunchest ally, *Melody Maker*, running a cover story titled "Suede hit America – America hits back!" suggesting that the band had come a cropper.

"I think what happened was the *NME* came over with us. And they were doing a piece on Suede in America," says Brett. "And at the time there was a lot of snappy rivalry between the *Melody Maker* and the *NME*. And I think *Melody Maker* discovered that the *NME* were doing a cover feature on Suede in America and so they did one the week before basically saying that Suede were fucking up. It wasn't true, we were just starting to play there."

Phill Savidge handled the crisis with typical aplomb. "I remember people ringing up and they were saying, 'Well, I see Suede aren't cracking America like they did Britain.' And rather than me going, 'Oh my god, it's all crumbling!' I just went, 'Isn't that great news? They don't get it and we do. Doesn't it just show you that Americans have got no taste?' And I think some people were like, 'What?' They expected us to crumble in the face of adversity. And I'm glad I did that because they were like, 'Yeah, why am I slagging them off when I should be supporting it?'"

All seemed to be back to normal when Suede headlined the *NME* stage at Glastonbury a few days later. It was a spectacularly confident performance, betraying none of the difficulties of recent months. The audience reaction was astonishing and their enthusiasm was rewarded with a rare Suede encore. Rather than deliver an old favourite as most bands would do, Suede chose the opportunity to unwrap one of their most striking creations to date. "Still Life", in this incarnation – just Brett accompanied by Bernard battering an acoustic guitar – was musically a sequel to "The Next Life", though lyrically it continued Brett's fascination with the plight of the average housewife as begun on "Sleeping Pills".

It was an awesome moment which Phill Savidge clearly recalls. "The *NME* had put them on the cover with 'Carry On Camping' or something, which was Brett and Bernard on the cover together for the first time. And I remember standing next to John Mulvey and saying, 'Aren't they absolutely astonishing?' And he said, 'Yeah!' And I said, 'Cover next week as well?' And he said, 'Yeah, alright then.' And I was just thinking, 'We could just go on like this for ever, every week because they're just so great!' And obviously they didn't put them on the cover, but it was a nice moment."

They followed Glastonbury with a short, six-date tour of Japan. Much of the travelling was done by bullet train and the fan hysteria was whipped up by Japanese radio leaking the details of stations where the band would be interchanging, ensuring a frenzied mob greeted them wherever they went. Charlie Charlton remembers the trip fondly: "The tour was great but the overriding memory of it is sitting in the dressing room listening to these little Japanese girls sat in the car park singing 'Animal Nitrate', like a chorus of three-year-olds. Definitely melted Bernard and Brett's hearts. It was such a sweet, sweet moment."

Accompanied by his girlfriend Elisa on the Japanese tour, Bernard seemed in far better spirits, though his disquiet with the seedier side of the business was made clear in an interview with a Japanese fanzine: "Please always love our music and only what we say in our music above everything around us. Then remember that music is only a start in life, not the whole story."

On July 12, Suede staged a genuine "event", a fund-raising collaboration with filmmaker Derek Jarman, who had made his name in the '70s
with the über-camp *Sebastien* and the apocalyptic punk nightmare
Jubilee. Having gone on to shoot music promos with the Smiths and Pet
Shop Boys, two of the prime influences in Brett's original "Guitar player
wanted" ad, a collaboration with Suede seemed inevitable. By this time,
though, Jarman was desperately ill, a victim of the ravaging AIDS
epidemic. "Basically, he was on the way out at that point in time, and he
knew it," says Charlie. "So he was casting around for people to work
with. We liked his stuff. We met his people on the 'So Young' video and
we wanted to do something a bit special."

As well as performing to a backdrop of Jarman's Super-8 home
movies, the band also invited several special guests to take part. The
extravaganza, held at the Clapham Grand in London, began with "The
Big Time". In Brett's place stood Avi from Sharkboy, recently signed to
Nude. Many in the audience initially mistook her for Brett in drag.
Other members of Sharkboy contributed trumpet and cello while, later
in the set, Siouxsie Sioux and Bernard played an acoustic duet of Lou
Reed's "Caroline Says" and Chrissie Hynde joined the whole band for
"Brass In Pocket".

"We were starting to feel a little bit constricted by being just a four
piece band," explains Brett. "I think we were starting to want to do other
things. I'd met Chrissie Hynde before at a photo-shoot. She was really
cool so we gave her a call. I think we were collaborating with Siouxsie
and Chrissie Hynde, sort of people from maybe a different generation
because we'd always had a sense that Suede didn't want to be seen as
part of a pack. People have interpreted that as snobbery but it was just a
desire to be doing our own thing, being in our own little world."

Derek Jarman introduced the show with a rapturously received
speech on the age of consent. "He wasn't in great shape," remembers
Charlie. "We weren't even sure if he was coming down to the gig
because he was so ill at the time. And he sat in the box. Then right after
the show he came back to say hi to the band. There's that fantastic
picture of Bernard just beaming and Derek happy as Larry, but an old
guy on his way out. It was a genuinely special moment."

Phill Savidge remembers the show feeling markedly different from
your average gig. "It was very grand. It felt like they were doing something important." John Mulvey agreed, with another ecstatic review in
the *NME*. "As a huge, celebratory version of "So Young" flounces out,

with producer Ed Buller on piano and Brett balancing on his monitor and lashing his mic lead round in a wide arc, all the reasons why Suede matter come flooding back, all that ambition, ego, drama, vitriol, passion, controversy, pure naked thrills...this is Suede proving they can triumph over the sideshows with real *hauteur* and rampant excitement. Impeccable, just impeccable."

Aside from a rare outing of "High Rising", "Still Life" was the only new-ish song played at Clapham, but there were many more in the pipeline. Rare home demos from July '93 expose the extreme differences in the working methods employed by Bernard and Brett by this time. Bernard would craft immaculate multi-track demos, putting down layers of guitar and keyboard parts over a drum machine. In the main these tended to be very similar to the end results. Brett, on the other hand, preferred to ad lib spontaneously over the top, unleashing a stream of (un)consciousness which he would later tidy up and make sense of on an old manual typewriter. His voice would be vari-sped to make hitting the high notes easier, at the same time making him sound as if he was on helium. In fact, helium was probably about the only thing he wasn't on. Yet the means continued to justify the end, for it's arguable that songs like "Stay Together" (sample lyric: "I was born in a nuclear storm, out of my head in a tiny home"), "Losing Myself" ("New Generation") and "Jazzy" ("Black Or Blue") were unlikely to have emerged by more traditional methods. Only one song from the period was shelved. "We Believe In Showbiz" was based on an interesting keyboard backing from Bernard, reminiscent of the theme tune from *World In Action*. Brett's vocal, though, featured some histrionic screeching that would test the patience of even the most devout fan. Never one to avoid recycling, he would re-use many of the lyrics in "Europe Is Our Playground" years later.

The first new song to be recorded properly was an eight-minute epic which would serve as an interim single to bridge the gap before the next album. The sessions were fraught with tension and what was supposed to be a quick two or three days in the studio ended up lasting a fortnight. "I'll admit that when we recorded 'Stay Together' I was stoned 24 hours a day," Bernard told *Vox* a year later. "My dad was dying. I was having a shit time. I was getting up, going to see my dad and then coming to the studios at midday, working until midnight. It wasn't nice. My father was dying and I had to make a record. He told me to do that. It was a real-life decision, a million miles away from pop music and the press.

Whatever I did on 'Stay Together' was the A to Z of the emotions I was experiencing...defiance, loss, a final sigh."

Then, on September 8, Suede won the coveted Mercury Music Prize, widely regarded as the only award worth winning, based as it is on music rather than backslapping. The awards took place at the Savoy Hotel. Bernard was absent, visiting his father in hospital, but his presence was keenly felt. Accepting the award, Brett immediately announced that Suede would be donating every penny of the £25,000 prize money to Cancer Research. "Bernard and I have both been seriously affected by cancer," he explained. "There are a lot more needy people out there in the world than us."

Despite this noble gesture, Brett maintains that Bernard never discussed his father's condition with the rest of the band. "He didn't talk about it to anyone. He never opened up like that. It was strange because when we won the Mercury Music Prize we'd said that if we won it we were going to give it to Cancer Research because of my mum and his dad...you know. That was quite an emotional moment. There was a lot of shit going on with the band and Bernard didn't turn up to the ceremony. His dad dying and stuff was all part of the process that it was turning a potentially happy moment into something potentially very sinister for him."

Simon Gilbert insists he knew nothing of Bernard's father's illness until that moment. "We didn't think we were gonna get it so we got absolutely caned off our minds," he remembers. "And then we gave it away to cancer, which is the first time I heard about Bernard's dad. I remember thinking it was great that they were giving it to cancer research because of Brett's mum and I think Brett said 'Bernard's dad's got cancer and my mum died of cancer.' And I thought, 'Really? Fucking hell.'"

Bernard's father passed away three days later, just as the band were about to begin their second American tour. While Bernard and Brett's partnership had long been largely professional, based on a mutual appreciation of each other's considerable talents, it is understandable that this tragic event marked a rapid deterioration in the band's relationships. The first week of the tour was cancelled, with the band flying back to London from New York. When the tour did resume, Bernard distanced himself from the rest of the band far more noticeably than before, even travelling separately.

Meanwhile, eager to press on and "crack" America, Brett, Mat and

Simon indulged in probably the worst excesses of their career. "Everybody else was out partying and enjoying the rush of success and he was obviously unable to enjoy that because of what was going on with his father," admits Brett. "And he was missing his girlfriend and so it basically contributed to him feeling very alienated from the rest of the band. He started not travelling with us. That was all a bit weird. Bernard was actually travelling with the Cranberries on their bus and hanging out with them. Also, Alan was out there with us and Alan was obviously my mate, whereas maybe if Alan hadn't been there I would have hung out with Bernard a bit more. Maybe he felt that there was another person missing that he could have spoken to. It's not until you see it with a bit of perspective that I kind of realise I could have dealt with it better."

"I can't really understand why we went on with it," reflects Mat. "It had reached that extreme that we just kept on going. All that happened in the band's life, we kept on going. When things fucked up, we kept on going. So that's what we did. Whenever we'd had a problem before we just played more or wrote more and we just didn't know that that wasn't the way round everything. The whole band had been virtually founded on a state of aggressive denial, 'I'm not gonna worry about it, I'm just gonna get on with it.'"

The tour itself was a hit and miss affair, with expectation far lower than for June's mini-tour, with the press and the public suffering from hype fatigue. The first show in Seattle, birthplace of grunge, Suede's musical antithesis, was undoubtedly one of the worst in the band's long history.

"Seattle wasn't very good, only half full," remembers Simon. "Mat and everyone went back to Jim Rose's house afterwards and they were all hanging things from their bollocks and I was really pissed off that I didn't go!"

Whether due to pig-headedness, antipathy or indifference, Suede neglected to play "Animal Nitrate", the closest they'd had to a US radio hit. "The thing that everyone forgets is that the first album actually did really well in the States," adds Charlie Charlton. "It did 150-odd thousand copies, which for a UK band that hadn't toured at that point in time is really good. But what happened is that Americans are not the most sophisticated consumers and they bought into the press that was coming out of here and *Billboard* was writing about this thing that was coming over to the States. And once they'd done it once with us, they thought they could do it with everyone. So every month there was a new great white hope and most of them were rubbish. And Americans just went, 'You know what, this hype thing doesn't work for us, forget it.' Therefore, it was over. So America's always been a weird deal."

Suede's co-headliners on the tour, the Cranberries, were meanwhile enjoying huge success with their latest single, "Linger", and understandably attracting a bigger crowd in some instances. "Then that whole myth about the Cranberries started, about us having to swap over and us support them and all this shit," says a noticeably aggrieved Brett. "That only happened at one gig. It turned into this ridiculous myth and the truth was somewhere in between, it really was. I'm not saying that we were bigger than them out there, but it was pretty equal and the gigs we were playing out there were pretty exciting."

Despite closing the show, Suede certainly played second fiddle to their Irish co-headliners in Las Vegas, where many of the audience left before the end. Tensions were by now beginning to reach boiling point. "I remember this huge argument in the dressing room," confirms Saul Galpern. "Fucking this and fucking that – a lot of swearing going on, a lot of arguing, a lot of shouting and Bernard and Brett were just shouting at each other. It seemed to just take a turn. For whatever reason he didn't feel part of it any more. He seemed to have lost the plot a bit. He seemed to be on his own. In America he was in hotel rooms on his own and he wouldn't speak to anyone, including me. And I was the enemy as well and I never really knew what I'd done to be so hated. The whole thing seemed unreasonable. Fucking weird."

Alan Fisher, who maintains he got on well with Bernard, often handing tapes between him and Brett when the two weren't speaking to each other, recalls a similar tale: "When we were in America he just flipped. He said 'You two drug takers!' – and he's sitting doing charlie – 'You drug takers!' And we thought, 'Oh my god, the guy's lost the plot!' Pointing his finger, 'You two!' he went into his room. 'Come and sit down and listen to this record!' He was really scary. At that point he got taxis separately to the gigs and stuff. And he toured on the other bus with that Irish band."

"The rest of the band were getting off and getting fucked up and enjoying it and partying and being a rock'n'roll band," continues Saul. "And Bernard wasn't, he was going to his bedroom and playing his guitar. He didn't like it, he just thought it was a bit false and not real, he wanted to do music all the time. Bernard just wanted to be in the studio 24 hours a day."

Revealingly, Bernard later told *Guitarist* magazine, "There was one point in Las Vegas where I could hardly leave the hotel room. I just sat there on the fourteenth floor with my Walkman and my guitar, completely unable to have fun. It can send you mad, it really can. I just wanted to be here at home writing a song, or stuck in the studio sorting out the string section or something. And there were things within the band, like people getting off their faces on days off. I wasn't in a very good state of mind, and it all kind of disgusted me. Sometimes it was fine, but sometimes it made me feel sort of dirty."

But Bernard certainly wasn't the only one whose state of mind was in question. In an interview with Jon Savage for *Mojo*, Brett described a dream about a character called Little Boy. "I asked Mat about it and he told me that Little Boy was the name of the bomb they dropped on Hiroshima. We were flying over the Nevada desert where they did all the nuclear testing. I turned and looked out of the window and, no joke, there was a mushroom cloud there. It was actually caused by a big fire that was going on in the desert. It was one of the most frightening things in my life."

Brett now attributes such visions to cocaine psychosis. "I was starting to see things, not having eaten for four days," he admits. "But I remember that really freaking me out." This nuclear paranoia and sense of impending Armageddon would shape much of Suede's forthcoming material.

Brett celebrated his twenty-sixth birthday the next day in Phoenix, Arizona. There was a sweet moment when Bernard played him "Happy Birthday" on his guitar with the entire crowd singing along enthusiastically, a gesture repeated ten days later for Mat.

The band were especially well received at two shows in LA at the Hollywood Palace, where the crowds were even madder than they were in England. But Brett betrayed his misgivings about America in an interview with *Swayed* fanzine after the first night. "I sometimes think the kind of thing we do will never be successful here because in a way you've got to be quite blank. The kind of bands that are successful here are straight down the middle, which is no criticism of them. I think REM are a brilliant band. I think U2 are quite a good band as well. But they're very straight. They don't deal with the slants of life in which we do. I'm not sure we're going to appeal to someone in the Mid-West or somewhere like that."

Sure enough, while the big cities on the East and West Coasts were quick to embrace Suede, many of the other towns were less welcoming. Simon described the Santa Fe show as "The worst I've seen while being in the band". Then in Atlanta, they suffered the ignominy of having to open for the Cranberries, going on stage at 7pm. By New York they'd had enough and the last few dates of the tour were cancelled. Contrary to popular opinion, it was the rest of the band, not Bernard, who made the decision.

"I said it was because of me," says Simon. "Us, not Bernard, had decided we would cancel the tour, I think because Bernard was becoming unworkable. We couldn't function, he was becoming intolerable. So I said it was because of me, I said I wanted to cancel it. He said, 'Why are you cancelling this tour you fucking cunt?' And I had to lie. I said, 'Well, you know…'"

Brett remembers the final gig vividly. "It was actually one of the most violent and insane – and I think powerful – gigs Suede have ever done, right at the end of the tour when Bernard was splitting off from the rest of the band. I don't think we'd spoken to him for a week. It was quite an incredible gig. We managed to channel all of our anger and all our frustration into something quite good. It felt almost strangely focused. I remember it being mad, evil, nasty but actually really good."

The band had only carried on as far as New York because all the Sony big-shots were based there, supposedly eager to meet them after the show. "We had every one of the top brass from Sony there," remembers Simon. "I think this was when Bernard was so fucking wound up, he was going behind Mat's back, sticking the Vs up at him in front of the crowd. It was really intense. You could see his hatred for the rest of us. And it looked like the audience had started fighting and Bernard stood at the front of the stage going, 'Raaaahh!' Just going insane. And we came off stage and I remember seeing all these people from Sony just completely flabbergasted and they couldn't speak to us!"

"They wouldn't come back stage!" confirms Mat. "To be honest it was pretty dramatic. It must have been like going round to someone's house and seeing them split up in front of you and have a screaming row, like *Abigail's Party*. It really was. I think we could all deal with indifference and somebody disagreeing with the way you lived your life, but it was a pretty hate-filled gig. It was a really simple thing. His dad died, he was having a horrible time, and none of us dealt with it."

"The reason we came home early was more to do with the fact that I nearly went insane," Bernard told *Guitarist*. "My dad died, so I had to fly home. Then we started again a week later and even though the shows were better, I just couldn't cope. Playing 'The Drowners' night after night... I realise you have to play your singles but it's very difficult to feel you're not just going through the motions."

By this time Brett had moved out of Moorhouse Road into the basement of a gothic mansion at Shepherds Hill in Highgate, replete with stained glass windows and big wooden beams where, in his own words, "I scrambled my brain on acid, coke and E and out came *Dog Man Star*." The house was owned by a religious sect called the Mennonites and Brett would often hear them singing their hymns while he was writing and/or partying downstairs. Although Alan Fisher officially lived there as well, he spent most of his time back at Moorhouse Road where his girlfriend Astrid was now living, leaving Brett to live a nocturnal existence largely on his own. "I deliberately isolated myself, that was the idea," explains Brett. "It was like, 'I'm gonna go up to Highgate and write a fucking album. I'll see you later everyone!' So I spent a lot of time on my own just watching *Performance* every day of my life. I was starting to go a little bit nuts. I was kind of having visions about songs. Lots of the songs were about visions, songs like 'We Are The Pigs'. I was actually having visions of Armageddon and riots in the streets and inventing insane things, living in this surreal world."

Brett cites William Blake as a big influence on his writing style at the time. He became fascinated with his use of visions and trance-like states as a means of creation. Brett claims that much of the torn, fragmented imagery on songs like "Introducing The Band" and "Killing Of A Flash Boy" were the result of letting his subconscious take over. He eschewed all literature except for books on sex and witchcraft and became seduced by occult master Aleister Crowley and his most famous protégé, film director Kenneth Anger and their pursuit of dark hedonism. Crowley advocated the practice of "Magick", in simple terms the power of mind over matter.

"It was part of having a very fertile imagination," continues Brett. "I was kind of aware that everything was getting slightly strange. I was quite into all these people that had visions and were slightly off their nuts, people like Lewis Carroll. I was into that whole idea of becoming the recording artist as lunatic. I was quite into that extremity, but I was definitely living it. It was good fun!"

He remembers doing a bizarre interview with the *NME* where they asked him to name his favourite recording artist of all time. While the other interviewees volunteered the usual responses like Lennon, Jagger, Dylan, etc., Brett's nomination was a creature he'd invented called Jaquoranda. "I was deadly serious about it," he laughs. "It had a deer's head and wore a sari!"

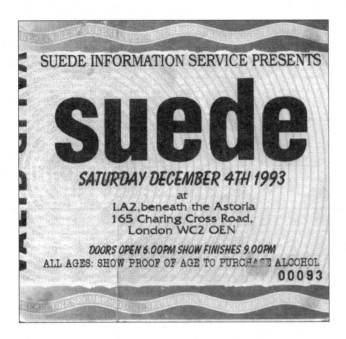

Even Alan was aware that his friend was going slightly off the rails. "He was pretty cut off from reality up there. That's probably why *Dog Man Star* is quite dark and heavy because it was actually in the middle of nowhere. There were no all-night 'offies'. At eleven o'clock it was like, 'I'll go out and get a bottle of wine.' So I actually had to pour a glass of wine and hide the rest in the cupboard because he'd just drink it like Ribena... Honestly, it was like *Withnail And I*, it really was."

As with the first album, drugs, though looming large, weren't the only influence. Brett again had a strong-willed philandering female muse to inspire him. "Daddy's Speeding" may have been a drug-induced fantasy where Brett thought he was James Dean's son, causing the fatal car crash by persuading his old man to take an overdose, but songs like "The Asphalt World" had a firm basis in reality. "That was about my girlfriend at the time, Anick. She had a girlfriend as well, so it was about this sort of triangular relationship we had. It was a very real story, so again there's a sense of truth in the song."

Many of Suede's most obvious love songs, including "So Young", "Stay Together" and "The Wild Ones", were inspired by her. "She was a tempestuous little thing," says Brett. "I got back late once and she'd put a brick through my window. She used to do mad things. She used to go nuts sometimes."

"Black Or Blue" was another true story set to music. Brett remembers constantly spending his evenings in the local casualty department at the Whittington Hospital in Archway after he and Anick had had yet another argument. "It was like that Smiths song, 'Friday Night In Outpatients', it was actually like that. Literally, every time," he says. "I wouldn't hit her or anything like that, but I'd grab her or something and she'd be like 'Oh you've hurt my hand' and she'd demand to be taken to hospital and she'd go to the doctor, 'He hurt my hand!' and the doctor would go 'There's nothing wrong with you, go back home and stop wasting our time!'"

Brett remembers another incident where the police actually arrived at the door after a neighbour had become worried by the violent rowing. "She was rolling around in the garden in Highgate and someone had called the police because they thought I was raping her or something and she ended up shouting at the police and the police trying to arrest her!"

The band resumed touring in November, although the first three weeks of their scheduled European visit were cancelled for reasons no one seems to remember, though the consensus is "Probably Bernard".

Simon vividly recalls rehearsing new material for the tour at Greenhouse studios in Old Street. "We were doing 'Losing Myself'," he remembers. "Bernard was being really authoritarian about how the song should go. I was doing the roll at the end, before it kicks off to the end part, and Bernard said, 'No, don't put it there, put it halfway through.' And I said, 'No it's better here,' and he said, 'Just do as you're fucking told!' And I just threw my drumsticks at him and they missed and hit his guitar, so he goes, 'Oh, you just can't be bothered, can you?' and walked out. Mat and Brett were in the control room and didn't know any of this was going on. So I went in there and said, 'Listen, it's been nice working with you two but he's a fucking cunt. I'm off, goodbye.' And I walked out the door. And Mat went, 'No, wait!' And I got in my car and went back to Gloucester Road and locked the door and took the phone off the hook and thought, 'Fuck you all. I've had enough of you all.' Little did I know that Brett and Mat were trying to ring me all night and they were really worried because we were supposed to be going to France the next day."

By the next morning Simon had calmed down sufficiently to put the phone back on the hook. It rang immediately, Brett urging Simon to come back. "So we flew over to Paris and Bernard was already there," continues Simon. "And I saw him and he saw me and we gave each other a knowing nod as if to say, 'Let's leave it at that and let's not talk about it.'"

The tour had been slashed to just four French dates, notable for live premières of "Trashy", "EAG" and "Losing Myself" – later retitled "This Hollywood Life", "We Are The Pigs" and "New Generation" respectively – plus the forthcoming single, "Stay Together". The live version of this was very different. Much had been made in the press of Brett's so-called rap at the end of the song. In reality it was another stream-of-conscious ramble that proved impossible to replicate live, so Brett wrote a more structured spoken word rant, climaxing in a shriek of "Whipping up a storm like a fucker from the dead!" It's a shame that this vastly superior vocal part didn't make it to the record. "For lots of that single I was exploring ideas of doing things more off the top of my head," explains Brett. "In the same way that the music was quite out there, I was trying to turn my consciousness off a little bit and that kind of manifested itself in the lyrics. It's probably why I don't like the song so much actually. It doesn't mean that much to me. It's a vaguely tragic, doomed romantic love song, but it doesn't have a huge amount of meaning. But that was how it was written, the talking part. It was me sort of chatting and feeling the music and reacting to the music. But as soon as we started playing it live, we were rehearsing it and I just thought, 'This just sounds crap, me talking! It needs to have more sort of form.' So I wrote a part."

And did he get into any special heightened state of consciousness for the recording? "This is where you want me to say I was in the nude," laughs Brett. "I can't remember to be honest. I was probably off my face. I was most of the time during those days so I wouldn't have put it past me."

The same new songs were played to a UK audience for the first time at a special Christmas show on December 4 performed exclusively for the band's burgeoning fanclub at the LA2 in London. Despite recent difficulties, Suede pulled off one of the finest performances of the Butler era in a mammoth 17-song set. Highlights were the three acoustic songs in the middle of the set, notably "Oboe" – soon to surface as "Stay

Together" b-side "The Living Dead" – for which Bernard sported a festive Santa hat. They climaxed with the definitive live version of "Stay Together", bolstered by Ed Buller on keyboards and guitar tech Peter Sissons on second guitar. "God knows if anyone heard what I was playing but I got it right," remembers Peter. "I was just strumming along, there wasn't anything clever about what I was doing. The band said it was the best they'd ever heard it but I don't expect that was through any of my guitar doodling. I think Bernard enjoyed just having someone to duel with, which was quite interesting."

Instead of the usual support act, the show was opened by the fans themselves after Bernard suggested a Suede karaoke. It proved to be hugely entertaining for the band as well as the audience. Brett remembers it being a very happy occasion. "I think we'd had a few problems recording 'Stay Together' with Bernard but I remember it being a fun night," he says. "I remember Bernard bringing his mum along and I kind of met her for the first time, which was really nice. My dad came and Steve Sutherland came. And there was a good feeling. We felt we were in a good place creatively. We'd done 'The Living Dead' and 'Dark Star' and stuff. So there was a good optimism about everything ahead."

They played their final show of the year at The Forum for new London alternative radio station XFM on Christmas Eve. "I remember I was wearing some stupid choker, that was probably the low point of the evening, what I was actually wearing," Brett groans. "I remember seeing pictures of myself and thinking, 'What the fuck am I wearing that for?'"

Brett immediately flew to Mauritius with Anick to stay with her family over the festive season. "It was a real extreme eye-opener," he says. "We went and stayed with her family and they were actually living in serious Third World conditions. Just a real eye-opener to go and live in this corrugated iron shed in Mauritius. The sort of side that if you're a holidaymaker you don't really see of places like the Caribbean and the Indian Ocean, that was quite extreme." 1994 would be an extreme eye-opener for entirely different reasons.

have you ever been this low?

SUEDE'S STAR CONTINUED TO RISE as 1994 dawned and expectations for their hugely anticipated interim single, "Stay Together", reached fever pitch. The band were everywhere, having eaten up the end-of-year polls – particularly *Select*, where "Animal Nitrate" was Single Of The Year – and Brett graced the covers of monthly magazines like *Vox* and *Sky*, almost unprecedented for a single with no parent album. Simon Gilbert was also in the news after making a speech at the House Of Commons on the gay age of consent, in the company of Stephen Fry and *EastEnders'* Pam St Clement. "I met Chris Smith [at the time the only openly gay MP] and he gave me a kiss goodbye in front of all these photographers, and he made a point of doing it as well," laughs Simon. "And I met Pat from *EastEnders* who was lovely and she was trying to get in all the Suede pictures. But it was really nice to see the whole band there in support. Even Bernard turned up, which was really nice."

Simon had actually been to Parliament before, to lend his support during a press conference for Youth Against Racism where Pete Shelley and Brett were also in attendance. "That's the night I went into the House Of Commons and suddenly remembered I had a little silver bowl of coke attached to my key ring. I got through the door and saw that they had all these metal detectors and people with guns and thought, 'Fucking hell, this is a bad idea.' So I put my keys through, and this bloke with a gun picked up the bowl and goes, 'Oh, what's this?' And I said, 'Just a novelty key ring.' And he said, 'Oh, quite nice,' and gave it me back! So I ran into the loos and did the whole amount in one go, just to get rid of it!"

Suede were now undoubtedly the most talked about and sought after band in the country. David Bowie had approached them to record one of his songs for a retrospective concept album (either "Time" or "Lady Grinning Soul", though in the end the project was abandoned), while Mike Leigh, riding high on the success of his classic *Naked*, was rumoured to be filming Suede's next video. The band also made two memorable appearances on *Top Of The Pops*, the first in the company of old acquaintances Elastica, making their *TOTP* debut with "Line Up", the second as a tribute to Derek Jarman who finally succumbed to his illness on February 21.

"Stay Together" itself arrived on Valentine's Day as a fully formed, four-act, eight-minute fantastically ostentatious classic. The single easily won Singles Of The Week in both inkies, the *NME* commenting that "Luxuriating in the ambitious, dramatic, exhausting spell of this makes everything else sound like so much ephemera. Like most great things it leaves you utterly silent."

Crashing into the charts at number three, the song was easily their biggest hit so far, yet the band remained strangely subdued about it. "It's reacting against ourselves to a certain extent," Brett told the *NME*. "The title is incredibly blank but it's how I felt at the time. The ideas in it are very clean, getting rid of all the bits of Suede that have been jumped upon and over-emphasised."

Aside from "So Young", none of Suede's previous singles featured their titles in the choruses. Charlie Charlton remembers Brett choosing "Stay Together" as a conscious decision to display some kind of solidarity within the band. Despite this, disagreements abounded. Simon Gilbert's diary reveals that Bernard even had a problem with the lyrics:

December 20: *Bernard objects to the lyrics in "Stay Together". Here we go again! Lyrics not to be printed on cover of single in case his mother reads it. "16 tears" obviously paedophilic!*

Suede have since distanced themselves totally from the song, an aversion usually attributed to problems with Bernard at the time. "I have no nice feelings about it probably because it was the time that things were going off," agrees Simon. "Once I'd got my drums done I walked out of the studio and didn't come back. Things were turning a bit...sour."

Phill Savidge has a different theory: "Brett has no feeling for it because it's about a girl that he has no particular feelings for, and he can't believe he wrote it about that girl, Anick. And I think it's as simple as that and that's why he's not interested in that song. I think it's amazing."

Another criticism is that, at eight minutes, it's overlong and over-cooked, a perfectly good tune being swamped with too many ideas. Bernard admitted at the time that there were almost fifty different tracks making up the record. While Brett has been particularly dismissive about the song in the past, his vitriol for it seems to have faded slightly. "I don't think the fuss about 'Stay Together' was justified, I think that was just hype," he shrugs. "I just find it a bit bombastic. I don't think the lyrics are that good either. It's okay, you know, it's okay. I think the b-sides are much better." On this, almost everyone agrees.

"The Living Dead" and "My Dark Star" remain favourites of the band and their fans and both songs still crop up on Suede's setlist from time to time. "The Living Dead" is a heart-aching, finger-picking, acoustic duet, often assumed to be about heroin addiction due to lines like "Where's all the money gone, I'm talking to you, all up the hole in your arm, is the needle a much better screw?" In fact, the song concerns Kevin, from Moorhouse Road, and his boyfriend Andy, who had gradu-ated from snorting to injecting cocaine. "They were lovers and they used to spend a lot of time shooting coke up, so it was about them," explains Brett. "It was inspired by them. They were really fun people. The song's very tragic but they weren't tragic in that sense. They eventually died of AIDS, which is a tragic thing to happen, but my relationship with them was they were my mates." Incongruously, for such a beautiful ballad – or perhaps not, considering its subject matter – the song was recorded in a toilet. "I'm not sure if it's the final version you hear," says Brett, "but there was definitely a version where Ed wanted to do just a live version of the song with natural reverb from the bathroom."

Again, Bernard took issue with Brett's lyrics. "I remember him having a real problem with 'The Living Dead'," confirms Mat. "With him saying, 'I've written this really beautiful piece of music and it's a squalid song about junkies.' And that was always part of it, he had a more monkish streak than the rest of us. We were much more prepared to take anything that was given to us. Literally, it did used to be like that. You'd go off stage and someone would just stick a pill in you. Partly he thought it detracted from the music and partly he just didn't like the scene."

Fortunately, there were no problems with "My Dark Star" which, if anything, was even better, Brett casting himself as a twenty-first-

century John the Baptist, predicting the coming of a new, female Messiah. "It's about the rise of the Third World and rearranging the hierarchy of international power," he expounded at the time. "It's about all those incredible people from these distraught countries, like Frida Kahlo. You can almost see it in their eyes, the beauty and the dark power that's never been tapped before."

If this sounds slightly pretentious, Brett now admits that he didn't really know what he was on about either. "I did start going off on one a bit," he grins. "It was all part of the insanity of living underneath this tribe of religious lunatics in a gothic mansion spending most of my time taking acid and ecstasy. I don't really know what 'My Dark Star' is about. There's not a neat little story. But I think it's still a good song. Not every song has to have an actual story."

To promote the single, the band embarked on a three-date mini-tour of unusual venues. "We always avoided the big sheds because we didn't want to be just another band. And so even when we were selling quite a lot of records, we were still playing these weird little places, and selling them out in about two seconds flat. I think if we could do it all again we probably would have done it in a different way because I think you need to grow, rather than constantly keeping it small and keeping it special, which I guess is quite nice."

Brett had always wanted to play Worthing because of the line in "The Next Life" and so the tour began at Worthing Pier Pavilion. "We did this sort of 'By The Sea' tour – Worthing and Blackpool and Edinburgh," says Brett, realisation slowly dawning. "Edinburgh's not on the seaside is it?" he laughs. "That didn't really work did it?"

On the way back to London after the first show, the band were pulled over by the police, who had presumably recognised Brett from the front cover of *Vox*, on which he was boldly quoted as saying "I told Morrissey to come round for an E!" "Simon was driving me back from Worthing," remembers Brett. "We got stopped and I think they searched us as well. Fuck knows how they didn't get anything 'cause I'm sure we had loads of stuff on us." One story is that Simon hid the stash in his mouth, but Brett smiles at this suggestion. "I've been stopped by the police before and Simon's been there and Simon's actually just thrust stuff in my hand, so I doubt if he put it in his mouth. He's not quite that courageous. This was a different incident but he just shat himself and put everything in my hands. But, yeah, they stopped us and they definitely knew who we were. Maybe they followed us." And did Morrissey ever take Brett up on the offer to come round for an E? "No, he didn't actually, miserable bastard."

The next morning Brett and Bernard were booked to do an interview for the *Ozone* in Highgate Cemetery. "I'd been up all night and I got a phone call from Brett at about seven in the morning going, 'Can you pleashe do the interview with, hic, Bernard?'" remembers Simon. "And I went, 'I've been up all night as well!' But to be honest I thought, 'Well, at least I sound better than him.' So, anyway, I went up to this thing in the morning and the first thing Bernard says is, 'Fucking typical, he's out of his head on drugs!' And I said, 'Yeah, really bad isn't it, shall we do the interview then?' Bernard was getting really pissed off with people doing drugs, especially after the 'Stay Together' video, because it was just chaotic, far too much. We turned up and the director's this crazy American guy who was sweating and dribbling with stuff coming out of his nose at 8 o'clock in the morning! And so consequently we bought three grams of coke!"

Brett did turn up eventually and then presenter Zoe Ball, being no stranger to late nights herself, carried the interview with typical aplomb.

The next gig at Blackpool Tower Ballroom, home to *Come Dancing*, was recorded by 1FM, capturing a band seemingly heading for the stars, road-testing material for their forthcoming album in versions occasionally quite different from – and often vastly superior to – the final results. Saul Galpern noticed Bernard starting to take centre stage around this time. "He'd deliberately make mistakes when he was playing the guitar and play the wrong key, which I thought was quite cool and quite edgy."

"I changed all the guitar solos because I love music too much," Bernard explained to *Vox*. "I don't want to be bored by it, like I'm bored with 'The Drowners' now. I hate it. It doesn't mean anything to me."

At the time the band described Blackpool as the best gig they'd ever done. Alas, the next evening's show at Edinburgh Queens Hall would be very different. Brett awoke on the tour bus to the sound of fans playing Suede songs on an electric guitar through a tiny battery-powered amp. Stepping off the bus, he paused briefly to sign autographs and pose for snaps, before darting into the venue. Noticing the dearth of security, the fans gingerly followed and were treated to renditions of "I Am The Resurrection" and "Lithium" during the soundcheck before finally being kicked out. (Yes, I was one of them, having recently started a fanzine, *Suave & Elegant*, detailing my trainspotter-like passion for the band.)

The tension-fuelled gig, plagued by technical hitches with the band looking like they were about to kick the shit out of each other at any moment, is described in detail at the beginning of this book, which is a rejigging of the original *Suave* review. To us mere fans the show was amazing, but the band disagreed. At the aftershow, where Bernard was conspicuous by his absence, Mat told us, "We thought we started off shit-hot and went downhill…we just really fucked up."

Brett still remembers the evening with a notable tinge of sadness. "The Edinburgh gig was just a mess because we were falling apart," he sighs. "I was really pissed off about that whole night. I just got the sense from my point of view it was just Bernard attention seeking. I remember bounding on to stage and really being up for it and the crowd being up for it and just wanting it to be a great night. And I get the sense that Bernard saw me interacting with the crowd and wanted attention of his own and started pretending or exaggerating technical problems. From my point of view that's what happened. And I think that's always a real shame."

No one knew it at the time, but this would be the last time Bernard Butler appeared on stage with Suede. There was no big bust-up after the gig. Bernard stayed in a hotel with his girlfriend while the others travelled back to London overnight on the sleeper bus. "We would always sulk with each other, that's probably where the problem lies," reflects Brett. "I was never confrontational. I'm not saying everything was all his problem. A lot of the problem with our relationship was that I didn't get things out in the open. His way of communicating tended to be pretty aggressive and I'd always avoid confrontation because I couldn't really face being shouted at for ten minutes."

In the preparations for this book I met Bernard to ask him for his participation. He politely and perhaps understandably declined, while asking me not to repeat any of our conversation. But I hope he will forgive this one indiscretion. "Brett and I only ever had one proper fight," Bernard told me. "Perhaps if we'd actually beat each other up like the Oasis brothers we'd still be together."

For now, Suede had a more immediate problem to contend with. An American jazz-folk singer called Suzanne de Bronkart had filed a lawsuit against the band on December 5, claiming she was legally the first person to be called Suede in the US. Having released two albums on her own Easily Suede Music label – a staggering 2,800 copies altogether – she claimed that the music industry and public were confusing her with the hip new British band of the same name. Speaking to the *Washington Post* she said, "When some of my fans saw the Columbia album in retail outlets with 'Suede' in bold print across the top, they thought I'd finally gotten a major record deal. When they took it home, they were quite surprised."

Saul Galpern had already considered the problem of other acts possibly using the same name and early on spoke to Sony Business Affairs to have them register the name worldwide. "They said, 'Don't worry about it, it won't be a problem,'" says Saul. They couldn't have been more wrong. Ms de Bronkart wasn't for turning and after offering a cash settlement, had to change their name permanently to "The London Suede" in America. It's a situation that still seriously embitters Brett. "I've actually always really enjoyed playing America, I really love playing there. The only thing that stops Suede playing America is the fact we had to change our name. And I couldn't go over there and play under the name The London Suede because I was just too embarrassed by it. It's as simple as that. Our first album did about 150,000 over there, which is not bad for a debut album. That was before we had to change our name."

Rehearsals for the next album continued at Jumbo in Dollis Hill, a cheap old studio which the band liked because it had a window which looked over the railway. "The whole thing with Bernard was we'd fall out and then get back together," says Brett. "One of my strongest memories of Bernard was him playing the piano to 'The 2 Of Us' and I think his father either had just died or was incredibly ill. I remember him playing it and it being really emotional. You could actually see him channelling his sadness into this song and I just felt it was so beautiful and so powerful. It was everything that was good about Bernard, the way he could actually write such incredibly musically powerful things. That's the memory I'd like to remember of writing *Dog Man Star*, it being such a beautiful melody that I couldn't fail to write something really powerful to it."

On March 2 Bernard made his last public appearance as a member of Suede, as special guest of the Manic Street Preachers who were playing a benefit for Cancer Research at the Clapham Grand. The rest of the band were in the audience. "Obviously, he was just getting frustrated, he was trying to express himself outside Suede as an individual rather than as a four-piece band," says Brett. "I don't really remember much about it. They played 'The Drowners' and I think Bernard played on 'Motorcycle Emptiness'."

It wasn't the first time Bernard had appeared on stage without his band mates. He had previously jammed with Teenage Fanclub as well as adding what the *NME* referred to as some "interminably out of tune doodling" at a Gigolo Aunts gig at The Powerhaus back in November.

Chased by rumour and conjecture, Suede took refuge in Master Rock Studios on March 22 to begin recording their second album. At the same time their old rivals Blur were bouncing back with their biggest hit so far, "Girls And Boys". The subsequent album, *Parklife*, went to number one a few weeks later. Saul Galpern clearly remembers the first time he heard it. "I was on holiday and I came back and I was in the control room talking to Ed and I didn't know the intercom was on," says Saul. "Bernard was in the booth playing his guitar and I said to Ed, 'I've just heard *Parklife* by Blur. It's a fucking great album.' And Bernard went fucking mental. 'How fucking dare you say that, get fucking out of here now, fuck off!' I always said Blur's next album was going to be huge and part of the reason was to up the ante, you know, and also because from a professional business point of view I could tell it was going to be huge."

Simon Gilbert's diary, gives a stark countdown of a band heading rapidly towards disintegration:

April 12: *Bernard and Charlie had a secret meeting where Butler said he wants the office run like Apple, i.e. secret. Well, we're like the Beatles really, we don't really like each other. It's only a matter of time.*

April 14: *4 tracks of drums have to be re-done. If we'd done it the way I wanted to maybe we wouldn't have to do it again. Fuck 'em all!*

April 16: *I have stopped doing drugs. I'm too paranoid.*

April 26: *Bernard was tolerable. Actually quite nice. Got drums done for "Losing Myself". ELO in next studio.*

May 11: *Charlie says he quits. Bernard doesn't want to sign management contract.*

*Charlie tries to play game with Bernard by standing up to him, by saying he'll
quit to see what happens.*

May 12: *Charlie tells me all. Charlie mustn't back down. Bernard is insane. He
must be brought into line. Bernard phones Charlie and he hasn't changed his
mind.*

May 13: *Went to New Cross to see Oasis with Bernard and Elisa.*

May 16: *Butler shouts at Charlie, 'Just you wait you northern git!' It's actually
now amusing me. Every day is becoming a chapter. A showdown is on the way.*

May 17: *Charlie phoned at 9am. I demanded a meeting.*

May 19: *Crisis over. Bernard says he'll sign after meeting with Kaz and Charlie.*

May 24: *Brett's in the studio.*

May 25: *Today Bernard got married to Elisa!*

Bernard's marriage to his long-term girlfriend Elisa somehow seemed to
consolidate his separation from the rest of the band. Then out of the
blue, he appeared on the front cover of *Vox* with the tag line, "Brett
drives me insane!" Coming from someone whose aversion to doing
interviews was well known, this was unexpected to say the least. It
seemed he'd chosen to vent all his burgeoning frustrations with the
band in public. "I wish I was in the kind of band where we could impro-
vise over and over, but when you get someone like Brett on your hands
it's impossible, because when he gets bored he simply puts the microphone down and ends the song," he said. "He's not a musician at all. It's
very difficult for him to get around anything that isn't ABC."

Saul Galpern had the dubious honour of warning Brett about the
article. "I do remember having to read it out to him over the phone,
Brett was in the studio at the time, so I started reading it word for word.
And all Brett would say was, 'That's not very nice is it?' And I said, 'No,
it's not!'"

The *Vox* article marked a turning point for Brett. This really was the
beginning of the end. "Everything was kind of going all right up until
then," he says. "I remember being really hurt by that and angry, the way
he passed off my contribution as simplistic and he seemed not to recognise the worth of what we'd done together. I think the biggest tragedy is
that Bernard didn't realise how special it was and I thought that was really
sad. I was kind of disappointed in Bernard to talk to the press and not be
sussed enough to realise how they were going to twist it round and obviously turn it into a big story and try and create a rift between us."

Having told none of the rest of the band about his wedding plans,

Bernard did invite them for a post-ceremony drink that night. But for Simon Gilbert, the *Vox* article was the last straw. "I just thought, 'I'm not going anywhere near you after you've said all that stuff about Brett as well in the magazine.' And everyone else went and I thought, 'Well, how on earth can you go, especially Brett? How can you go to his stupid wedding thing?' I was really pissed off."

The article may have had one redeeming outcome, however: it spurred Brett on to one of the most magnificent performances of his career. "The morning I read that interview, I was recording the vocals for 'The Asphalt World'," he reveals. "So I remember trying to channel all this hurt that I was feeling and the iciness I was feeling into the vocal. Maybe that's why so many people like that song so much, because there's an edge to it."

Remarkably, Bernard seemed to recognise the error of his ways and apologised to Brett soon after. "I think he came round with Charlie and apologised. And we decided, right, let's stop fucking bickering, we've got continents to conquer. That was the crux of where it led to. I remember saying to him, 'Look I accept your apology. I think you're fucking stupid doing that, don't do it again. Let's fucking get on with it. Let's stop internalising all this frustration and fucking channel it and use it against everyone else.' I was so frustrated by that whole concept. The fact that Bernard seemed to want to take his frustrations out on the people he should have been with. It was such a self-destructive situation. It annoyed me that all of the people we were competing with, the other bands that were on the scene that were nudging up to us, would all be rubbing their hands thinking, 'I can't believe it's so easy, that Suede are fucking imploding!'"

> **June 6**: *Brett is completely pissed off at the studio. Understandably.*
> **June 7**: *Meeting at studio with Brett, Saul, Ed, Charlie and myself.*
> **June 8**: *Charlie went to see Bernard – 'Brett's obviously a paedophile because he asked 'Lisa her age, on her birthday!'*
> **June 9**: *Spoke to Bernard. Seems he has snapped out of it. For now.*
> **June 10**: *Butler is apparently recording all his telephone conversations.*
> **June 11**: *E x 4. Coke x 1. Acid x 2.*

It was "The Asphalt World" that would trigger the next big argument. The version that finally made it on to the album clocks in at a lengthy nine minutes 25 seconds, but Bernard's initial creation was double that, although he now disputes that he ever wanted the song to remain that length. "Contrary to popular myth I never wanted the song to be longer," says Bernard on his website. "There are tape edits on it but there are on lots of those songs. It's not unusual to change structures as the recording progresses. Anyway, the mix is horrible and doesn't really get the whole dynamic of the song as much as it could. The reverb is just embarrassing to me and the first half of the song doesn't bring out the foreplay and the beautiful words enough."

This isn't the way the other members of Suede remember it, however. "He says that he intended to edit it, which seems like a strange way of going about it," says Brett. "There was a lot of conflict between Bernard and the rest of the band about that song. No one else wanted to do a song that was that long. It was going to be gargantuan. It was about eighteen minutes. There was a huge chunk that we took out. It was a lot of atmospherics and stuff. I just felt it was going too far. I was all for the album being out there but I just felt this ridiculously long version was just boring. But Bernard was very determined – he's always been quite stubborn and single-minded – he was determined that it would be long. I don't ever remember him saying, 'We'll edit it down.' It was always going to be eighteen minutes or whatever."

"I resented the way that song became viewed as a deliberate guitar wank-off and the focus of where I wanted Suede to go," continues Bernard. "It wasn't. I was just into the idea of songs going beyond the three-minute pop discipline, passing through musical time zones and seeing how the atmospheres could change and what you could do emotionally with all that space. I recorded the basics for it with just Simon and we went through quite a lot just looking at each other to produce all the highs and lows, mapping out the bare bones of the song. I knew what Brett had written for the verse and chorus parts but expected he'd use the middle section in the same way as he used the outro of 'Stay Together'. In the end I think the fact that it remains instrumental in that section gives the whole album a meditative moment which sums up a lot of the darkness and fraught emotions of the rest of the record."

The arguments over "The Asphalt World" spilled over on to the rest of the album as Bernard became progressively more dissatisfied with Ed Buller's production, eventually insisting that Ed should be sacked. He would produce the record himself. "He said it to me on the phone, 'I don't want to work with Ed Buller any more. I wanna produce the album.' It

147

became a big sticking point. That was the end of it," remembers Saul Galpern. "He changed his phone number, he wouldn't answer the door, he just disappeared, wouldn't come and finish the album and it all got a bit mad. This had gone on for months and months. I think Bernard thought, you know, 'I write the songs!' And I said to him, 'Brett writes the top line, he writes the melodies and he writes the lyrics, that's quite an important part. In most people's minds it's the most important part.' I think Bernard was embarrassed by Brett. I think he was embarrassed by his voice sometimes. I think he was embarrassed to be in the same band."

Despite this, Saul maintains he was very fond of Bernard and empathised with a lot of what he was going through. "I don't think he enjoyed the way it went. I don't think he enjoyed that Brett was getting the limelight in lots of ways. It was all very strange really," says Saul, shaking his head. "The whole thing was really weird. It was a shame because it was such a unique partnership. In some ways you're thinking this is good because you always hear these partnerships have friction, but if only people knew how tense it was at time. He made it impossible to stay. He used to shout on the phone to me and threaten me, 'If you don't fucking do it I'll fucking do this,' bizarre things, he made life so difficult for everyone it was not nice. There was no sense of reasoning at all. It was impossible to reason with him. It was impossible to have a conversation with him. There was so much angst and so much negativity. Ed Buller claims he's got several phone calls where there was the sound of scratching knives on the phone and it was allegedly Bernard. The other story was that he had files on all of us, he'd make files up. I don't know how true it is. It's one of the stories that at the time seemed believable."

June 14: *Photos on Regents Park house boat. Bernard ignores everyone. The last day I ever saw Bernard Butler.*

June 16: *Ed Buller is now Butler's number one enemy. Today Charlie went to studio. Butler says that Ed has to go. It's either Ed or him. Butler then storms out and goes home. He then phones Charlie. 'He's got to go. Tell Brett to be on my side!' Chaz goes to Brett and tells him both sides of the argument. Butler phones Brett and says to Charlie, 'What are you doing, let me speak to Brett!' He speaks to Brett. 'He has to go, Brett.'*

Brett: *No, we need a producer.*

Butler: *Come on, have faith in yourself for once. We can produce.*

Brett: *No, we need Ed.*

Butler: *You're a fucking wanker!*

Brett gives the phone to Charlie, Charlie saying 'It's me now, it's me now!'

Butler: *You're all siding with Brett, all of you. You never listen to what I say. Well listen to this, Suede are finished.*

He then puts the phone down. He then phones back later and says, again, 'It's him or me.'

Brett was determined that he wasn't going to be bullied and called Bernard's bluff. Saul recalls meeting with Brett, Ed, Charlie and Ros Earls (Ed's manager). They tried one last time to persuade Bernard to stay. "There were phones going down every minute and he was shouting, going mad and insane... 'Fuck this! I'm not gonna be part of the band any more!' This was it, this was the final thing I think round at her house, Brett had decided that's it."

June 17: *Meeting with Charlie and Brett at Charlie's. Same conclusion as yesterday. He is to go after album is finished.*

June 18: *Gay pride. Introduced the Beloved. Off my tits and shitting myself.*

June 19: *Gary [Stout, Suede's engineer] refuses to work with Bernard and Julianne [Reganne].*

June 20: *Butler has left knife-sharpening on Gary's answer machine.*

June 21: *Butler has his telephone number changed and they're ex-directory. He hasn't returned Charlie's calls since Friday.*

June 22: *Charlie went to his house and dropped a note through his door. No word from Bernard the next day.*

June 23: *Charlie gave Bernard final letter after speaking to Kaz. Went to Kaz's in Golders Green.*

June 27: *Cunt phoned Kaz. Wants us to re-record 'Banana Youth' as he knows how he wants the song to go. Sent him tape of 'Banana Youth' to go to another studio. He says it's crap and wants to finish it himself, and 'The 2 Of Us' in another studio. Or he wants to do it with Gary in Master Rock. He rings studio and speaks to Charlie, who refuses to budge. He says he'll do it if Saul gives him permission to work with Julianne.*

June 29: *Bernard complains. "I'm not in Simon's wordsearch in the fanzine!" Bernard starts recording in other studio.*

The popular myth is that Bernard's guitars were left outside Master Rock for him to collect the next day. "To be honest, I always felt that was a silly story," says Brett. "Maybe they were put outside the control room for him to pick up. They certainly weren't chucked out on the street.

Bernard was never chucked out of Suede, let's make this clear, he chucked himself out. He orchestrated all of these things where there was no other decision but for him to leave. And he made me make that decision. He didn't actually say 'I'm leaving'. He made me make an impossible decision. I felt as if I was being bullied into making an impossible decision. I felt as though if I hadn't stood up to his bullying, I don't know where it would have ended."

> **June 30**: *Bernard phones Charlie after receiving the tape. 'Leave me alone. I'll call the police!'*
> **July 8**: *Bernard Butler has left Suede.*

For the three remaining members of Suede it was a huge weight off their shoulders. "It was a big relief to be honest," agrees Brett. "It was hell for a few months, it really was. It wasn't enjoyable. It was an awful, awful, awful, horrific few months, just really tense."

"It was a blessed relief," agrees Mat. "It was getting to be everything was a band-ending decision and one of these days it was going to happen. To be honest he wanted to go. He kept saying things and just trying to find a way to end it. The point of being in a band is that you're doing something you like and enjoy virtually all of it. It's the world's greatest job stroke lifestyle. And if you're not happy being in what at the time was the world's coolest band, then what is the point? It's not like any of us were doing it for the money. We'd never had any money and we didn't have any money then. We were doing it because it was always what we wanted to do. And if he was hating it that much, then he was better gone."

They celebrated by playing an impromptu version of "The Girl From Ipanema" with the Kick Horns, the brass section who had just added their parts to "New Generation". This wasn't quite the end of Bernard's involvement with Suede, however. He was still contractually obliged to finish a few of his parts on the record. Unsurprisingly, this didn't go quite as planned. "He wouldn't come in and do the recording," remembers Saul. "There were one or two guitar bits still to be done. They asked him to come in and do something and I think he went to put down his guitar parts to one song but he wouldn't do it at Master Rock, so they had to book another studio where no one was there except him."

One particularly macabre story is that Bernard spent a day in the studio laying down an unrequested backing vocal along the lines of

"You're all going to die!" "That's actually true," confirms Brett. "I can't remember exactly what he was saying. It was on 'Black Or Blue' and this was after he'd actually left. We basically sent him to a studio and said, 'You are required legally to finish this album off. Go and finish your parts to "Black Or Blue".' And I remember him sending back this thing which was him talking down the mic. I can't remember the exact words but it sounded vaguely threatening. Obviously, he'd just left the band and 100 per cent in his heart hated everyone involved with Suede."

Throughout the compiling of this book, Brett regularly emailed me facts and stories which have proved vital in providing the detail of the story. His thoughts on Bernard are, I feel, worth printing in full:

"I think now finally the dust has settled I can talk about this objectively. Firstly, I will say that I have always thought it was a real tragedy that Bernard left the band. The work we did together was very special, untouchable in many ways. I think part of the tragedy is that he possibly never fully realised this. The rivals that we had at the time couldn't have believed their luck that this untouchable creative force seemed to be internalising their anger and conflict rather than harnessing it as a force to stride even further away. Maybe it was always supposed to be one of those special flashes of creativity like the Pistols, which explodes and then dies, but I always thought there was plenty of gas left in the tank.

"The insanity of celebrity and our rapid rise to fame definitely distorted and exaggerated any differences there were naturally between us. I think Bernard started to kind of demonise me as the fame-hungry fop, seeing my integration with, and manipulation of, the media as something that was diametrically opposed to the purity of his musicianship. Yes, I was enjoying the ride that I thought I had earned but I have honestly never cared for anything else above the music. I also believe that Bernard himself was becoming unwittingly influenced by the intense praise and adoration. Under such conditions confidence develops into arrogance and control into paranoia. It is a basic human response that everyone involved was guilty of. Under these conditions Suede kind of divided into two camps: Bernard and everyone else.

"The breaking point came during the making of *Dog Man Star* when Bernard became increasingly unhappy with Ed Buller's production. In hindsight I agree that many of Ed's mixes did not do justice to the songs but at the time it felt like a childish power struggle. I was wrong to disagree with Bernard about Ed but right not to be bullied by him. When he gave me the 'It's Ed or me' ultimatum I chose Ed because I felt

Bernard's basic unhappiness was too deep to be solved by such a simple decision. I assumed that next I would be confronted with 'It's Mat or me' etc., etc.

"Basically, what I'm trying to say is that I don't think there was anything anyone could do to keep Bernard in Suede. We all tried and we all failed because he was unhappy and at the time I think he just wanted to go. I have always respected him as a musician and an artist and frankly learned a lot from him. We were once friends. I think both of us could have dealt with the situation better.

"I wish him well and would like to speak to him again. It's just that we literally haven't bumped into each other in nine years."

Suede fan Nathalie Fraser happened to meet Blur at the Nyon Paleo Festival a month after Bernard left the band, and they were clearly taking some comfort from the guitarist's untimely exit. "I took the opportunity to ask Damon about Bernard's recent departure," says Nathalie. "He claimed he had done a little dance, which if I remember rightly was demonstrated as 'Parklife'-esque running on the spot but rotating 360 degrees."

CHAPTER TEN
so young

ON THE MORNING OF July 16, as the rest of the music business were ligging at the final day of the Phoenix Festival in Stratford, Phill Savidge received a phone call from Brett. "I lived round the corner in Highgate and Brett had been up for two days and I think he had done a colossal amount of E and he wanted to get some spliff, just to chill out," says Phill. "Why on earth he called me I don't know. I went round on the Sunday around lunchtime and it was quite an expansive flat. Brett had a weird harpsichord thing that he was composing on, but it was like a bomb had hit it or something. There was a massive living room with clothes everywhere, drugs everywhere, CDs everywhere, fags everywhere, and just Brett and Alan, who had, I think, been entertaining a couple of girls. There was a note in the kitchen saying, 'Thanks for a great time!' signed by two girls."

Phill could immediately sense something wasn't right. "I could just tell, Brett thought he was losing something and he was a bit scared that he'd fallen out with Bernard and he didn't really know whether it could go on any longer. The album was ready to go but with no guitarist, the person who'd written it with Brett. At that point it was quite harrowing really. I think Brett had spent such a long time trying to make it, since 1989 or whenever the formation was, and he just thought, 'Four years, an amazing album about to come out, and that's it.' And for some Suede fans that was it. That was quite a strange few weeks."

"It was pretty gutting," agrees Alan. "Highgate was a pretty dark place to be anyway and at that point I could see Brett had a lot on his mind. All his life there's always been these sort of lunatics in his life. I mean there was his dad and then the girl he was going out with at the time, Anick. It was a pretty heavy situation with that as well, she was an absolute nutcase. There seemed to be a load of lunatics around him. And the next thing Bernard leaves. It's like, 'Why am I plagued by these fucking madmen in my life?' He wouldn't talk about it but you could see he was thinking, 'Oh my god, I've got to finish the album,' and it was in the middle of the album. Maybe it was good that he left when he did 'cause it would have burned out anyway because it was quite a fast number, but they still had another album in them, they were still to reach their full potential. But if it hadn't happened then, it would have happened at some point because, as we've all seen since, Bernard's a pretty hard person to work with."

Backstage at Phoenix Festival, the rumours were rife. First thing on Monday morning, Phill received a phone call from Tommy Udo at the *NME*: "Bernard's left Suede!"

Phill was caught on his toes. "Some gossip had got out basically. And I wasn't prepared. It was big news, obviously, so we had to put together a statement. And at that point I thought we could either crumple and go, 'It's a bloody nightmare!' or we could really milk it and we actually got the cover of *Melody Maker* the following week. So I thought 'Is it all over for the best new band in Britain?' was better than a little news story saying 'Bernard's left Suede'. I just felt that Suede were a significant band so there was no point in just having a tiny puff of smoke, it should explode and then go on to the next level. And obviously then there was an obsession about who was going to replace Bernard."

The news was finally broken to the public two days later when Phill's press statement was read out on 1FM's *Evening Session*: "Suede are not splitting up and have no intention of doing so. However, Suede and the guitarist Bernard Butler parted company earlier this month while completing the band's second album in North London. Suede's as yet untitled album is currently being mixed by Suede and their producer, Ed Buller. Relationships between Bernard and everyone else in the Suede organisation had been breaking down in recent months. There were a number of differences of opinion and it would be fair to say that these were of a personal, rather than a musical, nature."

But how could Suede possibly carry on without Bernard, the song-writing genius, Johnny Marr of his generation? His own statement was a cryptic "I'm not insane and I am happy".

As self-appointed Suede fan representative, I made a point of calling Nude Records to find out what was going on.

"Is it true that Suede are splitting up?"

"Erm, who is this?"

"I do a Suede fanzine called *Suave & Elegant*. Are Suede splitting up?"

"No, no. The guitarist has left, that's all. They'll get another one."

Despite such official bravado that it was business as usual in Suedeworld, the truth was somewhat different. For a start, the album itself was still to be completed. And although Bernard had finished most of his guitar parts, there was still much to be done. There was one song, originally called "Banana Youth", that Bernard didn't appear on at all. The remaining trio recorded it three days before the end of the sessions. "We just got in a circle and played it," remembers Simon. "It was like being the Beatles, great."

The song is now better known as "The Power". Brett played acoustic guitar and an unknown session player provided the electric part, copied note for note from Bernard's original demo. "I think listening back to it, it could have done with a bit of Bernard's tension," reflects Brett. "It's a little bit pastiche, a little bit too '70s-sounding, a little bit light and throwaway. And definitely with Bernard it would have had more darkness and it could have done with that."

Asked about it on his website, Bernard's opinion of "The Power" is remarkably similar. "I left behind a pretty well mapped out 4-track demo from which the guitar parts were copied valiantly. I think the chorus is too jaunty and the whole doesn't have the emotional well of the other songs. Oh, and did I mention too much reverb?"

There was a great deal of nipping and tucking still required as well as the majority of the orchestral and other session parts. Impressively, Brett saw it as a challenge rather than a chore. "There was enough stuff recorded for it not to be daunting," he says. "I just remember being really happy that we had the album almost recorded and thinking, 'Wow! I can do what I fucking want with this record, I can actually turn this record from being potentially an unlistenable load of nonsense, which to be honest it was heading towards, and actually rescue it.'"

In addition to trimming "The Asphalt World" to half its original length, several other songs underwent some radical editing under Brett's guidance. "Things like 'Wild Ones' used to have a completely different ending," he reveals. "It used to have a coda which was a new musical part and that was how we rehearsed it and how we recorded it. And after Bernard left I put this new part on – 'Oh if you stay' – and the song would have been very different if it hadn't had that part, it wouldn't have been as poppy. And for me I brought it back from that sort of brink."

As well as the Kick Horns brass section there was a variety of other session musicians involved. "We had this guy who played the zither, a dulcimer thing and that was on 'Black Or Blue' and he played the flute too," says Brett. "We'd spent years as a guitar, bass, drums four-piece and it was really exciting to be exposed to these other instruments and enjoy them and that's possibly why the album sounds a little bit over-done and over-produced and over-orchestrated because we were really seduced by that."

Famously, they even invited a tap dancer to perform on one of the tracks. "That was one of Ed's ideas," grins Brett. "He just had this mad vision that we should have the sound of a tap dancer on 'The 2 Of Us'. He could hear a rhythm and it was just one of those things that was just laughably crap."

Most impressive of all was the 72-piece Sinfonia of London orchestra who played on the album's cinematic grand finale "Still Life", conducted by Brian Gascoine, brother of *University Challenge*'s Bamber. "I can't remember if we did the orchestra on 'Still Life' after Bernard left or before," ponders Brett. "I can't imagine if Bernard was there he would have wanted the orchestra to be quite so bombastic. It sort of sounds like the arrangement was possibly conceived after he left."

The final mixing was completed on July 27. Brett was in general very pleased with the results. "I'm not saying I did a perfect job on *Dog Man Star*, but as far as I'm concerned it could have been just really flabby and had too many ideas. I just trimmed it down and tried to make it more coherent. I think listening back to it you can sort of tell that it was finished off by someone who wasn't Bernard."

That same week *Melody Maker* ran the following advertisement in their musicians wanted section: "Name band seek rhythmical lead guitarist. Influences: Cocteaus, Suede, Beatles. Send photo, details & experience (if any)."

With the album in the bag, the search for a replacement for Bernard began in earnest. A couple of not too serious suggestions had already been considered. "The guy from Gene [Steve Mason], I thought he would have been good. I don't think I ever told the band that!" laughs Saul Galpern. "The bloke from Tiny Monroe thought he was gonna get it because he kept hanging around the studio. It was kind of embarrassing."

Part of the huge influx of new British guitar bands following in Suede's wake, Tiny Monroe had supported Suede at their Worthing show earlier that year and Brett had invited their guitarist, Richard Davis, down to the mixing. "I remember giving him a call and saying, 'D'you fancy coming down?' and vaguely thinking he could be a replacement," says Brett. "I don't think we even played with him or anything. I remember he came down to the session. I remember him in the control room when we were farting around. I'd invited him, but I don't know what the fuck I was playing at."

Neither did most of the rest of the western world, because Bernard wasn't just an unusually gifted guitarist, he was one half of a unique songwriting partnership – and in many people's eyes, easily the most important half. The common perception was that Bernard wrote the music, the thing that mattered, while Brett flounced around in a blouse, slapping his arse in a faintly embarrassing manner. Bernard was Suede, surely? And whatever the remaining members of the band might claim – that they would carry on and everything would be fine – the musical antecedents were not good. When Paul McCartney quit the Beatles, John Lennon's mate Klaus Voorman was touted as his replacement, an idea that thankfully vanished as quickly as it appeared. By far the closest parallel was Johnny Marr's exit from the Smiths. To the horror of the faithful, Morrissey, Rourke and Joyce limped on for a few weeks, recruiting the bloke from Easterhouse to record some b-sides for a just-completed album. "Anyone who says the Smiths have split up will be severely spanked with a wet plimsoll," quipped Morrissey. The sessions were aborted before anything was completed. When they did resurface for a farewell gig with part-time Smith Craig Gannon in Johnny's shoes, they had the decency to call themselves "Morrissey", for a Smiths without Marr was no Smiths at all. Why should things be different with Suede?

"I was fucking shitting myself," admits Saul Galpern. "I knew that Brett was extremely talented and a fantastic songwriter and they were insistent that it would be the same, they'd just get somebody else in and that would be that. Deep down my own thoughts were different 'cause I'd seen it before and I know historically how it works."

Yet despite the incredible odds, the notion of packing it in is one that Brett Anderson seems to have never even vaguely contemplated. He now admits to a certain amount of sheer bloody-mindedness in his determination to soldier on. "I remember Bernard saying to Charlie,

'Oh, I'm going to finish your band' or something like that and I remember thinking, 'No, that's not going to happen.' I felt that the band had a spirit that was bigger than that. Maybe in a way if we'd parted on better terms we might have called it a day with Suede, we might have gone and done something else. But there was a sense that, 'No, you're not going to decide this. I decide this, when it's ready.'"

While the music press were taking bets on whether the band would approach Johnny Marr, Craig Gannon or some other celebrity guitar-slinger for hire, Suede were set on finding an unknown. They would find their new guitarist in exactly the same way they found the old one, through an ad in the music papers. The reality wasn't quite that simple, however. As the tapes started flooding in, auditions began at Southwark Street in South London. "They were a bit grim," remembers guitar tech Pete Sissons. "We kept wheeling in these hopeless cases of people who tried to dress the part rather than play the part. It was pretty sad. I mean, I was worried because they were trying out this guy who came back a second time who could just about play the songs but made it look really, really hard. He just wasn't the right person, but perhaps they were getting a bit desperate."

Brett remembers finding the auditions unexpectedly depressing. "I kind of assumed that there were lots of people out there that could play guitar. I guess I was going through a phase of going, 'Well, Bernard's just a fucking guitarist!' D'you know what I mean? It was that kind of pig-headedness, just trying to blindly convince myself that anyone could do it, which was completely wrong and stupid of me because Bernard wasn't just a fucking guitarist, he was much, much more than that. But at the time I was being like, 'All you have to do is bang a few strings together!' It was kind of like that, but the reality of it was quite difficult."

Other than Tiny Monroe's guitarist, there were surprisingly few applicants from established bands. One exception was the guitarist from Birdland, a kind of non-political proto-Manics who'd made a brief splash in 1989 in a flurry of bleached hair and synchronised pogoing. "He sent a tape in. I don't think we auditioned him. I don't think we were that impressed," says Brett. "I actually quite liked Birdland. I can't remember if it was technically we didn't like it or we just didn't like the idea of having a member of Birdland."

One hopeful who got as far as an audition was Drew Richards from an up and coming outfit called Feline. What Suede didn't know was that Drew also moonlighted for *Melody Maker*. His experience was plastered over the next week's issue along the lines of "I nearly joined Suede", with a crude montage of his face stuck over Bernard's in an old press shot. "The funniest thing about that story though is that we actually came across this bootleg Suede T-shirt in Italy, which had a picture of him on it, which was hilarious," laughs Brett. "The one picture in the world with him in it. He didn't fit the bill to be honest."

Mat Osman remembers one applicant who couldn't play the guitar at all, though he didn't appear to think this would be problematic. "A guy sent in this letter saying, 'I understand you recently lost your lead guitarist. I am not a guitarist. I play the clarinet. But I think I could probably replicate a lot of the lead lines on the clarinet.' And then rather than a tape, 'Here is a picture of me with my clarinet.' Bald guy, beard, topless, clarinet. For ages we were like, 'We should get him in, we should at least try him, it would be a nice day!'"

As the auditions dragged on with no end in site, the "ghost" Suede had the usual round of interviews to contest with. "We had to remain as unflustered as possible and just defend the three remaining members of Suede," says Phill Savidge. "We were promoting the album at the time and we only had three quarters of the band. So it was quite a difficult thing to do and we had to focus on Brett even more than usual, because any picture of just the three of them would look like there was an arm missing."

In the midst of this Brett, Simon and Charlie flew to the States with the *Mission Impossible* type goal of persuading the US media that even though they were no longer called Suede, had lost the guitarist who'd written all the tunes and had no idea who his replacement would be, the future for the band was bright and everyone should buy their new album.

Brett and Simon probably didn't help matters by trying to score drugs the moment they boarded the plane to New York. They met two fans on board who offered to find them some cocaine. "They came to the hotel with us and said, 'We'll pop out to Times Square and get some'" remembers Simon. "And they came back an hour later and said, 'Oh, we couldn't get you any coke, but we got you some speed balls,' and we said, 'Go on then, whatever.' And we tried a couple of lines each and nothing happened and thought, 'Oh this is fucking rubbish!'"

As the two fans of The London Suede left, the speed balls – a dangerous cocktail of cocaine and heroin that led River Phoenix to an early grave – started to kick in. "I thought I was gonna die, quite honestly," says Simon. "Brett did as well. All night we were phoning each other up going, 'Are you still alive? Are you still alive?' We were projectile vomiting. Brett's room was covered in puke, all the walls and everything. And we were supposed to be doing interviews the next day, and we were just a wreck. We were an absolute mess."

The interviews were thus conducted with a bucket strategically placed between the pair. "We had to say we'd had some dodgy prawns last night," laughs Simon, "and we were puking up in between interviews – it was just hideous – and vowing never, ever to do heroin again!"

They managed to stick to this resolution for almost 48 hours. The next evening they attended the *MTV Awards* and witnessed Michael Jackson kissing Lisa-Marie Presley. "We got some coke that night and I remember ending up at the aftershow party and me and Brett just crawling on the floor," says Simon. "Everyone else had gone home. We were just crawling on the floor looking for drinks or something, out of our minds."

While the two members of The London Suede disgraced themselves in front of their US record company, an unexpected believer in the threadbare thesis that this was a band with the world at their feet was Kirk Hammett of metal gods Metallica, who proclaimed himself a huge fan of the band. For Suede's US press people at Columbia, this was a godsend. American music mag *Huh* had a regular feature where two mutual fans from different bands met for an informal chin-wag. An interview was duly set up at Kirk's house in San Francisco. "So we arrive at this big horror house, really posh," remembers Simon. "And you walk in and there's all these oriental rugs everywhere, it was all gothic and you can tell this bloke's got a lot of money and it's what a typical rock star would buy. And we did the interview and then all his friends came over."

The two parties got on like a police car on fire and, in one of Suede's least-known and briefest incarnations, Brett, Simon and Kirk jammed "Metal Mickey", "Ziggy Stardust" and "The Passenger" in the basement. The party went on long into the night and, so the story goes, once the cocaine had run out, a bag of heroin materialised from somewhere.

"I remember at the end of it getting really paranoid and thinking they were just laughing at me and Brett, all these rockers," laughs Simon. "His front window was smashed and he said one of Mötley Crüe had come round the night before and just fallen into the glass. It was all very rock 'n'roll!"

This was probably one of Suede's earliest encounters with that darkest of narcotics, though it certainly wouldn't be the last.

Back in London, with the album release only a month away, the auditions trundled on with no end in sight. Brett and Simon were meeting with Charlie in their offices in a rambling old warehouse in Old Street when they heard an instrumental version of "My Insatiable One". Simon immediately presumed it was an old demo he'd forgotten about. In fact, it was a tape from a fan who'd missed the ad in *Melody Maker* but read about Bernard's departure and sent a tape straight to the fanclub. "It sounded great," says Brett. "It sounded as if he could actually play, so we gave him a call."

A female voice answered the phone. "He's not here," she said. "He's just gone down to the shops to buy some guitar strings."

Suede took this as a good omen. "Ask him to give us a call."

"Oh, by the way," came the reply. "Do you know how old he is?"

They hadn't even considered this. "No."

"He's seventeen."

The son of a lawyer and language-studying housewife, Richard John Oakes was born in Perivale, West London on October 1, 1976, making him Suede's third Libran. He moved to a tiny village in Somerset a year later before settling in Poole in Dorset at the age of five where he lived with his mum, dad, brother, sister and a cat called Morrissey. He was a typical music-loving teenager, brought up on his parents' record collection of the Beatles, Bob Dylan and Caravan before developing a keen interest in spicier post-punk pioneers like the Fall, Magazine, Siouxsie & The Banshees and Public Image Ltd. He loved the stark, uncompromising sound of PiL's guitarist, Keith Levene.

"I'm still ripping him off, I'll happily admit," smiles Richard, "because I don't think it's a bad influence to wear on your sleeve. I remember arguing with my friend Pete because he was into U2 and I hated U2, and I used to say that the Edge had ripped off Keith Levene and he used to get really annoyed!"

Richard had played guitar since he was 13, had also taught himself bass and was more than adept at tinkling the ivories. "I stopped at grade four or five because the moment the music gets too academic or too theoretical I go off it," says Richard. "I did music GCE at school, which to be honest is piss easy. But music A Level I didn't want to do because all of a sudden it's all about studying Latin."

In their early teens, Richard and his friend Pete started a band called The Electric Daffodils who played one gig at a family do. Since then Richard had been in an eclectic string of bands including the school jazz ensemble and a covers outfit called Anomie who rattled off note-perfect renditions of indie staples by the Stone Roses, Blur and, handily, Suede. He'd been to his first pop concert just over a year before at Poole Arts Centre, little knowing he'd soon be filling the shoes of the lanky fretman on the right. "I was a Suede fan. I loved the first album, but they were the kind of band I thought could do better."

Richard was enjoying the summer break before going back to school to do A-levels in classics, history and French when he heard that Suede were looking for a new guitarist. "I used to buy the *NME* and it said on the news page the band are still looking for a new guitarist, so anyone who wants to fill Bernard's shoes should send a tape to this PO Box address. And it almost seemed desperate in a way. They weren't looking for the new Johnny Marr. This plea was open to absolutely anybody. And that's what kind of inspired me to send the tape because I thought, 'Well, I'm anybody!'"

He was actually about to go on holiday to France for a fortnight when the band asked him to audition but realised this was too good an opportunity to miss and took a trip to London instead. He had a startling level of confidence and ability for one so young.

On hand at the band's rehearsal rooms was ever-faithful guitar tech, Pete Sissons, the first person to witness the new line-up. "It was just unbelievable watching him play," remembers Pete. "He just walked in and said, 'Right, who do I give this to, to tune?' trying to be a bit cocky. I think he knew he was up for the job."

The band launched into a version of "Heroine" which Richard had learned from a bootleg of the Blackpool show. Brett, Mat and Simon instantly knew they had found their man. "I think the thing that I liked about Richard was that he was never really fazed by it," says Brett. "He was very young and very inexperienced, but it was never like *Jim'll Fix It*, for him to play guitar with his favourite band. He came along and played and I just thought he was a great guitarist. I've always had quite a lot of faith in my gut instinct about things. I've never been a technical person, I didn't know whether he was technically good at the guitar. But it felt good, so we said, 'Yeah, let's do it!'"

"I remember listening to the guy in before me playing 'Pantomime Horse' and thinking to myself, 'I really could do much better than this,'" says Richard. "It wasn't an arrogant confidence – I was shitting myself – but even being nervous I thought I could play better than that. It was very much a case of keep your head down, play the songs. I remember at the end of 'Metal Mickey' Brett kicked over his mic stand because he was so excited. To my young innocent eyes I thought, 'Wow, they like me,' but I still didn't really think they'd ask me to join."

---

suede will be having a very special surpise **party** to celebrate the release of **dog man star** at RAW (underneath the YMCA, 112A Great Russell St., London WC1) on **Monday** evening, **October 10th,** 1994. We're trying to keep it quiet so the papers don't find out hence the very short notice.

Doors open at **9:15pm** and **the band will be playing a very short set** at about **10:30pm**. This will be Richard's debut UK live performance and a fine opportunity to share a glass of fruit puch with the boys! After the performance the party will then continue until 2am!

Fanclub members and one guest will be admitted on a first-come, first-served basis until the Club reaches capacity. Unfortunately, we cannot guarantee admittance as we have no way of knowing how many guests will turn up. Basically, please don't travel any great distances to attend only to be turned away. (There's always the fanclub gig in December).

Please bring your membership card (if you've got one) and some form of identification as this is a bit of a special event and as capacity is limited we want to make sure that only you, the genuine fans, and your guest are admitted.

Barely able to conceal their excitement, the band gave Richard a copy of the forthcoming album and asked him to come back in a few days to see how he coped with the new stuff.

Saul Galpern had been tipped off that this could be the one and came along to see for himself. "I couldn't believe it, the confidence oozing from this young guy," says Saul. "He was strutting his stuff and playing all the Suede songs absolutely perfectly and I thought, 'Fucking hell!' And Brett was like, 'Yeah, imagine what it'll be like when he starts writing songs.'"

"I remember thinking, 'This isn't just Suede, this is an industry person,' looking very serious, dressed in his blue suit and white trainers. I remember thinking he looked like Rab C. Nesbitt!" laughs Richard. "I don't think he spoke to me. And at the end they said, 'Are you up for joining?' And I said, 'I'll have to ask my parents!'"

Charlie accompanied Richard to Waterloo station and had a long chat with him while waiting for the train back to Poole. This was likely to be the biggest decision he'd ever make. A-levels and university would go out the window and his parents were all too wary of the dangers of the rock'n'roll lifestyle. Suede's reputation was hardly chaste. But they all realised that if he turned down this chance he'd regret it for the rest of his life. Suede had a new guitarist. And a future.

"Brett did an amazing thing," reflects Phill Savidge. "He kept it together and he found Richard. The Stone Roses and the Smiths, they split and they were all over the place, but Brett kept it together. And then '17-year-old prodigy', that's quite a nice story isn't it?"

The rest of the Oakes family returned from France on August 28 and Richard spent two whole days with them before being whisked off to London to perform his first duty as a rock star by appearing in the video for "We Are The Pigs".

"It was really strange," says Richard. "I'd been hired for my musical ability and the first thing I had to do was be a model, basically. I remember watching the video back and thinking, three members of Suede, fine, and then some kid at the end, trying his best to look hard, and it just didn't work. I remember laughing myself!"

Suede's comeback single was released on September 12. A clarion call to violent insurrection, "We Are The Pigs" was beautifully enhanced with "Peter Gunn"-style brass and a children's choir aping Pink Floyd's "Another Brick In The Wall". It also featured some of Bernard Butler's most impressive guitar acrobatics to date, which only served to high-light the gaping hole he'd left behind. Richard had a lot to live up to but the band were at pains to impress their utter confidence in his abilities. "If we hadn't found anyone good enough then we wouldn't have taken anyone, it's as simple as that," Mat told *Select*. "If it had taken a year to find someone then we would have taken a year. This is the only band me and Brett have ever been in. It's all we care about."

Alas, it seemed that the rest of the nation cared slightly less, becoming slowly gripped in a fever of laddish nationalism, hinted at on parts of Blur's brilliantly conceived *Parklife* and consolidated by the arrival of five comedy-louts from Manchester called Oasis. A kind of idiot-friendly Stone Roses, Oasis bludgeoned sophistication in favour of undeniably catchy tunes about the joy of fags and booze, a much easier concept to grasp than the nuclear wind blowing away Brett's sins, or whatever he was on about. While Oasis's debut album, *Definitely Maybe*, hogged the top of the album charts, Suede's new single peaked at a worryingly shy 18, plunging to 38 the following week. Even Suede's staunchest allies, the music press Mafiosi, seemed to be shifting allegiances, one journalist noting, "This would have been single of the week were it not exactly the same as the last nine."

Hardly Suede's most commercial offering, the choice of single had been a subject of heated debate. "I remember some guy from Sony coming along to meet me at Nude Records and literally begging me to let them release 'New Generation' as the first single," says Brett, "and I said, 'No, it's going to be "We Are The Pigs".' Being slightly off my head had its good points in that it created an album like *Dog Man Star* but had its bad points in that I had zero business sense at the time. I was convinced that 'We Are The Pigs' was this huge, brutal chant and I wasn't listening to the

actual song. It probably would have made more commercial sense to release "New Generation" but I didn't feel it had the drama and the power that represented *Dog Man Star*. It was a good pop song but that was about it."

"At the time it was the band against the world," adds Saul Galpern. "They were in a fighting mood, no question. Any decision made was from them. They'd decided 'We Are The Pigs' was the first single and they were like, 'I don't fucking care what you think,' so I said, 'You know what, I'll support you all the way.'"

"We Are The Pigs" did serve its purpose in as much as it introduced Richard Oakes to the wider world via *Top Of The Pops*, though as he was simply miming along to Bernard's playing, the big question – can Brett's Little Dick cut it? – remained unanswered.

"It just shows ignorance can be bliss sometimes," reflects Mat Osman. "I don't think we realised what a big step it was to take on someone with no experience who was still at school. I don't think he knew quite what he was letting himself in for. But it was lucky that neither of us did otherwise we just wouldn't have done it. And we'd be playing with some grizzled old session man regaling us with his tales of Eric Clapton!"

At the beginning of October, Suede crossed the Channel for a few days promotional activity in Paris. Richard's first live appearances were two French radio shows, Bernard Lenoir's *Black Session* on October 4 and *Top Gear* on October 6. His first "proper" gig was a special show for the French fanclub on October 7 at Passage du Nord Ouest. It was less than a week after his eighteenth birthday. A popular story is that the rest of the band treated him to his first E as a typically Suedey coming-of-age present, though Richard remains appreciably coy about the topic. "Don't put that in," he laughs. "The only thing I'll say about drugs is that I realised very early on in my Suede career that drugs weren't going to do anything for me, that's all I'll say. I don't want to go into the details of how I found this out! I'm not a drug-orientated person. Just booze. And lots of it. I can out-drink the band."

After this rite of passage, Richard made his UK debut on October 10 at the Raw Club in the bowels of the YMCA off Tottenham Court Road. Another secret showcase for the fanclub faithful, it was a safe yet auspicious inauguration. "To say that Richard doesn't have Bernard Butler's hip-swinging, hair-threshing style would be unfair. But, as yet, he has no discernible style of his own," observed Simon Price in *Melody Maker*. "It'll come. As it is, he spends tonight with his face 100 per cent veiled by his fringe, crouched over his fretboard, concentrating on a note-perfect replication of the Anderson-Butler back catalogue. The boy done good."

He certainly had, though he was determined to keep his feet on the ground. "Everyone patted me on the back afterwards and said, 'Well done, you must be the bravest kid in the world,'" remembers Richard. "But I had closed my mind off to all that. If I'd let my guard down for a second it probably would have scarred me for life. I remember people saying, 'You're so mature,' and it was printed as well – 'He's got the demeanour of a middle-aged man' – but I had to in a way because if I'd been a starry-eyed kid I would have been sucked in and spat out the other end."

The most notable aspect of the Raw Club comeback was not the new boy, but the change in the rest of the band. Even Mat "Emotions Man" Osman was visibly laughing throughout. "I remember the first couple of gigs with Richard being really exciting," says Brett. "It was really nice to play in a band that felt like they were fucking enjoying it, for the first time in a couple of years. After all the grief we had with Bernard towards the end of his time with Suede, I remember Richard playing like he was enjoying the songs. And that enthusiasm spread through the band and we were all enjoying it, with a great album ready to come out, and we were just happy we got our shit together."

Simon Gilbert agrees. "I remember phoning Saul at the height of Bernard's madness and saying, 'Either he goes or I go,' and Saul said, 'Don't be stupid, you're only the fucking drummer!' And I remember doing the first gig with Richard and thinking, 'Yeah, I am only the drummer but I'm still in the fucking band.' I was really proud. Everyone thought we were either finished or out of action for a good couple of years. And we turned it round that quickly. It was up yours the lot of you!"

Dog Man Star finally hit the shelves that morning. Those three little words had been mysteriously appearing in graffiti-sprayed letters all over London, and particularly in close proximity to journalists' drinking dens, over the previous few weeks. A Suede spokesman put this down to over-zealous fans, but the other story is that members of Creation band the Telescopes had been slipped a back-hander of £50 and a couple of grams of speed.

Brett spoke about the title as a kind of shorthand Darwinism reflecting his own journey from the gutter to the stars. Fans noted the similarity to experimental film-maker Stan Brakhage's 1964 classic, *Dog Star Man*. "The film wasn't an influence but I obviously dug the title," Brett now confesses. The suitably sombre cover images of a bloke with a bare bum sprawled on a bed were lifted from another of Brett's old photo books. Taken by Joanne Leonard in 1971, the front cover picture was originally titled "Sad Dreams On Cold Mornings" and the rear photo "Lost Dreams". As for the contents, the dozen songs housed within were "Surrounded by the white heat of something close to genius", as John Harris put it in his effusive *NME* review. "Put it down to wild ambition, disdain for the limits that strait-jacket most young people with guitars, a crazed wish to equal the achievements of their forebears," he continued, before brilliantly pin-pointing Suede's influence on the current musical climate and their subsequent rejection of it. "Suede have set up modern life as an endless comic opera, a seaside postcard dipped in cheap lager and Coca-Cola. They've given up trying to root themselves in it, and wrapped themselves in alien robes, icy European futurism, lank-haired American cool... And sure, in times when sincerity and echo laden drama are so out of kilter with a culture whose abiding motto is 'irony or death', anyone who does this, and makes Great Art out of it, will be ridiculed. So scoff, chatterers. Suede Mark 1 have made an album that will regulate your laughter to trifling background noise. You're a fool, Bernard Butler. You really are."

Phill Savidge remembers constantly badgering John Harris about what mark he was going to give the record. "*Dog Man Star* is, I think, the pinnacle. It's not just the best Suede album, it's one of the best albums ever released. At that point I was hanging around with John all the time. I used to ring him up and go, 'Is it 10? It's 10, it's got to be 10!' And he said, 'Well, it could be 10.' 'It's got to be 10,' and he'd say, 'Well maybe it's 10,' and I said, 'This album has got to get 10!' And it came out and it was 9 and I said, 'Why did you bottle it?' And all he could say was, 'I don't know.'"

Phill points to a music industry joke about what journalists really mean by the marks they give records. "Nought out of 10 means 'Look at me!' and 1 out of 10 means 'Look at me!' and it goes all the way through to 7 out of 10 – 'I'm friends with the band!' And then it goes to 10 out of 10, 'Look at me!' and that's kind of what 10 out of 10 means."

But whatever the actual marks, the press were almost totally in agreement that at last Suede had finally made a record that more than validated the hype. "Butler may never be heard of again. Suede may never make another decent record. Or both parties could evolve into megastars of the twenty-first century. It simply doesn't matter, because with *Dog Man Star* the group has vindicated just about every claim that was ever made on their behalf," gushed David Sinclair in *Q*. "A long, sprawling and not entirely flawless album, it will be hailed in years to come as the crowning achievement of a line up that reinvented English guitar-band rock'n'roll for the 1990s...for the most part, *Dog Man Star* is a triumph. Listening to how far on this has taken from their first album, it now seems faintly ridiculous that Suede were once branded as '70s revivalist or bracketed with the Auteurs as serious competitors. It's our loss that Butler and Anderson will not be working together in the foreseeable future, but at least with this album as their swansong no one can say it was a partnership that failed to deliver the goods. The hype stops here."

But Suede had made a name for themselves with a string of brilliant pop singles and the public were not quite ready for a Suede concept album concerning warped Hollywood iconography and doom-laden premonitions of Judgment Day. *Dog Man Star* entered the charts two places lower than its all-conquering predecessor – held off the top by

REM's latest and Bon Jovi's greatest hits – and for all its merits sat uncomfortably on the sidelines of the cheery Britpop beerfest.

"It didn't sell as well as the first album. It didn't sell as well as I thought it deserved," says Brett. "I thought it was quite an extraordinary record and the sort of thing a band should be doing on its second album, making bold leaps and being out there and not too safe. I felt that it didn't get the commercial success it deserved, it got the critical success. I think a lot of people thought the band had split up because Bernard had left."

The subtext was that the band was over because the talent had gone. "I think a lot of the media had over-read Bernard's role," Brett continues. "I'm not trying to under-read Bernard's role, but they'd almost assumed that Bernard did everything, which really wasn't the case. Yes, I was writing to his music but within the chords of his music there was a million possibilities for melodies and it was actually finding the right one. And of course things are suggested by the chord changes and stuff like that but what I was doing within the Anderson-Butler relationship certainly wasn't just writing the lyrics. It was writing the topline which was, like you say, what the milkman whistles."

The *Dog Man Star* tour began at Preston Guildhall on October 26. To a backdrop of specially commissioned arthouse films by Derek Jarman's production team, a leaner, meaner Suede came to the fore, Brett in particular ripping into the songs like a hellcat on heat. At the first couple of shows he uncharacteristically stage-dived into the audience, re-emerging bloodied and shoeless. While it made for a terrific spectacle, there was a nagging suspicion that the twin distractions of background movies and a rabid, hyperactive Brett were compensations for Richard's inexperience. Bernard Butler spoke in the press of being replaced by "a talentless clone". Yet Suede's one ray of hope was the grudging acknowledgement that, yes, the boy could play.

Among the many devout fans determined to follow Suede, pilgrim-style, to as many of the shows as possible was Victor Aroldoss, then still at school. He'd been introduced to the band by his cousin Subodhini. Both were typically obsessive fans who'd already met the band a few times including Richard's *Top Of The Pops* debut and the recent Raw gig. But it was a chance encounter with their ex-guitarist that would lead to Victor really getting his foot in the door with Suede.

"The day before I went to Preston, from overplaying my copy of *Suede*, I went to go and buy it again from HMV. And walking down

Oxford Street, who should I see but Bernard," remembers Victor. "And I thought, 'Oh my god, I have to say something!' So I went over there and said, 'Oh. Bernard, I think you're brilliant. I love the album and good luck with whatever you want to do.' He was quite friendly to me at first but then said, 'Well, you shouldn't like them. Brett sleeps with children and they all take crack!' And it was one of those conversations when I was totally gob-smacked. He said, 'You shouldn't like them, they're not nice people, they all take drugs,' and I didn't know anything about drugs at the time. And it was quite weird because it was these people I'd met three or four times and they seemed really nice. Even when I've had encounters with him since, you always feel sorry for him, he always portrays himself as the victim. It's really weird."

Victor very nearly abandoned his plans to follow the band on tour but, as the tickets had already been bought, Subodhini was able to change his mind, and they bumped into the band again outside the venue. "I told them I'd met Bernard and he'd been really horrible about them," continues Victor. "And that was the best thing you could have said. If anyone wants to get in with Suede, go back to 1994 and slag him off. And they went, 'Oh brilliant!' After the gig Charlie got us backstage and Brett jumped over the sofa to talk to us and Richard obviously didn't know a lot of people so he always talked to us. Then we started doing loads of gigs on the tour."

Victor soon found himself accepted as part of the band's inner circle of confidants. "I went by myself to meet them when they did 'Wild Ones' on *Top Of The Pops*," he explains, "and me, Brett, Richard and Mat went to an antiques

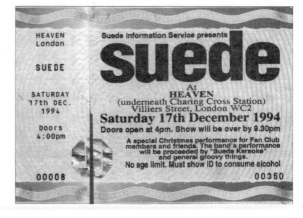

fair and went to McDonald's and stuff and Brett was and always really has been interested in my opinions of the music as well."

Suede released "The Wild Ones" on November 7. Brett spoke of wandering around Highgate for three hours feeling like he'd just done an E once he finished it, and it remains one of his favourite Suede songs.

With one of their most straightforward lyrics and an uncharacteristically light, breezy feel, it had been whispered about in terms of becoming Suede's first transatlantic number one. Sony even commissioned a six-figure video (Suede's most expensive ever) by Howard Greenhalgh who the band had met on their New York promo trip when he won MTV's Best Video Award for Soundgarden's "Black Hole Sun".

"Filming the video was the worst day of my life," Simon told Simon Price in *Melody Maker*. "We did it on fucking Dartmoor, blowing a gale, raining…"

"…four of us and six models sitting in a Volkswagen camper van for 15 hours," continued Mat, "shivering to death. Then the rain would stop and I had to go outside, pull these silly poses and stand completely still. It's still one of my favourite songs, but it kind of died on the vine." Lost under the cloud of Bernard's departure, "The Wild Ones" stalled at number 18. "Possibly the best song of the week," admitted the *NME*, "but this week, the band recorded here really no longer exists."

"The Wild Ones" single's greatest significance, however, was that it introduced Richard Oakes to the studio for the first time. There were a couple of Anderson-Butler songs left over from the *Dog Man Star* sessions for b-sides, but Ed Buller felt that one of them, "This World Needs A Father", needed a bit more work. "Most of it was recorded but Ed decided it needed a Hammond organ," remembers Richard, "and because I was the new guy it was like, 'You have a go!'" As a result, "This World Needs A Father" is a real curio in the band's discography – the only Suede recording to feature both Bernard Butler and Richard Oakes.

Richard also added guitar to a new song, "Asda Town", which Brett had had kicking around for some time. "My hands were shaking but I did it in a couple of takes," he says. "Ed had worked really closely with Bernard so I wouldn't have found it strange if he'd looked down his nose at me, but he didn't at all. He was really encouraging. He was like a real mate of theirs, a real gang member for a long time and he helped me a lot. I did get to play some electric on it, a little bit of squealing at the end, but I'd had my experience in the studio and I was very pleased with it."

In contrast to their latest chart positions, Suede were still doing the business live and, equally importantly, enjoying the business of still being rock stars. "The morning of the Cambridge gig, I went round to Brett's because I was driving down there, and he was still in bed with some naked chick," laughs Simon. "And he just wouldn't get up because he was so off his tits. I was like, 'Please get up, we've gotta go to this gig!' And it took me hours to get him out, it was very funny. Anyway, I got to the gig, bought a gram of coke, tried to do a line and then dropped it all over my trousers!"

Suede were doing particularly well on the Continent where the music press had less influence. Many Suede fans didn't even know Bernard had left until they turned up at the gigs. Some didn't even notice then. Support on the first European leg of the tour came from Manic Street Preachers who, as well as covering "The Drowners", had previously demonstrated their appreciation of Suede by making "Metal Mickey" single of the week in *Smash Hits* and complimenting Brett and Co on looking like rent boys.

The Manics had also just released a brilliant but difficult album, *The Holy Bible*, and were suffering personnel problems of their own due to the increasingly wayward behaviour of troubled rhythm guitarist Richey Edwards. With a history of depression, drinking, eating disorders and self-mutilation, Richey had been in and out of hospitals and rehab clinics and had missed several of the band's gigs that year including the T In The Park and Reading festivals. "I remember Richey being very withdrawn," says Brett. "He was the only one of the band who wasn't very sociable. I think I spoke to him once. My memory of him is him just being withdrawn."

Richard Oakes remembers making an effort to speak to Richey after a gig in Oslo. "Richey obviously had all his problems and he was always quiet so nobody ever went near him," remembers Richard. "We were on our bus waiting to go and the Manics' bus was parked next to us and it was bitterly cold. And somebody from our crew came on and said, 'That guy from the Manics is sitting outside in his pants!' And everyone was like, 'Pffff, what a weirdo!' and I thought to myself, 'I'm going to go and talk to him!'"

Sure enough, Richard found the Manics' guitarist sitting outside in the Scandinavian winter dressed only in his pants and socks and a very thin cardigan. "I went down and said to him, 'Aren't you absolutely bloody freezing?' and he said, 'Yes but I want to be.' So I was like, 'Okay…are you enjoying the tour?' And he had this laminate round his neck with a list of dates and he pointed to the ones he'd enjoyed, this one, this one and this one. And he said, 'This must be amazing for you, you're so young, you've come straight from school, you've got your whole life ahead of you.' And I was aware the whole time that I'm having a great time on my first tour with Suede, this lot are on the point of breaking up, I'm speaking to the reason that they're breaking up. It was a strange juxtaposition."

Despite Richey's problems, Brett maintains the tour was an enjoyable one with the other band members getting on well with each other. "The rest of them were always very friendly," he confirms. "I got on very well with James, I know James quite well still, I bump into him in Marks & Spencer's quite a bit! I felt quite a kinship with the Manics at that time because I felt as though we were going through similar periods of our career. The whole cartoon Britpop world was just starting to happen and I think both bands felt it was complete garbage, bullshit, and it felt like we were exiles. It was appropriate that we were touring Belgium and Holland and places like that, like weird deposed kings."

Brett flew back to London the day before the Madrid show for a promotional engagement in London on Channel 4's *Big Breakfast* where he was to be probed "on the bed" by the late celebrity flirt Paula Yates. As the show was obviously filmed early in the morning, Brett surmised that his best option was probably to stay up all night. On the bed but off camera, Paula coyly whispered in his ear, "Would you like an E?" Brett's reply? "No thanks, I've already had five."

Simon vividly recollects Brett phoning Charlie in Spain to say that unfortunately he wouldn't be able to participate in that evening's performance. "I just remember Charlie saying, 'If you don't get on that fucking plane I'm gonna fucking walk out," laughs Simon. "And Brett arrived literally a minute before we went on stage. He walked through the door and went, 'Come on then!' And it was the most punkiest gig ever. It was just crazy, a really good gig."

At the end of November, they had a day off in Hamburg before their gig at the Zillo club. Following in the footsteps of the Beatles and countless other rock'n'roll bands, the members of Suede decided to let their hair down with a night out in the port's notorious red light district, the Reeperbahn. All of them, that is, bar Richard, who was exiled to his room and told he wasn't allowed to leave until he'd written a song. "It's totally true," laughs Brett, "we actually made Richard stay in. It was like a load of teachers forcing someone to do their homework – hilarious. And we all went off and got incredibly smashed on Jagermeister and watched a load of strippers and got chased out of various bars and Richard had to stay in his hotel room and write. And I remember him being so pissed off. 'Why can't I come with you?'"

When they came back, Richard had written his first Suede song. "That was quite a good moment actually," says Brett, "because it's sort of relatively easy for someone to play someone's lines, no matter how good a guitarist Bernard was and how difficult it was to emulate Bernard. I always felt the test wasn't the first live gig we did, it was the first thing we wrote together."

Richard's recollection is slightly different. "They went out to look at porn shops and I didn't really fancy that," he smiles. "I just stayed in and fiddled about with an acoustic guitar and came up with a couple of riffs, one of which stayed a riff as 'Bentswood Boys' and the other one turned into one of the songs I'm most proud of, which is 'Together'. And when that happened you could see the relief, it was like, 'It doesn't matter what anyone says, they can say we're finished if they want, but the reality is we can write with this new guy.' And a lot of the people around Suede as well taking me to one side and saying, well done, what a relief!"

Originally titled "Electric Cakes" after the rest of the band's affectionate nickname for the wee lad, it would soon be better known as "Together" (the other one, "Bentswood Boys", was initially "Acoustic Cakes").

"I like 'Together'," continues Brett. "I think it's a good song. I don't think the production's very good. I think it's a bit confused and too much reverb. But I remember feeling quite encouraged at that point."

Brett had to put a fair amount of work into Richard's creation to knock it into a fully functioning Suede song, however. "He'd written the chorus as the verse and the verse as the chorus and we had to juggle it around and stuff like that," reveals Brett. "But working with Richard has always been like that, it's never been as structured as working with Bernard. With Richard it's always been much more of a fluid sort of thing. Bernard wasn't really flexible in that way. For whatever reason, I mean Bernard didn't need to be flexible in that way because maybe what he wrote was more structured and fully developed. It's just a different way of working."

Suede debuted the song at yet another fanclub show, this time at Heaven underneath the Arches at Charing Cross in London, on December 17, the band all donning T-shirts with Polaroid photos of each other on them. Despite this obvious show of camaraderie, one couldn't fail to notice a certain tiredness in the band's performance.

Christmas brought a welcome break. Sheri Friers, who'd just landed a job as Saul's PA at Nude Records, was introduced to some of the band at a music biz festive bash. "Saul invited me out to come and meet everybody," she says. "Richard was there and we got on like a house on fire. He was young, I was young and we ended up drinking everyone else under the table! The next thing I know, everyone had left and Richard was on his own with no where to go so he ended up crashing at my dodgy flat in Kilburn. It was all so innocent – he was 18 and in one of Britain's biggest bands and I was 22 and getting ready to start my dream job. We stumbled back to my house and fell asleep watching telly. It probably wasn't the best way to start the ball rolling with Nude because the next morning my mobile went. It was Saul. He was trying to find Richard."

Sheri met Brett for the first time shortly afterwards one cold, January morning. "Brett came into the office and he looked really rough," she remembers. "He was sporting one of the band's 'Suede' mod-style bomber jackets, which looked hilarious on him. He looked like a marshmallow with two pegs sticking out the bottom. I asked him what he was up to and he said something about doing a photo shoot. I then asked if he'd come in to get his hair and make-up done for the shoot. I'll never forget his face when he said, 'No, I've just come from having the pics taken!'"

It was a knackered-looking Brett who appeared on Suede's first *NME* cover of 1995. Under a none-too-subtle headline of "Horse & Hounded" the interview stirred up dark rumours that Brett was in danger of becoming the latest in a seemingly endless line of rock'n'roll casualties. In short, Brett was accused of being a heroin addict. It was no great surprise that the source of this tittle-tattle was a certain Mr Albarn of Kensington Park Road, West 11, who'd spouted off in *The Face*, "I think heroin is shit, and I know for a fact that Brett is doing heroin."

Someone who perhaps had a more informed idea of what was actually going on than most was that other resident of Kensington Park

Road, Justine Frischmann. "Damon accused Brett of doing it when he was doing it and Brett wasn't," she says now, eyes rolling. "That was the ironic thing. I remember Damon accusing Brett of being a junkie in the press when Damon was doing it regularly and Brett wasn't. But therein lies the tale. That was just how it went. It was constantly the two of them, just ridiculous."

Brett's response at the time was classically ambiguous. "I don't give a fuck if anyone thinks I've got my head down a toilet with a needle up my arse," he told *NME*, "as long as I make good records." He was less woolly when it came to his opinion of the origin of such rumours. "I object to people attacking me, especially if when I go abroad I find that that same person is ruthlessly and relentlessly trying to assassinate my character all over the fucking world. I find that objectionable. Especially when made by a talentless public schoolboy who's made a career out of being patronising to the working classes." *Touché*.

Nevertheless, face bloated, eyes blood-shot and with a nasty-looking cold sore flourishing on the edge of his mouth, Brett certainly wasn't looking his best. So what was he up to? "I wasn't doing heroin," he says firmly. "I hadn't been introduced to heroin at that time." Brett then pauses, reflectively. "Actually, I tell a lie. I had done it, I'd done it a couple of times. I actually used to snort it, but I wasn't doing it at that time." He does admit to drowning his sorrows in a cocktail of cocaine and alcohol, however. "I was getting incredibly fucking drunk every night. A lot of it was escape. I was feeling incredibly fucking hounded by the press and feeling pretty aggrieved that I thought we'd done quite a lot of good stuff and we weren't really getting recognition for it."

He betrays an understandable hint of jealousy as well. "There were other bands that were sort of overtaking us and becoming press darlings and that was pretty frustrating, especially when I thought we'd made a couple of good records. But I wasn't doing smack, that's the truth. I didn't start doing it properly till the summer of 1997." Of which more later.

Suede propped up the third leg of the UK tour with a third single from the album. Nude and Sony finally got their way with "New Generation", although again not without a fight. Eager to put the Butler era behind them, the band wanted to make a statement with the Anderson-Oakes-penned "Together" as their new release. "They wanted it to be a single," confirms Saul Galpern. "There was a big debate about that." A compromise that it would be a double-A side was reached, although in the days of multi-tracked 2x CD formatting, this counted for little. "I tell you what, we'll put a little sticker on your 12-inch," laughs Saul, "all right? Byeee!"

By this time paranoia about Brett's drug use was epidemic. Sheri Friers remembers watching a rough edit of the video at Nude. "We all sat down excitedly to watch it. About half way through, Saul gasped and the tape was stopped and re-wound about five times. The problem? Brett touched his nose! In my naivety, I couldn't figure out what all the fuss was about but soon learned that there was a load of press fuss about Brett's increasingly public drug habit. Him touching his nose was a dead giveaway he'd been doing coke during the filming."

Victor Aroldoss was thrilled to be invited to hang out with the band at the shoot, which coincided with the publication of the *NME* hatchet job. "I remember them saying, 'We're not going to do any more press ever!'" he reveals. "And that's when I realised they didn't do scenes, they stayed in their own houses with their own friends, went to local pubs, never went to trendy bars. They went to Heaven a few times, did a few Es, but they were totally removed from everything else, the whole Britpop thing. They'd quiz me on the b-sides and stuff, Subo played it cool but I was a right fucking knob-end... In fact, after Heaven, Brett went, 'This is my friend Alan,' and I went, 'ALAN FISHER!' If somebody said that now you'd be like, 'Fuck off you freak!' I was really surprised they didn't. It's really easy for people who are popstars to look down on people, but they never did. It was cool."

"New Generation" reached a respectable if hardly dizzying 21, holding up well at 24 the next week as the band played two sold-out nights at London's Hammersmith Palais. One-time champion Steve Sutherland, now editor of the *NME*, voiced a certain dissatisfaction with Brett's increasingly blokey stage presence, a million miles from the androgynous snake-charmer of only a year ago. "He was dragging Suede into someone else's agenda," he wrote in *NME*, "and it wasn't a pretty sight."

Two days later Suede flew to the United States where *Spin* magazine had just voted *Dog Man Star* the ninth best album of the year, the only British record in their top 20. The latest American tour again started in the dodgiest part of Washington DC at a venue with no dressing room or separate toilet for the band. The curse of America returned when, after being pulled off stage by over-excited fans, Brett bust his ankle and had to hobble through the rest of the tour with the aid of a cane.

"America was phenomenal," says Richard Oakes. "It was getting more and more amazing, the further round the world we went it was just incredible. We did Washington first, terrible weather, freezing cold, jet lag, but I was having the time of my life and for no other reason than I was able to play the guitar to a bunch of people in America. And barely six months ago I'd been in the situation where nobody outside my bedroom was in the slightest bit interested in what I had to play on the guitar!"

By coincidence producer Ed Buller was holidaying in the States as the same time that the band had a few days off in Los Angeles, so a quick recording session was arranged to see if they could come up with a couple of b-sides for the "The Power", the proposed fourth single from *Dog Man Star*. As the only song on the album that Bernard didn't play on, it would be a symbolic full stop to that chapter of Suede's career. "The Power" was set for release on May 1 – at least that was the official story. "What we didn't know was that Saul had put us into the studio right in the middle of the tour in the hope that we were going to come up with a new single," claims Brett. "He said it was for b-sides but I don't think he had any intention of releasing 'The Power' at this point. And he'd wanted us to come up with a song like 'Together', which he thought could maybe be a new single."

Instead, they came up with "Sam" and "Have You Ever Been This Low", which even the most devoted Suede fan would be unlikely to consider as potential hits. According to Sheri Friers, Saul burst into fits of laughter the first time he heard them. "Sam", written wholly by Brett, was a saccharine love song detailing the minutiae of Brett's new girlfriend, Sam Cunningham, who lived on Lancaster Road and had a computer. He'd already waved goodbye to Anick in "Another No One" ("You'll have to find another no one to take the shit like I have, I guess this is the end") though the final version wouldn't surface for some 15 months.

"I met Sam in Notting Hill Gate around October 94," recalls Brett. "I think Alan knew her first, there wasn't any sort of formal introduction really. I really liked her unpretentiousness, that appealed, going out with someone down to earth after the embroiled torment of going out with this other girl."

"Have You Ever Been This Low", originally titled "Rocky" and one of the earliest collaborations with Richard, was a heavy, lurching tune with Oakes's trade-mark spidery arpeggios. "It's just a song about being pissed off with being on tour," says Brett, "which was pretty much where we were at the time. This was at a point where it was becoming really not much fun touring an album that wasn't made by the band. I felt as if I really, really was keen to get back and start writing with Richard and the rest of the band. You get locked into these tour cycles and you have to do things and it's pretty depressing going through the same fucking thing, walking on stage doing 'Asphalt World' every night."

"The Asphalt World" did, however, provide ample opportunity for Brett to walk off stage during the instrumental break, at which time long-serving drum tech Kimble Garcia would have a line of refreshments dutifully chopped out on one of the flight cases.

A trip to the Far East lifted their spirits somewhat. They even encored with an unplanned, unrehearsed version of the Sex Pistols' "No Feelings" in Tokyo. A particularly riotous party in Hong Kong ended up with Brett sleeping in the bath.

"We got to Japan and we did the first gig and there's two tiny little Japanese girls, with this huge banner, FUCK US RICHARD!, just months after he's been sitting in school with ink on his nose," remembers Mat. "So the first months must have been a blast."

On April Fool's Day the band returned to Europe. Supporting them were a Bristol outfit featuring one Alex Lee on lead guitar. Alex had joined Bristol legends the Blue Aeroplanes when, like Richard, he had just turned 18.

"I was in a band before them called the Coltraines with Joe Allen who went on to Strangelove and David Francolini who went on to do Levitation and Dark Star and we used to do gigs supporting the Blue Aeroplanes," explains Alex. "And they're like a YTS scheme for musicians in Bristol. If you're an aspiring musician you have to do your time with the Blue Aeroplanes and I did my time. They were a brilliant, brilliant live band. As soon as I joined they were just signing a major deal. I joined at exactly the right time. I left school and within six months found myself recording an album and touring with REM. At the end of the REM tour, at the beginning of 1990, we all ended up on stage together. REM became the extra guitarists. It was always a part of the Blue Aeroplanes live set that they'd drag up friends, musicians, journalists anything. You know, you'd drag a journalist up there to get a good review. And on the REM tour we had REM up there. It was absolutely brilliant. It was hilarious."

After such a prestigious apprenticeship, Alex set about plotting a Bristol supergroup of his own. "I knew Joe and Dave and when we got Julian, Jazzer, on guitar, it seemed that we had something," he explains. "I really had faith that that band had masses of potential, really talented, gifted musicians. If we could just harness that potential and make it something great. It didn't quite go according to plan, it has to be said, but we definitely had our moments."

Hijacking a Byronic local drop-out called Patrick Duff as their frontman, they became Strangelove and after less than ten gigs signed to Blur's label Food in 1992, releasing their critically acclaimed but commercially ignored *Time For the Rest Of Your Life* album in the autumn of '94.

"We arrived about the same time as Suede started," recalls Alex, "so I suppose we were perceived as outsiders who did our own thing. There wasn't a lot of great guitar music at the time, it was all quite baggy."

Strangelove were undoubtedly far more adventurous and ambitious musically than your average early '90s indie fare. They were due to begin writing their second album when Suede invited them to support. Charlie Charlton knew them from the time they supported Adorable, when he was acting as their tour manager. "That was a particularly chaotic tour. I remember Charlie getting really pissed off with us because we were really drunk one night," laughs Alex. "We nicked Adorable's van and decided to go joyriding and Charlie was chasing us around the car park with Adorable watching, laughing."

Strangelove determined, though, that the tour with Suede would be a much more serious affair. They would write their new record on the road, taking a box with a porta-studio, mics and a few effects pedals. "We lost that box within about three days of starting the tour," says Alex, "And once we found out that Suede had as hedonistic an approach to touring as we did, we realised we weren't going to get quite as much work done. There comes a point where you just turn into a bit of a monster on the road and you can't always harness the creative energy to write. It was a nice idea and we got some things done but soon we just realised it was going to be more fun just living it up!"

The two bands shared much in common – and not just a charismatic, floppy-fringed frontman and a taste for the odd nose-up. A mutual appreciation society of sorts developed. By the time they reached Spain, Strangelove were playing Suede's "Killing Of A Flashboy". Suede returned the favour by covering "She's Everywhere", then still under its working title of "Spacey Vibe Thing". By the time they got around to recording it, Strangelove would invite Brett to provide backing vocals, while Richard Oakes joined in on their astonishing 1996 single, "Living With The Human Machines".

"The Manics were good and they were fun to watch but nothing excited me that much until I saw Strangelove and they were just incredible," remembers Richard Oakes. "None of them hardly spoke. I remember trying to say hello to Strangelove and Pad wouldn't say a word, Joe wouldn't say a word. They were just like that. And John would get drunk and hug you. And so the only normal one in the band was Alex. Pad was insane at this point, a lunatic. He was pissed out of his face by mid-day, and hugging you, crying, saying 'I'm having such a nice time', and then when they were doing their soundcheck, screaming with anger into a microphone. He was really on the edge, pulling his hair out during shows. I found him thoroughly entertaining!"

Alex was surprised at how down to earth Suede were as people. "You couldn't escape them in the UK at that time so I was fully expecting them to be a right bunch of prima donnas," he admits. "I thought they were going to be a nightmare to be honest. There were quite a lot of emotional problems in Strangelove and Suede just seemed so much more together. We noticed things like they used to get changed into stage clothes before they got on stage. If anyone had a change of clothes in Strangelove, we'd be amazed!"

The two bands got on so well that on one night they formed an impromptu backing group for opening act Peter Stewart, a singer-song-writer friend of Brett's. "He got Julian on guitar, John on drums, Joe and

Mat, they both refused to play bass, so I did it instead," remembers Alex. "And then as backing singers Patrick and Brett came on with paper bags on their heads, just to freak out the audience! They snuck on and they were the backing singers. It could have been so insulting, but Peter Stewart loved it."

Brett indulged in some other extra-curricular activities on the tour, including an embarrassing appearance on French television. He was cajoled into dueting with Terence Trent D'Arby, resulting in two of the worst cover versions of all time, Neil Young's "Cinnamon Girl" and an almost inconceivably bad "Children Of The Revolution" by T-Rex.

Far more respectable, thankfully, was the duet Brett recorded in Paris with pretend Frenchie Jane Birkin, a cover of "Les Yeux Fermés" for a French charity album. Brett also put his more than adequate French to good use at the Paris show when a technical hitch led to a hastily improvised rendition of "La Puissance" – "The Power", in French.

Despite such distractions, however, the tour was beginning to drag for all concerned. "It didn't feel fresh after a while," agrees Brett. "We weren't particularly enjoying it. We were very keen to move forward and not to dwell on the last album."

The band had been playing "Together" live almost as soon as it had been written. The second Anderson-Oakes song, "Bentswood Boys", was given its first live airing at the Albert Hall in May, a charity event that raised £15,000 for Friends Of The Earth. Brett dedicated the song to Hayward Heath's sweet and tender hooligans. The concert, one of Suede's best of the year, was apparently Richard Oakes's one-hundredth. His entire family were in the audience, beaming proudly.

At a radio show in Israel a month later, Brett wheeled out a little number he'd had up his sleeve for some time. The first draft of "Lazy" had been written back in Moorhouse Road. It was a comment on the lifestyle he shared with Alan at the time, watching the nine-to-fivers scurry to and from work while they were off their nuts, a "Where The Pigs Don't Fly" Part 2. Even earlier was "By The Sea", unveiled for the first time at that summer's festivals. "I'd written 'By The Sea' and 'Lazy' years ago," confirms Brett. "I pretty much knew Bernard wasn't going to be in Suede for the rest of his life and I thought it would be good to have a couple of things knocking about. I remember being under pressure to write b-sides for maybe 'The Wild Ones' and I knew these songs existed but I just wanted to save them because I thought they were too good."

Vaguely concerned with a fantasy he and Justine had had about running away from it all, "By The Sea" was written while the band were recording the first album, perhaps explaining why its opening line is almost identical to that of "So Young".

"I remember writing it in Moorhouse Road," says Brett, "when I was very first learning to play a few chords on the piano. They're both quite simple songs. I think there's a point when you're not quite a master of an instrument and you can actually get something really beautiful out of it. I always felt that was the case with 'The Next Life'. Bernard wrote the music to that and I always thought it was a really beautiful piece of music because it was so simple – he hadn't mastered the piano. It was almost in that transition point before he'd become too knowing about the instrument."

"By The Sea" had its UK première on July 14 at Suede's final gig of the year, the headlining slot – despite some wrangling with Bob Dylan – at the Phoenix Festival near Simon's birthplace in Stratford. The minute the band walked on stage, the heavens opened. "I thought someone's really got it in for us!" said Brett, looking like a young Bryan Ferry in white shirt and black tie. But through the pouring rain, Suede were triumphant.

They celebrated in traditional Suede fashion. Victor Aroldoss remembers being slightly concerned by the excesses that ensued. "Phoenix was the first time I thought maybe they did a bit too many drugs," he remembers. "Simon had a suite and everybody was in there, and I didn't do any drugs and didn't really enjoy it, I was just sitting in the corner. There were these two scousers laughing, 'I had my finger up her arse and she was sucking me off'. So it was a pretty weird night and I was a bit dubious about it."

The band, however, thought they were perfectly entitled to let their hair down. Despite an *NME* photo-shoot set in a gentleman's lavatory – the inference being that Suede were down the toilet – their confidence was warranted by the fact that "By The Sea" was easily the highlight of the Phoenix set. "I'd really like to relax a bit," said Brett. "Just ease off and make some groovy, relaxed things. I think the next album will be quite simple, actually. I'd really like to write a straightforward pop album. Just ten hits."

Though no one in their right mind would have believed it, Suede would do exactly that.

CHAPTER ELEVEN
beautiful ones

DETERMINED THAT THE NEXT album would be a total contrast to the saturnine *Dog Man Star*, Brett moved out of his gothic manor house and shed his Dracula skin, moving into the sunny top maisonette of 106 Chesterton Road W10.

"*Dog Man Star* was such an extreme album, without a doubt the most extreme album we've ever made, that the last thing we wanted to do was do something even more in that direction," explains Brett. "So I wanted to get away from everything to do with it; the isolation was the main thing. So I moved back to West London. I was conscious as well of all sorts of things in my life changing. I'd split up with my girlfriend, Anick – and she was a lot of trouble – started going out with Sam, moved back round here and felt a bit more like a human being rather than a sort of vampire."

For Richard Oakes, who'd spent the few days when he was not on tour crashing on Charlie's floor, he found himself living on his own for the first time in his life. "We got back off the tour and I'd got my own flat, so I was completely self-sufficient now, had to learn to do the washing-up and wash my own clothes. I know it sounds silly but I'd never had to do that before!"

Armed with a top of the range multi-track recorder which had been used to record the tour for accompanying live video, *Introducing The Band*, Richard began obsessively poring over songs. "The first thing I did was this demo called 'Dreamy', which became 'Picnic By The Motorway', though it was known as 'Lovely Day' right up until we saw the finished album artwork," he remembers. "'Every Monday Morning Comes' was originally called 'Exercise in D', 'Jumble Sale Mums' was an early one called 'Sad' and 'Saturday Night' came from a demo of mine called 'Ballad Idea'. There were loads. That was an intense writing period. We'd hit something!"

Brett was very keen to involve Richard and bring him into his life at this point. "That was part of the whole atmosphere," agrees Brett. "He didn't take drugs and I'd be sitting there with Alan and we'd been up for days and I'd just invite him round. Alan was really instrumental, not in the writing of the songs but his enthusiasm for them. 'Get Richard round, I wanna hear that riff!' And so we called Richard and he comes over and there were these weird little scenes where we had these bits of songs and we'd sort of write them like that. It was quite magical in a way. And the way the songs were written in this weird, hedonistic atmosphere was sort of what the songs were about as well."

The most obvious example of this is "Beautiful Ones", which began as an infectious riff from Richard which the band then played around with at rehearsal. Brett and Alan were watching a video of the rehearsal and decided to call Richard round. He arrived with his best friend, Pete, who was staying in town.

"Alan and Brett were wrecked," remembers Richard. "They'd been up for a couple of days and they invited me round. And every time it got to the end of 'Beautiful Ones' neither Brett nor Alan could be bothered to lean over and press rewind, so Pete had to do it. We were both stone cold sober and I just invited Pete round for the gruesome spectacle of Brett and Alan completely off their faces. We ended up cramming into his tiny writing room, which was basically a cupboard, and he gave me a guitar and said, 'Play the riff.' And I played it and he'd sing over the top of it. We were all in there, Alan and Pete as well, crammed into this room, sweating buckets. But I knew we were on to a winner and that's how a song got written back then, so I was happy to drag Pete round there!"

Among the many visitors to Chesterton Road who inspired "Beautiful Ones" was Gary France, a hairdresser friend of Brett and Alan. "We had this band called Bruiser," laughs Brett. "We had a night of drug taking where we wrote about ten great songs, it was kind of a pisstake of Britpop, it was actually really funny." Among the Bruiser songs were "Kissus For My Missus" and "Santa Ain't A Wanker" and some of the lyrics ended up as the basis for "Beautiful Ones" b-side "Young Men".

On another occasion Brett and Alan were listening to a demo of "Lazy" for the umpteenth time at full blast when, through the din, they became vaguely aware of a knocking at the door. "There was this guy at the door going, 'Please, please, please stop playing the same song, my mother's just died.' It's actually quite tragic when you think about it but it shows you the extent of how we weren't connected with the real world."

It was around this time that I began working full time in the band's offices as general dogsbody, a dream come true for a naive Suede groupie. My introduction to the wacky machinations of Suedeworld was a phone call from Brett, taking a break with Sam in Barbados asking if I would mind doing his girlfriend's homework for her. Somehow I managed to wriggle my way out of this and passed the buck to the other Sam, Sam McCormick, who at that stage was the band's fanclub manager.

"She had to do a 1,000 word essay on Nicholas Roeg for the day after they got back," remembers Sam. "He told me he was faxing me the book list, and question, and asked me to write the essay. Given that I was at university myself at the time and writing my own essays, I told him I wouldn't be writing the essay. We ended up compromising, which meant that I had to go the library and bookshops, get the research material for her, and highlight all the relevant pages and paragraphs. She dropped out of the course a few months later."

One of my earliest errands was to buy a pair of jeans for Brett's young lady: white Levis 501s, size 10. Arriving at number 106 one sunny summer morning, I could clearly see Brett and Alan curtain-twitching at the top window. Yet despite ringing the doorbell for what seemed like an eternity and leaving numerous messages on Brett's answer phone, they refused to open the door. Eventually, I pushed the jeans through the cat flap. Alan later told me they'd thought I was Bernard come to pay a surprise visit.

Shortly afterwards Brett asked to arrange to have satellite television installed. The engineer had similar difficulty getting anyone to answer the door at the pre-arranged time, but after a couple of weeks this simple task was completed. Sky TV would prove to be a big influence on the next record, being name-checked in the revamped lyrics to "Lazy" and even giving the album its title. "Pop music took over. My diet at the time was cocaine, T-Rex, Prince, *EastEnders* and Sky TV," says Brett. "Watching *Sky News* was when I first saw the phrase 'Coming up', you know, as an advert for what they were about to show. Of course, I'd used the phrase a million times doing E, but I also liked the sexual implication."

Just six weeks after their appearance at the Phoenix Festival, the band were ensconced in Dave Stewart's The Church Studios in Crouch End, London, working on an early version of a new song called

"Filmstar", inspired by actors like Alan Bates and Terrence Stamp. Brett was enjoying the new freedom in working methods that Bernard's departure presented. "Some of the songs that I wrote with Richard on *Coming Up*, which are 'Filmstar' and 'She' specifically, were literally me going round to his place and singing the words and tapping my knees and him working out chords to it," he reveals. "So he didn't give me a demo for those songs. I'd go, 'I've got this song, She-ee, walking like a killer,' and he'd work out the chords to it 'Ding ding ding ding dit dit'. It sounds easy [but] obviously there was a bit more fucking sweat than that."

This new flexible approach rubbed off on the more upbeat nature of the new material. "I kind of like working like that," continues Brett, "because the whole of *Dog Man Star* was written by post pretty much. Bernard sent me a cassette and I'd spend a couple of months crafting them into whatever. There was no mutual exchange or anything like that."

During Suede's absence, the musical landscape had shifted massively. Previous support bands such as Pulp and Manic Street Preachers appeared to be stealing Suede's thunder and audience. Blur and Oasis were the new Beatles and Stones, regularly shagged in type by a fawning and predictable media cabal. Ex-Suedettes Justine and Justin were enjoying a number one album with the eponymous *Elastica* and Bernard had bounced back as one half of the inspired if unlikely partnership McAlmont and Butler. The frankly stunning "Yes" was undoubtedly one of 1995's greatest singles, and "You Do", purportedly a Suede song rejected by Brett, was almost as good. "I've had two top 20 singles," sneered Bernard. "What have they done?"

Symbolically, the week that Suede entered The Church Studios coincided with the beginning of the end for Britpop. Blur's "Country House" pipped Oasis's "Roll With It" to the top of the charts in a battle of the bands that made *News At Ten*. Assuming, as many others had done, that Bernard's exit sounded Suede's death knell, Damon and Co. required a new enemy to spar with. The "singing electricians", as Brett once put it, were the perfect foil. "As soon as Suede stopped being something to pick on, Damon started picking on Oasis," confirms Justine Frischmann, now the indie Posh to Damon's Becks. "Revenge and hate are often the best motivating factors."

The Machiavellian Albarn had deliberately shifted release dates to make it a head-to-head clash and the resultant hoo-ha temporarily masked the fact that both bands had accidentally released the worst singles of their careers. In a genius gesture, Blur's Alex James wore an Oasis T-shirt on *Top Of The Pops*. Oasis retaliated by wittily altering the "In the country" chorus of "Country House" to "I'm a cunt, me!" before exposing themselves further to abject ridicule with some ill-conceived mutterings. Blur supporters maintain that Liam understands Balzac to be French for scrotum.

A ceasefire in the Britpop wars occurred on September 4 when Blur, Oasis, Suede and the cream of the current indie elite were united under the common cause of each recording a special track for *Help*, the Warchild charity album to raise awareness and cash for children caught up in the war in the former Yugoslavia. Twenty bands had 24 hours to record and mix the songs of their choice, with the album released a record-breaking five days later. Suede chose the Elvis Costello/Clive Langer classic "Shipbuilding", made famous by Robert Wyatt. Brett described it as the best protest song of all time. "We've played it before at soundchecks but it was never really appropriate to record it until now. We didn't want to just knock off some chirpy pop song."

Suede were already considering changing producers and took the opportunity to work with co-writer Clive Langer and his side-kick Alan Winstanley, the legendary duo who had worked with everyone from Madness to Morrissey. Elvis Costello had been approached but was in France at the time, though he did send a good luck message to the boys on the day. The song was recorded at Olympic Studios in Barnes where the Rolling Stones had recorded "Sympathy For The Devil". James Banbury of the Auteurs added a touch of pathos with his cello while Guy Barker contributed a dazzling freeform trumpet solo. Richard played a beautiful new piano arrangement though lack of time scuppered any chance of adding guitar. But as Richard said, "The great thing about the track is that it sounds really Suedey and yet it doesn't have any guitars on it."

Suede's fine contribution was drowned out in the furore over three generations of Britpop icons – Noel Gallagher, Paul Weller and Paul McCartney – coming together for a pedestrian stroll through "Come Together". Not that this really mattered. The album sold bucket-loads, raising two million pounds in its first three days. In a happy extension of this spirit of *détente*, Noel Gallagher, at the launch for the album, told Richard Oakes, "You've got balls bigger than a buffalo."

Toward the end of 1995, Sam McCormick and I couldn't help noticing an extremely thin, chain-smoking young man dressed in a fur coat and shaking unnervingly, who would regularly visit the office with the apparent sole purpose of collecting money from Charlie.

"Who's he?" we asked one day.

"That's Neil."

The band's increasing use of keyboards on songs like "By The Sea" and "She" presented them with the problem of how to play them live. The answer, like the shopkeeper in *Mr Benn*, appeared as if by magic. Neil John Codling, Simon Gilbert's cousin, had recently graduated with a 2:1 in English and Drama from Hull University and was living around the corner from The Church Studios in Crouch End. Legend has it that he popped into the studio to borrow a jacket and joined the band by osmosis.

"Maybe it was fate," ponders Alan Fisher. "We were sitting in Simon's flat in Portobello Road and Neil was there and seemed to have all the qualities of a star. He was very Suede, slightly mad, ideal sort of Suede member. Neil picked up the guitar then started playing the piano. 'Anything else you can play?' And he started reeling off this list of instruments. And Brett's like, 'Simon, you know we've been having a meeting to talk about a new member, why didn't you mention your cousin could play all these instruments?'"

Neil's origins have been a matter of some dispute. "I did an interview with Simon Price once and he misheard me," laughs Neil. "He said I was from the affluent village of Tilling, which doesn't exist. I was born in exactly the same place as Simon Gilbert was, this maternity home just round the corner from where we grew up. It's in Tiddington and it's not affluent at all."

Neil's father was a civil engineer from Hartlepool, his mother a secretary from Redditch. They met somewhere in the Midlands while working for the local council and married in the early 1960s, when they had two children, Paul and Lynda. Neil was born much later, on December 5, 1973. His earliest musical memories are of a strange mix between classical and heavy metal, his father's taste for Elgar and the romantic classics sounds being not a million miles away from Brett's dad's passions. "I think they would have got on famously," agrees Neil. "If they'd ever have met it would have been like something out of *Ghostbusters*!"

Although his father could pass muster on the piano, there wasn't any great musical legacy in the Codling household. "My mum adored Deep Purple and Led Zeppelin, basically because she fancied Ian Gillan and

Robert Plant," says Neil. "Basically, anybody she fancied she was into. My brother was really into the Pistols and punk and Stiff Little Fingers and the Police. He's about the same age as Simon. We were just a stone's throw from each other so they were buddies."

Neil attended William Shakespeare's old school, King Edward V Grammar, an all-boys school with all the terrors that go with being in a single sex school. "It was fairly uneventful," shrugs Neil. "There's that programme on BBC2 at the moment, *In Search Of Shakespeare*, and they went to his old school and it's completely different from how I remember it. It was archaic. They had some government inspectors round when I was there and they said 'These boys are too cowed and repressed' and what have you. My brother used to get the cane a lot, for vandalism. I used to get slapped a lot."

Neil had always wanted to be a bass player and started playing in his early teens. Interestingly, his first band was named Strangelove. Heavily Floyd-influenced, they played "long, noodly songs" in a Baptist Church next to the Warwick bypass. Moving to Hull, he shared a house with Tom Watson who was then Union President and has since gone on to become MP for East Bromwich. Tom took Neil to the Union Bar one evening and introduced him to a friend called Nick Rogerson who just happened to be looking for a bass player for his band, Moist. Neil joined and soon started contributing his own songs. "It was a strange band," he remembers. "If you could imagine a cross between the Bonzo Dog Band and somebody on Acid Jazz."

Overviews of Suede have occasionally mentioned a band called the Fit Drunks, who Brett once named his tip for the top and of which Neil was supposedly a member. "That was a joke," reveals Neil. "Bob Dylan was once asked about his favourite bands and he said, 'Oh, the Fab Clocks and the Fit Drunks,' and it was in a book that Mat had and he said that the Fab Clocks was a fantastic name for a band. Mat was round here the other night and said somebody should still use that as a name for a band."

In July 1995, the week after he graduated from Hull University, Neil set off for London with his friend Jim. They had absolutely no idea what they were going to do when they got there. "We just got out of the car somewhere that looked London-ish and we got this place in Crouch End and it was the size of a shoe box. It was an absolutely tiny attic and we moved in there for that summer."

Neil's new digs at 149 Rathcoole Gardens were spitting distance from

The Church Studios, where his cousin's band were working on material for their new album. He'd seen them a few times. "They had an early review in *Melody Maker* that said 'lead singer Martin' and so that was all very exciting for everybody in the family," remembers Neil. "The first place I saw them was the Hummingbird in Birmingham when they were supporting Kingmaker in May 92. And that was insane because that was the back end of Fraggle Rock. It was all the Stourbridge thing, all shorts and stagediving. They played 'Pantomime Horse' and there were people getting on stage and leaping off in the middle of this incredibly quiet reflective ballad."

Neil had decided to try his hand at being a film editor and reckoned that wearing a suit would give him a better chance of getting his foot in the door. "I had to do something rather than live on the dole," he says. "So I thought if I looked the business I might have a better chance. I knew that Simon had a suit of my brother's, because when Simon was on tour my brother used to look after his flat when he lived in London and he'd left one of his suits at Simon's place. So the story is fairly accurate. I did actually go to borrow a suit."

Arriving at The Church Studios, Neil was given a camcorder by Simon and asked to film a few of the songs the band were running through. "They were doing 'Picnic By The Motorway', which was then called 'Lovely Day'. I heard the demo of 'She' and things. So that was fun. Nobody ever really talked to me much. Simon was affable as ever. Mat I don't think ever spoke to me for at least three months."

Neil began hanging out with the band more and more until eventually they asked him to come down to their next rehearsal at Backstreet on Holloway Road. "They basically made up a tape and said, 'Go away and learn that,'" says Neil. "'This needs a piano part, this needs bit of strings on it, this needs some backing vocals.' So I went down to a couple of rehearsals, it was just with the aim at that stage to add a bit of bulk to the sound."

The songs on Neil's "audition tape" were demos of "She", "Lazy", "We're So Disco" (a song from the Justine days which would go through many permutations before finally surfacing as the dubbed-up "W.S.D."), "Money" (which Charlie had flagged as the potential comeback single, a suggestion that Saul Galpern still finds incredibly hilarious), "Saturday Night", "Young Men", "Another No One", "By The Sea" (live from Phoenix) and "Together", in effect the first draft of Suede's third album. The band got as far as re-recording the drum track of "Together" before realising that a set of entirely new songs was preferable to re-hashing old ground. Reaction to this work in progress was favourable, if hardly ecstatic. "I remember thinking it was good," says Saul. "There was a shortage of singles, but they came later."

Pete Sissons agrees: "As soon as I heard songs like 'Beautiful Ones', 'Chemistry', 'Starcrazy'…just superb songs. There was no doubt. It took a while for these songs to come about, though. There was a while when I was hearing songs that became b-sides a bit too much, 'We're So Disco', you know. All nice enough songs but nothing that was quite sticking out. One day you'll go into rehearsal and it's a different story. It's classic singles flying out."

After two or three rehearsals Brett asked if Neil fancied playing keyboards on their live dates. "I went down to the offices in Old Street," Neil continues. "Charlie stared right through me and thought, 'What on earth are they doing with this specimen?' but had to acquiesce. So they put me on a retainer but I don't think it was ever with an aim to be a proper member, it was just making up the numbers as the keyboard player in the background."

Richard remembers an amusing piece of footage from Simon's video diaries of Neil's first rehearsals with the band. "Neil's playing the piano, and Simon zooms in on his hand and it's got 'Sign on!' written on his hand as he's playing," laughs Richard. "So he was already becoming a member of Suede and had to remind himself to sign on as well."

With a wage and a part-time post in the "Best New Band In Britain", Neil's luck was on the up. And Suede weren't the only ones to spot his potential star quality. "I was walking up Kilburn Lane, walking home and somebody stopped me," he recalls. "I was wearing that hounds-tooth checked jacket that Charlie really disliked, and this woman said, 'You've got a great style. We'd really like to use you for free and get a twenty-grand photo-shoot for nothing.' So I went down and did some Polaroids and then they phoned up and said, 'Yeah, it's this *Vogue* thing.' I didn't know what the fuck I was doing." The photos, of Neil sucking in his cheeks like he'd scoffed a particularly bitter lemon, were ostensibly for Italian *Vogue*, but inevitably resurfaced at the height of Cod-mania in publications from *Select* to *The Face*.

The jacket that had caught the fashion scout's attention would soon be appearing in Suede photos around the world, much to the chagrin of the band's manager. "Charlie phoned me up and said, 'Oh, the album's going great, you sound like U2 but you look like Sleeper, so lose the jacket!'" laughs Neil. "So every time I knew I'd see him, I wore the jacket to piss him off."

"We always used to congregate around Chesterton Road at that point," remembers Richard. "There was much more of a scene of people back then, you'd always see the same faces. Neil used to come round a lot, he was on the dole and just hanging out. And he was really nice and he looked good and everything. I could imagine him being in the band. He was a cool person. He used to play us some of his own songs, like 'Digging A Hole'. He used to sit down after a few beers and play it on guitar. He was into things like Scott Walker and would talk to Brett about that and things like Pink Floyd and it was obvious that there was a connection there. The way he came into Suede was so different from the way I did. It was much more, 'You've got a job to do. Here's your job. Can you handle this?' And then going on tour straight away. I didn't have to get integrated into Suede, I was just shoved in, in somebody's place. And Neil was much more able to get in there like roots growing into the ground."

Victor Aroldoss remembers Neil's arrival ushering a definite sea-change in the inter-band relationships. "Brett was really taken with Neil. Richard had been the centre of attention, and he wasn't after that," says Victor. "Richard sort of knew his place. He was like quiet little Richard and Neil was with the big boys. He'd socialise with Brett, he'd be the cool one and Richard wouldn't be. I think that's when Richard's confidence started going and what we've seen since is a steady thing from that, 'cause he was a confident, cocky little shit before that!"

Nevertheless, Richard and Neil hit it off, often helping each other out with their latest compositions. "Neil came round one evening and we got really drunk together," remembers Richard. "There's a hilarious recording of us doing the song that became 'Weight Of The World', with one of us playing piano really badly and Neil singing and there's like five tracks of 'waaaagh' at the end. We were obviously having a bit of a laugh with the multi-track."

According to Victor, however, the band slowly began to divide into two camps. "At that point it was very much Brett and Neil. Mat mellowed a bit and was with Richard a lot. There can be certain alliances with the band and Simon would fluctuate between them. There was sort of two sets. Mat didn't do drugs, I know he did earlier, but not since I've known them. Neil joined in and was sort of the golden boy. Around that time Richard met Alex [his long-term girlfriend] and just went into his own separate world."

Despite these tiny hairline cracks, it was with huge self-belief that Suede began pre-production for their third album, for some reason lumbered with the working title of *Old People Make Me Sick*, on November 23. Recording proper began at the Townhouse, Goldhawk Road on December 3, two days before Neil's twenty-second birthday.

With little to do in the studio, Neil asked to borrow Richard's drum machine and four-track recorder to potter about with over Christmas. "I did this demo of this thing which ended up as 'Starcrazy', or 'Tiswas' as it was then known," says Neil. "And I wrote it on the back of this thing that said 'Do not let your dog crap here, Haringey Council', a sign that was strapped outside, because I didn't have any paper. I wrote the chords down on that and gave it to Brett and he did 'Starcrazy' from it. So that was the start of becoming less of a keyboard player and becoming more a part of the band."

Victor remembers Brett being over the moon when he heard the first demo of "Starcrazy". "He was jumping up and down and throwing bottles of red wine against the wall, smashing them against the wall. From the outside it seems, 'Oh, I love myself so much,' but everyone thought they were really great tunes and was just excited about how well they'd done."

Neil was by now crashing at Mat's new place at 1 North Pole Road. "For some reason, which I never really fathomed, he used to be quite happy wearing underwear and boots and a T-shirt," recalls Mat. "That's how I remember him, wandering around the house in his underwear plus boots and he'd be brewing up some horrific potion, some Chinese herbal thing, and it just stank. And he was a strange character with bizarre diet fads and he was interested in things that none of the band were, like cricket and Shakespeare."

Neil's formal introduction to the outside world came on January 27 when the band played another of their legendary fanclub gigs. This time, more than 800 of the faithful were shoehorned into the Hanover Grand off Regent Street. The set was a lot shorter than usual, just nine songs. But it's no exaggeration to say it was one of the most important gigs of their entire career. "It was quite a trying experience for everybody," agrees Neil, "because this was Richard's stuff and the only one that anybody had heard was 'Together', so everyone was really nervous. It wasn't any harder for me than it was for the rest of them because they all thought, 'This is it, either we cut the mustard now or we don't know what's gonna happen.'"

The band, who hadn't released a single for over a year, proved they were still a force to be reckoned with. "No Bernard Butler songs. A set that says 'No need'," observed Steve Sutherland in *NME*. He seemed particularly taken with their new fifth appendage: "Sulky, skinny and dead-eyed as a fashion model, hands on hips, the occasional backing vocal, a pouty threat from *A Clockwork Orange*, an occasional pianist, an immobile show-stealer."

Simon Price, writing for *Melody Maker*, was similarly impressed. "There's a new fifth member, who has the face of Laetitia Sadier, dresses in regulation Suedewear and supplies everything from piano to handclaps. After some deliberation we decide it's a girl. Then Brett introduces it as 'Neil'."

For Neil himself, it was a most peculiar initiation. "This was still part of being absorbed into the band," he recalls. "And that was a strange thing because it's like, 'Where does this guy stand?' It's like, 'What the fuck do you do with your hands?' I hadn't thought about this shit at all. Every other time thereafter I had a keyboard to sit behind but I only played it on 'Lovely Day', which the *Melody Maker* for some reason thought was called 'A Terrible Mistake'! But I didn't have anything to do. And Hanover Grand is such a terribly narrow stage so, 'Oh, you're going to have to stand in front of Mat, right at the front,' and Brett and Richard are doing their stuff behind the monitors. I'm standing right at the front so that Mat doesn't whack me with his bass. 'What do I do with my hands?'"

The *Guardian's* Susan Corrigan didn't mention the new arrival, but did accurately pinpoint the radio-friendly, commercial appeal of the new songs; "Like the singer, the new compositions are pared down and direct, and they shock like a slap in the face. The lyricist has refined his approach…still consumed by love and obsession, but using the wisdom of maturity to make his lyrics simple and direct, Anderson triumphs over his words rather than being so obviously ruled by his thesaurus." After singling out "Beautiful Ones" and "Lazy" as pop hits-to-be, her review ended with an optimistic prediction: "Hindsight always looks kindly on the bands who stick to their vision. Don't call Suede's return a comeback – that happens this spring."

After being written off, rejected and ridiculed, Suede were about to pull off the most impressive resurrection since the boy from Bethlehem. The band oozed confidence.

"It was a really exciting time because it was a new kind of band," agrees Brett. "Neil had just joined. Neil would turn up and come and get off his face with us and Richard would turn up and Simon and Victor and people like that. There was a really cool, united band atmosphere, which I kind of miss now to be brutally frank. It did feel like a little gang, it was really exciting and the spirit of *Coming Up* came from that."

CHAPTER TWELVE
starcrazy

ONE MORNING IN MAY 1996 Charlie bounded into Suede's office like a Cheshire cat with a particularly large consignment of cream. "Listen to this," he beamed, jamming a cassette into the hi-fi, "and ignore the fact that it sounds like 'Heroes'!" The last number written and recorded for the album, the song was called "Pisspot", but would shortly be better known across the globe as "Trash". The quintessential Suede anthem, "Trash" introduced the new poptastic Suede in glorious Technicolor. The working concept about recognising an old flame in a porn mag originally kicking off with the couplet, "Saw your legs spread in a magazine, I never knew you did pornography," had been abandoned in favour of a brash celebration of the band and their fans. "Maybe, maybe it's the clothes we wear, the tasteless bracelets and the dye in our hair... We're trash you and me, we're the litter on the breeze..." It was the missing ingredient in an album that would re-establish Suede as a worldwide commercial and musical force.

"We were searching for the first single and we'd written 'Beautiful Ones' and we thought it was great," remembers Brett. "But the first single off the album, as well as being a great song, had to say something fundamental about the band and for me 'Trash' is THE Suede anthem in a sense. It says it all about what it is to be Suede and what Suede are all about. And because it was about the band it was sort of about the fans as well. And I felt as though I'd hit the nail on the head there and universally everyone around us said, 'Yeah, that's the single.' It was a very exciting time."

Released on July 29, "Trash" effortlessly shot to number three in the national charts, only held off the top spot by that summer's two heavyweights. Robbie Williams was at number two with his first solo outing, a cover of George Michael's "Freedom". Pole position went to the pop phenomenon of the year, five young ladies of indeterminate talent called The Spice Girls, with their indisputably brilliant debut, "Wannabe".

For Richard Oakes, it was probably the most exciting moment of his life. Having previously been perceived as either a joke or a whipping boy, he was now re-positioned as the saviour of the band's career.

"'Trash' got a review in the *NME* that said, 'This is a brilliant single, the b-sides are brilliant as well. Suede are back!'" remembers Richard. "We definitely had a real sudden image at that point. We all had leather jackets and dark hair and I can tell you that was actually spontaneous. I know Suede are such a stylised band in people's eyes, but look at us and look at a band like the Hives. They've got a stylist! But that never happened with Suede. I dyed my hair 'cause I felt like it. I understand the impact that had, though. People were like, 'Suede are back, look at them, they're all mean and fit and they've all got black hair and white faces and they've got this brilliant single!' And fine, because that was our biggest hit. 'Stay Together' got to number three and when 'Trash' got to number three I was like, 'If only it had got to number two!' But it sold more copies. It's our biggest selling single. And rightly so, it was a really good song."

After being out of kilter for so long, Suede had caught the *zeitgeist* perfectly. In many ways, they had inadvertently become the indie Take That, a kind of Dorian Gray-style mirror to the ubiquitous Spice Girls. Posh Suede, Neil Codling, was the band's teen heart-throb, giving Suede all-areas access to pre-pubescent magazines like *Just Seventeen* for the first time. It was a role he relished. "I didn't have a problem with it at all," he admits. "Richard didn't really want to do that sort of thing. That time was quite propitious for guitar bands, it suddenly did have some kind of credibility so you have to kind of milk it. You know, I used to do *Smash Hits* and stuff with people saying, 'If you got stuck on a desert island, which member of Take That would you sleep with?'"

To this new generation, for whom indie music might as well have been what Ghandi listened to on his Walkman, the burning question of the day was what was going to happen to the various members of Take That now that they'd split up. "I remember saying to *Smash Hits* that Mark Owen would become the new Norman Wisdom and I failed to catch on to the target audience," laughs Neil. "So it had to explain who Norman Wisdom was: 'Latvia's biggest star and the man from the late '40s early '50s who starred as a milkman who kept upsetting the apple-cart in various appalling Ealing comedies.'"

Suede's ubiquitous presence in teen rags like *Smash Hits* was indicative of a new mood. Thanks to bands like Suede, the alternative had become the mainstream, though this happy renaissance would soon disappear as real bands were rejected in favour of increasingly disposable pop pap, culminating in the woeful *Pop Idol* phenomenon which would come to dominate. "You used to get the lyrics to 'Every Day Is Like Sunday' and Neil Tennant used to write for them," reflects Neil. "It used to have a bit of acerbic wit and a bit of nous but now it's gone completely out the window."

By this time Neil had established himself as a fully functioning fifth member of the band. After the success of his first effort, the candy floss "Starcrazy", which Brett even talked about as a possible single, he'd begun work on a more weighty composition. "I did this demo round at Richard's and it was this fantastic, huge, multi-layered thing and then on the other side of it there was this crappy little rinky-dinky acoustic idea that I'd kind of abandoned," he recalls. "And Brett rewound the tape and played the crappy half-idea and wrote 'Chemistry Between Us' to that instead of this fantastic demo that we'd spent two days on."

Seven minutes long, "Chemistry" would become the album's epic centrepiece, while the abandoned master work on the other side of Neil's cassette would eventually resurface as "Simon".

Since his sweaty initiation ceremony at the Hanover Grand in January, Neil had played just two gigs, enormous outdoor festivals in Denmark and Spain. "That was my first time on a bloody plane, flying to Denmark," he recalls, still not quite believing his luck. "That was quite a thing. The rest of them, they'd seen it all before. Even Richard by then was jaded. But I was like, 'Hurray, I'm in the band, hurray!'" Within 48 hours, he was on *Top Of The Pops*.

Coming Up was finally introduced with a midnight gig and signing session at the Virgin Megastore on Oxford Street on September 2. The launch party was held at Heaven where guests were presented with a free Suede condom, a shrewd move considering the Bacchanalian excesses which ensued. The album shot straight to the top of the charts.

"At the time I thought it was exactly what it deserved," says Brett. "I totally wasn't surprised. Of course, I was pleased about it, but I thought that we were the best band around again, that we'd got our crown back after a couple of years of being down. I always thought of myself as a writer as quite untouchable at the time. I thought all the

other people, peers, other bands,
were quite good musically and
obviously good bands but what
they were saying was meaningless. I thought I was the only
contemporary writer that was
saying something."

Exactly as Brett had planned,
Suede had made an album of pure
pop thrills. Ed Buller's vision was
of a *Slider* for the '90s, although
Brett's personal favourite T-Rex
album was *Tanx*. "Ed was totally
up for it," says Mat Osman. "He
was really keen on using all those
devices: the big repeated end, the
handclaps, the straightforward
chorus, make it big and obvious.
Dog Man Star had been so

labyrinthine and we wanted something that was much more direct."

Suede were back. With a vengeance. "It was very strange when
Coming Up came out," reflects Neil. "It was battling against *Jagged Little
Pill*. It was a strange kind of time but it all felt right."

By now, rather than teetering, sacrificial lamb-like at the edge of the
stage with hands on hips, Neil had developed a stage persona all of his
own. Affecting a louche insouciance that would infuriate almost as
many as it delighted, he would saunter off stage mid-set, in a puff of
cigarette smoke, returning perfectly on cue to deliver a brief snatch of
piano. At more than one gig he even began reading a newspaper at his
keyboard, as if oblivious to the rock'n'roll circus caterwauling around
him. It was fantastic theatre, though not everyone got it. "We played
Dublin," remembers Neil, "the MTV thing at the Tivoli where they spent
all the money on some lights that didn't work, and this girl came up to
Richard and said, 'Young fellah on the organ, what's he got to be so
miserable about?'"

Neil's most important contribution, however, was bringing a
newfound sense of symmetry, which had been upset since Bernard's
departure. Surprisingly few people made the obvious comment that it
had taken two people to replace the mighty Bernard properly, perhaps

because against all odds, Suede really had arisen from the ashes of the Phoenix Festival. "I can't believe it's not Butler!" gushed the *NME* in the cover headline of the year. The band was properly united for the first time in years.

"I think the time around 'The Drowners' and the time around 'Trash' is when the band has, in its different line-ups, had that kind of real gang mentality," agrees Brett, "which I've always really envied when I've seen it in other bands. You know you see it in bands, like the Smiths and the Stone Roses in their heyday, where they're just a gang of guys who're hanging out together and making great music. There's nothing contrived about them, it's a very natural thing. And the music's a very natural expression of who they are as people and the clothes they wear is the same sort of expression, it's just a different kind of creative expression."

Suede's new regulation uniform of floppy dyed black hair, black Doc Martens and the ubiquitous black leather jacket was as serendipitous as the junk shop clothes of yore, as Simon testifies: "With the photo-shoot for the *Coming Up* album there were two black leather jackets at the photographer's studio, one was mine and one was Brett's. Nobody else had a jacket, so everybody wore ours."

It was a look that would be adopted by the disaffected youth of the UK and beyond. "I think we've always been the outsider band," Brett told Simon Price in *Melody Maker*, when asked about his new Pied Piper status. "It's partly because we are a strange band: all different ages, and heights, and sizes, we didn't all grow up together at school. It's more like a collection of…freaks, forced together under the name Suede. And it's partly down to me feeling like an outsider, which I have done all my life. And I think people who feel like outsiders empathise with the songs."

This celebration of the dispossessed was taken even further on Suede's next single. Saul Galpern remembers hearing it for the first time during the album sessions. "They hadn't demoed it, and they said, 'Oh, we've got a good one.' And then they wouldn't let us hear it for ages. When they did I was like, 'Fucking hell, that's really strong, what's that called?' 'Oh, "Dead Leg",' they replied."

Richard had been going through a phase of naming his latest compositions after playground tortures. "We'd just come home from somewhere and I was getting out of a taxi to get into my flat in Westbourne Grove and Mat said to me, 'If you don't write a pop hit tonight, I'm going to give you a dead leg!'" laughs Richard. "So I went and wrote the music to 'Beautiful Ones' and called it 'Dead Leg'. There was another one, 'Chinese Burn', which never got used, but which I'm gonna do something with it 'cause I really like the chorus. Then 'Wedgie', which became 'This Time'. And various other threats from the rest of the band. But the songs got written!"

In many ways the ultimate Suede single, and certainly one of the most enduring, "Beautiful Ones" echoed the moronic melodic genius of Strawberry Switchblade's "Since Yesterday" and, uncannily, the latest from Suede's closest rivals at that point, The Spice Girls' "Say You'll Be There". It was only natural that the two bands should appear on *Top Of The Pops* together on October 23. Charged with chaperoning Suede that day, Sam McCormick recalls the great meeting only too well. Neil Codling, it seemed, was determined to make the most of his new-found celebrity status. "Neil decides he's going to go on a bender," winces Sam. "He's on at me to get him some charlie, so I'm trying to get hold of some dealer all day, and having Neil pester me every ten minutes to see if I've sorted it."

For once the drugs never materialised but Neil, it seems, managed to enjoy himself thoroughly without them. "He's throwing chips at cast and members of *EastEnders* in the canteen," groans Sam, "flicking V signs at the camera during rehearsals – which results in Rik the producer taking me to one side and telling me that if he does it again he's off the show – and flirting with The Spice Girls."

By home time Sam had just about had enough of Suede's new pin-up. "He's refusing to get in a cab, saying that he's going to go out with the Spice Girls for the night. I tell him he can do whatever he likes, knowing that he's hardly any money and therefore no way of getting home once I've sent his cab away." At the end of her tether, Sam eventually left Neil to his own devices, only to be awoken by a call from him the next morning. He was in a dreadful funk. Somehow he had managed to get home, but had no idea how. More importantly, Suede's European tour resumed that evening in Hamburg and he had lost his passport.

"Bear in mind I'm on the phone so I can't see him," laughs Sam. "I tell him to look in his back trouser pocket. He pats his pocket and is mightily impressed that I have the ability to see down a phone line and find a missing passport. I remembered seeing it there the day before!"

Suede played more than fifty shows in the four months between the release of the album and the end of the year, as well as countless promotional engagements ranging from *TFI Friday* and *Later With Jools Holland* to the *Smash Hits Poll Winners Party* at Docklands Arena. "I didn't think the gigs were as good as the *Dog Man Star* days," reflects Victor Aroldoss. "They were quite an efficient rock band during *Coming Up*. I don't think they were as good live. Even though it was an amazing album, I didn't think it was as amazing as before, but surrounded by all the magazines and the chart positions, it was a roll…

"Neil was big time into drugs during the first half of the tour. And Neil wasn't the best person on drugs – he used to have panic attacks and stuff. When they did the *Smash Hits* thing they were completely off their faces. That tour was completely sold out, that was the height of it. Brett put his business hat on and distanced himself from partying with the band, still did drugs but did it with his own set of people. He didn't socialise with the rest of the band. So then Neil was on his own and did more drugs and got madder."

Despite the usual hard play, the hard work was beginning to pay off. *Coming Up* would turn platinum in January, eventually going on to sell more than half a million in the UK alone – roughly the sales of the first two albums combined. More significantly, it sold a further million copies and more around the rest of the world. "It's their biggest selling album and it's the album that broke them internationally," confirms Saul Galpern. "They toured a lot in Europe and did a lot of work there and it paid off. To their credit, Suede in relation to a lot of other bands in their genre at one point were bigger than Blur and Oasis and the Manics. It all came together at the right time. I knew it would be massive. It was always hard with Suede, though. I still think they're like the biggest underground band in the country. It was a hard struggle to do it, it was never easy. Every time we put a single out, there was an increase in sales but we had to spend a lot of money to keep it up there or it would drop away. They never ever had a record which just went off on its own steam."

It was this international breakthrough that would secure the band's longevity. While most British groups sell around three-quarters of their records in the UK and the remainder abroad, for Suede these proportions swung the other way.

"You first start and all you give a shit about is what people think of you in London," says Brett. "And as we went on and started to see the world and be exposed to different people, you don't see German journalists as such a joke any more. These people are fans of music and seeing the rest of the world did make international success really important and it was something we really concentrated on. The British music scene can be very fickle and very unforgiving and it's always been a strength of the band that we have had success abroad."

The year 1996 drew to a triumphant close with three sold-out nights at London's legendary Roundhouse, which had been in limbo since 1983. A converted steam engine workshop, this was where Jimi Hendrix and the Rolling Stones made their names and the Doors had played their only UK gig. On the final evening Suede were joined by the Pet Shop Boys' Neil Tennant – another hero from that very first "Guitar player wanted" ad – who sang on both the next Suede hit, "Saturday Night", and on Suede's blistering version of the Shoppies' own "Rent".

"I've always been a huge fan of the Pet Shop Boys," says Brett. "I think they're absolutely brilliant. Them and the Smiths and Prince were without doubt the best artists of the '80s. I've always loved the way they combine the incredibly slick and urbane with something very poetic. Songs like 'Rent', 'West End Girls', lots of the really big hit singles, they're not just throwaway pop songs. So I think we just called him up and said, 'Fancy doing this?' I'd met him before, the first time in New York when we were doing press for *Dog Man Star* I think. We got together in a hotel in Times Square and did a lot of coke together, it was quite a laugh. Every time Neil's around we always have a good time. He's one of those permanent friends. He's a smashing man."

"That was great," laughs Neil Codling. "Neil Tennant said, 'I've never sung with a pop band before!' and Chris Lowe corrected him. 'It's a rock band Neil, a rock band!'"

A huge celebratory party was held at Bagleys, an enormous warehouse building in the no man's land of goods yards behind Kings Cross Station, the VIPs ferried by a fleet of limos. Brett enjoyed himself so much he lost track of time and, as dawn broke, somehow managed to find himself locked in the building with his girlfriend long after the last revellers had departed.

"I think Sam and Brett were shagging in the toilets there and got locked in," laughs Victor Aroldoss. "Bagleys, as you know, is in the middle of nowhere and they had to climb through the window and dogs were chasing them. I'd already gone back to the house with Alan, and Brett and Sam were supposed to go on holiday to Barbados later that day and they came in and did more drugs and booked a cab to go to Heathrow at six. And it was really sweet because Brett was really off his face and we did Rohypnol so we were just spaced out and Brett said,

'Okay, we're gonna go, have a nice holiday and stuff,' and he kissed me on the head." Brett and Sam made it to Heathrow in the nick of time. Unfortunately, their plane left from Gatwick.

It was during one such absence by his lordship (as Brett was now increasingly known) that Alan made one of the biggest *faux pas* of their lifelong friendship: losing Brett's beloved cat, Missk. "We originally found Missk on the street when we lived at Moorhouse Road," explains Alan. "We'd got ripped off as usual. You know what it's like when you're buying drugs on the street. There's some black guy, 'Give us your money and you wait here.' That's why I got into dealing drugs, because I was bored of being ripped off. It was actually a lot easier to start dealing yourself. But yeah, we got ripped off and then we met this black cat and kind of lured it back to the house. Brett's in love with his cats. But yeah, he went away one time and left me in charge. After a couple of days I remembered we had a cat but I'd taken so many fucking drugs I couldn't even remember what a cat was. I knew it was black and hairy but it could have been anything in that flat. I was looking at cushions, staring at my black Doc Martens, thinking, 'There's the cat!'"

Eventually, a visitor to the flat pointed out to Alan that a pair of black Dr Martens was not in fact Missk. "We had this friend, this lovely mad kind of hippy woman," continues Alan. "She'd write poetry and talk to the cat. She noticed that it had gone missing. So I went out to try and look for it. I found this cat on the street. And I thought it was Missk. I thought it had a cold because it miaowed a different way and it had this kind of white patch."

There was an all too obvious reason why the cat looked and sounded completely different from Missk. "It was actually the wrong cat," Alan cringes. "I remember Brett ringing up and going, 'How's the cat?' 'Oh fine, got a touch of flu I think.' Then he came back and he didn't look happy at all. It was a genuine mistake but he was really pissed off."

This wasn't Alan's only cat catastrophe. "There were a few times," he groans. "We got another cat and it had gone missing as well. 'Why is the cat doing this to me? I'm sure it's doing this on purpose, trying to get me into trouble. They're all at it.' I went out on the balcony and it was literally stuck in the drainpipe up on the roof. So I called the fire brigade and I'm literally off my knackers trying to climb up the drainpipe and the fire brigade arrive and there's this big gathering of people on the street. You start to get really paranoid…but I'm a lot more together these days." Well, quite.

There was another cause for the creeping paranoia at 106 Chesterton Road other than curious looks from the neighbours and strange Bernard Butler look-alikes shoving mystery packages through the cat-flap. Brett's burgeoning fame brought with it the increasingly unwanted attentions of the celebrity stalker. While most were relatively harmless, simply camping out on the doorstep like well-to-do vagrants, a small group of girls turned nasty. The first we knew about it was when Brett's Sam called the office in tears. Some vandals had painted his name and address all around the neighbourhood. There were arrows from Ladbroke Grove right up to Brett's door accompanied by angry daubs including "Brett Anderson lives here!", "Suede is shit!", "Ring top bell!" and bizarrely, "Pulp Rules!" When the local council refused to do anything about it, Suede roadie Kimble Garcia was despatched to paint over the worst of it, but it was a thankless task. No sooner was the offending graffiti obliterated than more appeared. Things got even more sinister when flyers started to appear outside indie nightclubs with full details of how best to harass Suede's lead singer. Unsurprisingly, he eventually initiated plans to move house and the saga was immortalised in the song "Graffiti Women".

In early January, while Suede's wintry ballad "Saturday Night", an ode to Sam, was winging its way to number six in the UK charts, Suede enjoyed a balmy few days in the Canary Islands. "Why have you come to Gran Canaria?" they were asked at the press conference. "Free holiday!" replied Mat. This is the stock answer at virtually every press conference Suede have ever appeared at. To this day no one other than the band themselves has ever laughed.

Much merriment was had, including jet-skiing in the Atlantic and scoring the worst speed known to man. Backstage after the show, someone who wasn't feeling quite as excitable as usual was Neil Codling. "That was pretty difficult. I'd just got glandular fever or something like that," he remembers, "so things were grinding down. I don't know exactly when I got whatever I got but the six months following that everything was running down and I got really unable to cope with touring."

For now Neil's weariness was dismissed as payback for overdoing it slightly and the touring continued with the rest of the band in high spirits. They had plenty to celebrate. "Saturday Night" was the third top-ten single from *Coming Up*, making number six and being the first Suede record to cross over to mainstream radio. The album was doing the business across Europe, particularly in Scandinavia, where it turned gold in Finland, platinum in Norway and double platinum in Denmark and Sweden. "They went mad for it in Scandinavia," laughs Brett. "Maybe because they're all depressed sex maniacs or something."

A particularly exuberant Brett could be observed racing up and down the plush corridors of the Balmoral hotel in Edinburgh, bombarding his beleaguered manager with an endless stream of statistics-based questions.

"Charlie, how many albums have we sold in Spain?"

"Um, about seventy thousand."

"How many have we sold in the Philippines?"

"Er, thirty-five thousand."

"How many in Liechtenstein?"

Etc.

This latest stretch of the UK tour ended on February 15 with a date at King George's in Blackburn. It was a notable gig for many reasons. Brett made an impromptu appearance with support act Raissa, dueting on their wistful "Green As Sea". Suede themselves played "The Chemistry Between Us" live for the first time, something its composer was particularly chuffed about. "I really liked playing it because I got to play guitar on it," grins Neil. This also marked the first occasion where they played an entire album live.

Sam McCormick remembers the date for very different reasons, however. "I had to haul my arse up there to get them to approve the 'Lazy' artwork, and do some behind the scenes radio interviews for Mary Anne Hobbs on Radio 1 for a tour diary thing," she recalls. "They were meant to have been doing the diary all week but hadn't done anything, and the BBC wanted their dat recorder and material back to go on air on Monday night. I had to go round doing interviews with the band, Mansun [the support band] and fans to get something broadcastable. I even managed to get Brett, Neil and Rich singing "Beautiful Ones" *a cappella*. Got on the bus home after the show, listened back to it, everyone very happy with it, so I went to bed and fell into a very deep sleep."

Next thing Sam knew, they were in Maida Vale and it was time to get off the bus. "I walked into the lounge to find the whole place trashed," she groans, "after a massive fight that I had somehow managed to sleep through. A foot had gone through a stereo speaker, there's stuff all over the floor, and the BBC dat machine is in pieces after being repeatedly stamped on. I had to go out and buy a brand new dat player to send to the BBC with an apology that the tour diary had somehow been lost!"

Pausing only to spend a few days in the studio, Suede flew to the Far East for some of the most exciting shows of their career. Pandemonium was the operative word, riots almost breaking out in ultra-conservative Singapore and crowds mobbing them at Bangkok airport. The gigs were pure punk rock and to prove the point Suede frequently encored with the Pistols' "No Feelings". In keeping with this phlegm-speckled spirit, they also had their barnets ruthlessly shorn, the famed floppy fringes replaced by near skinheads. "We all had our hair cut by this woman who said she normally works in Hackney," remembers Neil. "That was quite bizarre."

"Brett's fringe was as much a part of Suede as he was!" bemoaned some fans, pinpointing this event as the Samson-like moment when Suede began to lose their power, an observation which in retrospect has at least a glimmer of truth in it.

The final show in Hong Kong would be the last by a visiting band before the colony reverted to the control of Communist China, after 156 years of British rule. It was also the island's first all-standing rock show.

The cropped crew's next duty was to film the video for the latest single on the seemingly never-ending *Coming Up* conveyer belt, Brett's "Theme From Scooby Doo" soundalike, "Lazy". Loosely based on *Performance*, the shoot saw Richard Oakes suspended from the ceiling by a bungee rope while the rest of the band were pumped full of laughing gas to give them a suitably demented cackle. Brett describes the video as his "cinematic nadir". He had already talked about Neil as being his own personal *Picture Of Dorian Gray*. "I just deteriorate behind the scenes while he stands there looking cool!" And nowhere was this more apparent than the scene where a split mirror contrasted half of one face with the other. Someone else who couldn't help noticing that Brett seemed to be hell-bent on replacing himself with a younger, better-looking version of himself was Justine Frischmann.

"It was funny to meet Neil. I think Brett really adored him because he saw a lot of himself in him when he was younger," says Justine. "Brett was absolutely stunning at 22, he was ridiculously good looking, just beautiful. He really was amazing looking. He really, really did fuck himself up with drugs. I think he looks really healthy again now, so it was temporary. But at the point Neil came in it was almost a reminder to Brett of what he'd lost temporarily."

Now a number one album recording artist herself, Justine had gone

With Derek Jarman at the Clapham Grand, 12th July 1993. "We weren't even sure if he was coming down to the gig because he was so ill at the time. He sat in the box, then right after the show he came back to say hi. It was a genuinely special moment."

Brett in classic arse-slapping pose: "There was something I quite liked about it, the ridiculousness. I didn't feel it was feminine in a soft way, it was quite aggressive, it was almost sexual."

Bernard and Brett in Paris, 1993: "In the early days me and Bernard were good friends and that's something people might not know now."

Simon Gilbert at the House Of Commons in support of equality for the age of consent, 16th January 1994: "Stephen Fry was there, and Pat from *Eastenders* who was lovely. She kept trying to get in all the Suede pictures. It was great to see the whole band there in support, even Bernard turned up which was really nice."

Producer Ed Buller adds some fairy dust at the Christmas 1993 fanclub show. "I've always really liked Ed. He struck me as someone who had a great enthusiasm for music and a great enthusiasm for Suede. I think as Bernard got more technically aware he very soon saw flaws in what Ed was doing."

Bernard's last stand, Queen's Hall, Edinburgh, 12th February 1994: "The Edinburgh gig was just a mess because we were falling apart."

Richard Oakes' worldwide debut, Paris, 7th October 1994. "At the end of the audition they said, 'Are you up for joining?' And I said, 'I'll have to ask my parents!'"

Richard pays his dues on the *Dog Man Star* tour. "It was getting more and more amazing the further round the world we went. Barely six months ago I'd been in the situation where nobody outside my bedroom was in the slightest bit interested in what I had to play on the guitar."

Brett and Mat with Nicky Wire of the Manic Street Preachers, Munich, 4th December 1994. "I felt quite a kinship with the Manics at that time. It felt like we were exiles. It was appropriate that we were touring Belgium and Holland and places like that, like weird deposed kings."

Brett, Richard, Simon and Mat, Europe 1995. "There was a really cool united band atmosphere, which I kind of miss now. It did feel like a little gang, it was really exciting and the spirit of *Coming Up* came from that."

Triumphant through the rain at the Phoenix Festival, 14th July 1995: "I thought 'someone's really got it in for us!'"

Neil Codling, the thinking fan's piece of crumpet. "I think Neil could've been a great popstar and a really great artist as well. He had that little spark, that little bit of creativity and little bit of stupidity in the right amounts."

Neil backstage at *Top of the Pops*, 23rd October 1996. "Neil decides he's going to go on a bender ..."

"... he's throwing chips at members of *Eastenders* in the canteen, flicking V signs at the camera and flirting with the Spice Girls."

Brett, with Tony Hoffer and Alex Lee in pre-production at the Depot, spring 2001. "It was a shame because we got on so well. Tony was really funny and a nice guy to be around. That was probably part of the problem."

Alex and Richard on the video shoot for *Positivity*, 25th July 2002. "I know Suede fans hate it with a passion but there's something I still feel is quite beautiful about the song."

Brett and Mat on the Great Wall of China, February 2003. "China was an amazing place to go. For a lot of the kids it was their first ever rock show and they experienced rock'n'roll madness!"

Brett and John Hurt give a little bit of attitude, 27th August 2003.

Suede, 22nd August 2003.

through a similarly meteoric rise to international superstardom, exacerbated by a touring schedule that made Suede's look like a picnic and a boyfriend who, in the words of her best song, was "Never Here". The catalyst for looking up her ex was a nightmare in which Brett had died and she hadn't even been invited to the funeral. "I woke up in tears and I just thought, 'Oh, my god, I haven't even seen him for like four years and he lives round the corner,' and I just called him up. I said, 'I've just had this really fucking weird dream about you.' It took me all day to get hold of his number because we didn't really have any mates in common any more. I went to see him and just had a real laugh straight away. It was all like water under the bridge, all the shit that had gone on."

And so the two ex-lovers began hanging out together again, and were even spotted sharing a weekend break in Dublin, causing no small amount of gossip among the music biz coterie. "We're just really good friends," Brett told *Select*. "I hate the thought of investing all this time in someone and they just disappear, and all that time slips down the drain. They remain in your memory. If you go out with someone 'for ever', then you should stay friends with them because there's obviously a bond there."

"I met Sam, his girlfriend," continues Justine. "Thought she was amazing, she was wicked, really got on with her and the three of us just started hanging out. We were living round the corner, only two streets away from each other. A lot of what I went through in Elastica, part of the problem for me was that I didn't have anyone to talk to about what I was going through, apart from Damon, who was on his own little planet and was never really around, touring and working constantly. And when the whole touring thing came to an end I was suddenly sitting on my arse in Notting Hill with nothing to do. And it occurred to me that Brett had gone through a lot of the same stuff so we had a lot in common. We had a lot to talk about."

The rekindled relationship was made public on April 5 when Suede played a very special fanclub gig at The Forum, with a set comprised entirely of b-sides. Justine could be spotted on the balcony, dancing and singing along with "To The Birds", the song that used to close the set when she was in the band but which Suede hadn't played for nearly four years.

As for the gig itself, they didn't come much more legendary. "Still they talk of it in bedsits after a hard night's shaking their meats to less sordid beats," marvelled Mark Beaumont in *NME*, "stacked up, shacked up and shivering at the memory. London's Kentish Town Forum awash with a sea of riotous Terylene and nostalgic reverie. Remember Brett's spine-melting solo spot? The most uplifting encore since Jesus claimed he could do more than just the loaves trick? How about the moment when Neil Codling realised that he had to do precisely arse all for the *entire gig*? Better than Radiohead at Glasters, they conclude." And they weren't far wrong.

From that moment, Justine was never far away. "She's not getting back in the band, no matter how hard she tries," Richard Oakes told me on one occasion, and I wasn't entirely convinced he was joking. "She's an old friend of Brett and Mat's so I was happy for her to be around," says Richard. "Whether she's a good influence on Brett is something I won't comment on. I did see him in a state at one point because of her, but we won't go into that!"

According to Victor Aroldoss, this was when the cracks – and the crack – began to become visible. "The b-sides gig was a really, really good show. Justine was there and everybody was vibed to see her. It was like having ghosts laid to rest. But that's when it all started going wrong. I remember going to a club afterwards and someone caught Justine, Sam and Brett in a cubicle with a Polaroid camera. I've no idea what was going on there. This was when Brett was in his own gang and having Justine around reinstated that it was his own gang."

Sam McCormick remembers Justine's Siren-like effect on Brett when the band travelled to Braintree Arena, a misleadingly named venue that was literally a large cow shed replete with mud. "We're all sat in the lounge talking about films," says Sam. "*Forest Gump* gets mentioned, a film that we all hate, and that Brett has professed his hatred of. Justine announced that she really liked the film, and thought we were all wrong, at which point Brett suddenly changes tracks and says: 'Actually, I don't think it was that bad either,' leaving the rest of us looking incredulous!"

Justine even joined the band on stage that night, bellowing through a microphone during "Implement Yeah", a Fall parody from Suede's embryonic years. "We did it ages ago, before Bernard joined, I think," says Brett, "when me, Mat and Justine were just farting around doing nothing. But she's not getting a writing credit if that's what she thinks!"

The lyrics had been updated to include the saga of Saul Galpern's recent encounter with the Fall when he had discussed the possibility of signing the curmudgeonly Mancunian for a second time. Mark E. Smith had been visiting the Nude offices when, unimpressed by what he took to be Saul's lack of enthusiasm for his latest *meisterwerk*, scribbled a few choice obscenities in Saul's diary. The revamped Suede lyrics thus read, "That boy Smith called Saul a Scotch homo, a bald, insane, satanic romo!" The offending words were distorted on the recording by some studio trickery and Mr Galpern has remained blissfully unaware of the horrible truth. Until now.

Back in Braintree, as the band hopped on to the bus, Sam McCormick made an interesting discovery. "I was doing a last minute check of the dressing room just before we left the venue," she remembers, "and came across some needles at the back of the room that had just been left there. Don't know if they were Justine's, though."

While Brett has always had a phobia of needles, it was clear he was beginning to dabble in the hard stuff. "The first thing I heard was crack," says Victor, "which was just a different version of coke which everyone was using anyway so that seemed fine. It just got progressively worse. Nobody ever socialised with each other. Neil stayed by himself and was strange and she came to Braintree and she did 'Implement Yeah'. Brett was so happy to have Justine back in his life. I remember Sam Cunningham telling me that she came back to the house one day and found the two of them in bed together."

In May, Suede crossed the Atlantic for one last stab at bringing the disobedient dog to heel – as Brett had once put it. The opening shows in Canada and New York were excellent, but by Boston the band's enthusiasm was waning. "He sucked singing 'Saturday Night'," says one fan. "He gave a half-assed performance 'cause he was pissed. He sat down and said the words. The crowd kinda sucked too."

Whether this observer means "pissed" in the UK "drunk" sense, or the US "pissed off" sense, the band had a perfectly good reason not to be cheerful when, not for the first time, their equipment was stolen after the show. The culprits had broken into the compound, hotwired the truck containing all of Suede's gear and coolly and calmly driven off into the night.

"We were touring with the Longpigs," remembers Richard. "I used to really like some of their stuff and they were a good live band. They were a bit wild at that point. That guy Richard Hawley was a bit of a character. We'd just done a gig in Boston, went to bed and woke up in the morning and Peter van der Velde [tour manager] was sitting in reception on the phone frantically and he called us all down to reception and said, 'The gear's been stolen.' And we were like, 'What's been stolen, the snare drum and...?' 'No, the whole truck's been stolen, the truck with everything in it from a secure car park in Boston.' It was graduation day and the hotel said, 'A lot of trucks get stolen because there are a lot of trucks on hire and they've got students' whole lives in them so it's a regular occurrence.' And we were like, 'But we've got hundreds of thousands of pounds worth of equipment,' and not only us but the Longpigs as well, who hadn't had massive hits so some of their equipment was borrowed and it was like, 'What do we do?'"

While the crew desperately scrambled to replace the missing loot, the band heroically soldiered on, playing the next couple of shows acoustically. Ironically, they turned out to be two of the best-received shows of the entire tour.

"I have to say it's a large part of the reason we haven't gone back," admits Richard. "It's not just that we don't sell any records. We don't sell any records in Germany but we go there, but it just left such a bitter taste. And it's a shame because we have got fans there. I think doing a one-off gig in New York and a one-off gig in Los Angeles would be a great thing to do. We wouldn't gain anything from it and we'd lose money but they haven't seen us for years and we've got so much better live since then."

Suede spent the summer headlining virtually every major festival in Europe and the *Coming Up* world tour finally ended with a headline appearance at Reading on August 22. To celebrate, a fifth and final single was lifted from the album and "Filmstar" became yet another top ten hit. As with the rest of the campaign, the artwork was overseen by Peter Saville who had made his name as in-house art director at Factory in the '80s, but had been largely absent from the music side of design until *Coming Up* repositioned him in much the same way it had done the band. As an in-joke, Brett and photographer Nick Knight suggested featuring Peter as the suave cover star. "I was press-ganged into 'Filmstar' by both Brett and Nick, who thought it would be amusing," Peter revealed on a recent website Q&A. "I disagreed. I felt it would look egotistical. Also, the character description was 'washed up, failed filmstar'. The lack of budget for a suitable model sealed my fate."

Suede ended their year of triumph in grand style. "Suede have never looked so current, so alive," raved Robin Bresnark in *Melody Maker*. "It's been said already how much they've changed but, tonight, Suede seem to have stopped changing. They have arrived. You can tell by their bewildering confidence, by the way they don't appear to be trying, yet not one second falls short of electric."

Midway through the set, Brett introduced a "very special" guest, "Ms Justine Frrrrrrrischmann!"

"What Justine's appearance says about her love life God alone knows," continued the *Maker* review, "but what it signals about Suede's current state is clear. This is a band so comfortable with their past – and, thereby, their present and future – that they have started to exorcise their demons by sharing a stage with them and hugging them silly. Remember? This is a band who have arrived."

The rumour mill went into hyperdrive when Brett and Justine checked into the Ramada together, the Reading hotel where the entire music industry spends the bank holiday weekend. Simon Gilbert had a better idea than most what was really going on. "I remember walking into the dressing room and Justine was there because she was gonna do 'Implement Yeah' with us, all very exciting, and I walked in and there they were doing a quick bit of smack before the show. And I thought, 'Oh who cares, it's none of my business.' And then it sort of snowballed from there. You didn't see Brett that often after that. He wasn't around. He wouldn't go round everyone's house and have a laugh and get some coke and go down the local pub, the Cock And Bottle. He started getting a bit distant, he wasn't part of the gang any more. And that was smack. That's what it did."

What smack did was almost destroy the band. Suede, who had pulled off the seemingly impossible with an astonishing run of five top ten hits and an album which had made them a truly international success for the first time, were about to disintegrate in a squalid horror show which would make the drama of *Dog Man Star* seem like a trifling tiff.

CHAPTER THIRTEEN
crackhead

SUEDE'S FINAL PUBLIC ENGAGEMENT of 1997 took place a week after Reading in the plush surrounds of the Grosvenor Hotel on Park Lane when they were again nominated for the Mercury Music Prize. This time the award went to Roni Size, something Richard Oakes was delighted about. He'd placed a wager on Size winning. After a dignified rendering of "By The Sea", they retired to their suite for a *Select* photo-shoot. Not unnaturally the magazine wanted the band's two pin-ups, Brett and Neil, on the cover, something the rest of the band weren't too happy about. There was an unwritten rule that it was either Brett or the whole band. "They'd been burnt before having two members on the front," says Victor, "and I think they knew this could go tits up. But at that point Brett really didn't care about his career. I think that was the one time when Suede wasn't the most important thing in his life. Before, it was. Seeing him watching his videos and things you could tell it was the most important thing in his life…now it wasn't, it was drugs, and the band was on the periphery."

Brett and Neil stole the cover of November's *Select*, under the banner "I've tried everything". The article celebrated the release of *Sci-Fi Lullabies*, a 27-track double CD of the pick of their b-sides, which obliterated any hint of unease in the Suede camp. It was a gesture of staggering confidence. "No other band could get away with playing an entire set of b-sides," frothed one reviewer of that year's fanclub gig. And few other bands could get away with releasing a double album of what was usually regarded by mere mortals as filler and throwaways. So stringent was Suede's quality control that they had released surprisingly little cack over the years, throwing away gems like "Killing Of A Flash Boy", "Together" and "Young Men" with almost reckless abandon.

Perhaps the highlight of the compilation was Mat's first co-write, "Europe Is Our Playground", which started off as a chord sequence he'd tinkered around with on an old electric piano and titled "Sombre Bongos". Originally a b-side to "Trash", the band re-recorded it for the album to represent its epic live incarnation.

"I was absolutely thrilled," beams Mat. "It was amazing. I couldn't even talk about it. There's always been really good songwriters in Suede who just do it like making a cup of tea. I've seen Richard and Alex and Bernard do it and it's incredibly frustrating to be honest. I'd always felt the competition was too great. I felt like Ringo. And you don't want more than one 'Octopus's Garden' on the album!"

Even with the evil advent of multi-formatting – releasing several version of the same single – Suede's standards had held up admirably. "Basically, you're asked to produce four new songs for each single and it's actually quite hard work," Brett told *NME*. "We've managed to do it pretty well so far and I think the quality control we've had on each formatted record has been excellent. But it's just one of those things. If you're competing in this marketplace you've really got to compete, simply from a business angle. All the early singles, none of them were formatted. 'Stay Together' would probably have gone to number one if it had been."

One of the few songs not to make it on to the compilation was "Digging A Hole", the first of a handful of numbers penned and performed entirely by Neil Codling and thus, arguably, not a Suede song at all. "Well quite," concedes Neil, "especially when it's the keyboard player. If Richard had done his solo songs it would have made more sense but it's kind of like the guy who's wheeled in. But with *Coming Up*, if you're doing five singles and you're formatting them then any songs that are kicking around you're grateful for, especially when you're touring a lot of that time. I'm sure there's a bit of debate either way among fans saying stuff. It's perfectly legitimate for people to vent their spleen about it. At the time you just think, I've got this song and we need some songs and that's what happened."

Also left well alone was the eight-minute "Feel". "That was our first impromptu rehearsal room jam, called 'Shitbag' back then," says Richard. "Should've kept that name!"

Of the 27 songs that did make it on to the album, it was hard to pick out highlights, such was the bounty of brilliance on offer. It also show-cased a frighteningly detailed chronology of Suede from the small town beginnings of "Where The Pigs Don't Fly", through the sudden rise to "The Big Time", the drugged out bliss of "High Rising" and the downside in "The Living Dead", via the highs and lows of touring in "Europe Is Our Playground" and "Have You Ever Been This Low" right up to Brett's brush with the paint daubing "Graffiti Women". It was practically an Encyclopaedia Brettanica.

"This is truly as good as most Greatest Hits albums," declared John Harris in *Select*, while the *Melody Maker*'s Simon Price sighed dramatically, "The man who is tired of Suede b-sides is tired of life."

Unfortunately, insiders were beginning to suspect that the man who was tired of life was Brett Anderson. By the time of his next public appearance he was a changed man. Suede had been asked to contribute a track to another charity, in this case the Red Hot Aids Charitable Trust. The album, *20th Century Blues*, featured interpretations of songs written by quintessential English fop Noël Coward. Suede chose to update "Poor Little Rich Girl", an arrangement mostly down to Neil Codling, experimenting with the electronic sounds that would form the basis of the next album. Backing vocals were provided by sometime support act Raissa, adding some much needed colour to what was otherwise a bit of a dirge. The gala launch took place in the swanky Park Lane Hotel on January 15, 1998, where guests paid £300 per ticket to see acts like Robbie Williams, Elton John, the Divine Comedy, Pet Shop Boys and Suede. Anyone paying especially to see Suede would have been perfectly entitled to demand a refund.

"The Noël Coward thing was really bad," remembers Victor Aroldoss, "that's when I thought, 'Fucking hell, there's something wrong.' They looked a state, they looked really bad. For part of the song Brett didn't mime. I thought, 'How unprofessional!' I really lost a lot of respect for him then. I thought, 'What's the fucking point?' That sort of upset me. It was just really horrible seeing him not give a shit. I think Rich had really big problems then too."

It was a testing time for Neil Codling too. "I felt really rough that day and that was when Brett was singing 'blurgh' – just wouldn't sing – and the camera had to focus on Mat and that was trying for everybody, mostly Mat. They kind of hung around and met Chris Eubank and he was going, 'Oh yeth, I'm a very big fan of your music,' and all that stuff. I remember sitting in the corridor with Mick Hucknall, talking to Brett, and Elton John walking past and I was sitting there up against the door with everyone doing lines in the room and I was just going, 'Ugh, it's too hot, I can't cope!' so I went home really soon after that and they carried on having fun."

"Before we even did that thing I'd done a load of crack so I didn't know what the fuck I was doing," Brett grimaces. "Drugs were starting to get very, very in control of me. Smack is the ultimate one like that. I think the reason so many people get hooked on it is it seems so inoffensive. It's like smoking a joint or something minor like that. All of a sudden a month later you're crawling up the walls, but it doesn't seem like a big deal at first."

As someone who'd spent the last eight years of his life doing drugs, particularly when the experiences, good and bad, were so closely intertwined with his art, Brett had convinced himself he could handle it. "I actually thought this could be an interesting new chapter," he admits. "I could maybe explore something of myself as an artist doing this. It might bring out something different in me. I didn't want to make another *Coming Up* even though I loved the record. I wanted to go somewhere else with it and I thought it could maybe open certain doors for me. But in the end it just makes you completely flaky and selfish."

Perhaps fortunately Suede bowed out of the limelight for more than a year. When they did resurface, it would be as a shadow of their former selves. Neil Codling spent the best part of the year in bed. "We were doing some demos with Dick Meaney for *Head Music* in March and I got a cold and ended up spending the next five months in bed," he reveals. "I spent five months just sitting or lying in bed, just couldn't do anything. In '98 I was literally in bed for five months. And that was my big sabbatical and they carried on writing and then started recording at Air studios and that was the next thing I was involved with at the time, where George Martin was driving around in his big Rolls Royce."

Brett, now living in a basement flat in Westbourne Park Villas, had become a virtual recluse. "I went to their house once," remembers Victor Aroldoss. "That was a conscious effort to socialise again because they never really socialised with anyone unless you were a crackhead. Sam, especially, was in a really bad state. Brett was hanging around with really awful people, really, really horrible people. You'd go into this room and really hate them immediately. It just wasn't fun any more. Drugs are fun when they're fun; they're not fun when it's serious like that. We saw less and less of Alan. Brett saw more and more of Justine. I think the three of them, Brett, Sam and Justine, were just spiralling out of control. I think something had to give. And it did give."

It was around this time that Mike Smith from EMI Publishing introduced Justine to '60s' chanteuse Marianne Faithful with whom there were obvious parallels. "I put her in touch with Justine and she did some work with Justine and Brett," he reveals. "It didn't come to anything, unfortunately. It was during the long period off that both Suede and Elastica enjoyed at the end of the '90s. And you throw somebody like Marianne Faithful into the middle of that, it was never going to be the wisest move. But her and Justine seemed like a match made in heaven. And I think Justine in particular found a great deal to identify with in Marianne, having been going out with a rock star. And on the back of that they did some recordings. I never heard them. They did some recording but it was very much on portastudios and round at people's houses. I think Marianne was frustrated. She didn't find the whole process particularly together."

This was perfectly understandable. Chris Mackay, a close friend, and occasional Suede fan, recently reminded me of an episode which summed up Brett's hermetic existence at this time: "It was a quiet Saturday afternoon, certainly summer, I was in Suede's office stealing CDs when the phone rang. It was Brett desperate to know if there was £800 in cash in the safe because he didn't know how to use a bank card. Next thing I knew we were in a cab to west London on a mission of great importance and some secrecy. The cab pulled up outside Brett's flat and the curtain twitched and shortly an ordinary looking man in a baseball cap and shades climbed into the front seat. 'Alright mate,' he said. It was Brett in disguise. Within moments we were briefed on our mission and the cab drove some fifty yards down the street and pulled up outside a hi-fi shop. David went in with the cash and it was my job to lift the smallest stereo known to man into the boot of the cab. To this day I don't think anyone saw us. Fifty yards later, Brett was unloading the stereo. 'I'd invite you guys in,' he lied, 'but the flat's a bit of a mess.' 'Is that it?' asked the taxi driver, agog. 'Yes,' I replied. It was a day I'll never forget."

While it seems obvious that Brett was fast losing his grip on reality, Mat Osman admits that for a long time he remained largely unconcerned about his singer's latest hobbies. "It's difficult to tell when things become a problem. There's always been a load of drugs around Suede, not just the band, but all the people we're involved with, so it's hard to tell if a line has been crossed... Brett's a strong personality and I never really saw him as a person who would have a problem with drugs. I'm not moralistic about drugs, I wouldn't say this one's bad, this one's okay.

More than anything there started to be a whole load of people he was associating with who I just couldn't stand. They had nothing to do with the band, nothing to do with anything but drugs. They were drug buddies. This just seemed to be a pure drug thing. The rehearsals got more and more difficult. You couldn't get him up."

It was during a rare visit to Westbourne Park Villas that Richard Oakes realised that he and Brett were heading in very different directions musically and otherwise. "I was still going about it as enthusiastically as I did when we did *Coming Up*," he says, "but with about a tenth of the result. We got 'Everything Will Flow' written right at the beginning and I was thinking, 'Oh this is good.' And I went round to his house with a piece of music that eventually ended up being 'Leaving' and he was writing 'Hi-Fi', bashing away at this keyboard, very focused on what he was doing but oblivious to the rest of the world because he was so unbalanced. I'd get him something I'd just written, I'd give him a tape, and I often wondered whether he actually listened to it. He was so into what he was doing."

Richard was well aware that the next record wasn't going to be a traditional guitar record, but while Neil was becoming more and more interested in synthesiser experimentation, it left Richard in a bit of a pickle. "It kind of meant that I didn't really know what to write, because I always write on guitar," he admits. "I always write from a fairly straightforward classic point of view. I always write imagining a verse and a chorus. Neil was far more...he'd write vibe pieces. And he was doing some great stuff. He did the demo for 'She's In Fashion', which was called 'Gloopy Strings'. It was like something out of *Doctor Who* at that point! He did a lot of really innovative stuff and I was really into it as music, but there was no way I could have written like that. I couldn't find my way around a sampler. I knew how to play the guitar but, especially with Brett, that wasn't what he wanted to hear."

Oblivious to the concerns of his colleagues, Brett was still full of enthusiasm for the next album, soaking in a huge range of influences. He became increasingly excited by dance music and hip hop. "One night me and Justine did some E and she played me Tricky's 'Black Steel'," he remembers. "I simply couldn't stop playing it. I loved the dark groove and the voice but most of all I loved the words. They seemed to sum up generations of racial anger. They were written by Public Enemy."

Suede's recent excursions to the Far East proved hugely influential.

"While we were touring *Coming Up* in Asia I started to read a lot about Eastern philosophy and began to practise meditation," he says. "There were no religious implications, only philosophical ones. The concept of ultimate enlightenment, Satori, was very seductive."

"Everything Will Flow" is an obvious example of this fixation with the karmic laws of cause and effect, but Asia had a musical impact too as witnessed by the bent string motifs of "Indian Strings", "She's In Fashion" and "Everything Will Flow". "The initial concept for 'Indian Strings' was to get that tinny Bollywood string sound," says Brett, who had also begun devouring literature for virtually the first time in his writing career. "I read *The Outsider* by Camus around 1998. It's bleak, blank, observational style made me want to write in a less romantic, flowery way. I later discovered Michel Houllebecq, whose obsessions with sex and depression seemed to mirror my own."

He had converted the summer house at the bottom of his garden into a studio where he wrote the bulk of the material that would form *Head Music*. "Can't Get Enough" – his personal "Lust For Life" – and "She's In Fashion", based around a loop called "Gloopy Strings", were both based on tapes sent by Neil, while the deeply personal "Indian Strings" and "Down", about his slide into crack addiction, were solo works. "These songs were the first I had written using eight-track rather than four-track portastudios and these songs were the first I had written around technology like Juno synths, loops and drum machines rather than acoustic guitars and pianos," he says. "I was trying to do Prince, Tricky and Krautrock. A more accurate title for the album would have been *Crackhead Music*."

"Brett used to be quite productive on drugs," concedes Victor. "He used to phone up late at night and play me songs down the phone. The magic was still there. The demos for 'Everything Will Flow' and 'Can't Get Enough' were great. I think they've always been quite an honest band. Their songs have always been a true reflection of where they are at."

While this is undoubtedly true, lyrics like "shooting up sugar" (later subtly altered to "shaking up sugar") and "she cooking up crack giving us heart attack" suggested that where Suede were at wasn't a particularly pleasant place to be. For Richard, in particular, the rehearsals were a nightmare. "I remember for quite a few of them, having to make sure that I was semi drunk just in order to turn up," he confesses. "It's a sad thing but I remember thinking, 'I'm gonna have a shit time, I'm not enjoying it, so I'd get a bit of cider down me and then it won't seem so bad.'"

Richard remembers one rehearsal in '98 when they were working on a very old song of Brett's called "God's Gift". It had actually been the very first song Brett, Mat and Justine had played to Bernard at his audition in 1989, though it wasn't until the release of "She's In Fashion" that it would surface as a b-side. "I remember playing it and Brett being so out of it he was singing Cyndi Lauper's 'Time After Time' without realising it!"

One of my most vivid memories in eight years of working for the band is of a visit to Mayfair Studios in Primrose Hill in June 1998. The band were still unsettled on which producer they wanted to use for the next album. They had decided to move on from Ed Buller who had moved to the States and whose involvement on *Coming Up* was largely to provide some consistency between Suede's mark one and two. They had already tried out a version of "She's In Fashion" with Steve Lironi and were now working on a test-run of "Savoir Faire" with Steve Osborne, who had proved his mettle with U2, Placebo and Happy Mondays. Arriving at the studio I was met by Sam and Alan, huddled round a bong, which they eagerly offered me a quick puff on. Naively assuming it to be a hash pipe, I took them up on the offer and was surprised to experience a sensation akin to inhaling several bottles of poppers at the same time. This was my first and last personal encounter with crack. Reeling from the giddying nausea, I then had the misfortune to witness Brett bouncing into the room, dressed only in what appeared to be a hideous pair of shell-suit bottoms. His torso, while muscular, had the consistency of wet putty. He immediately grabbed a guitar and shouted, "Hey, listen to this," before launching into a tuneless embarrassment which in retrospect I suspect was "Electricity" b-side "Killer". Noticing my lack of enthusiasm, he summoned Richard and Simon, who had both been skulking nervously in the shadows, for a run through "Down", which was admittedly miles better. But Brett wasn't convinced. "Don't you like the new happy me?" he frowned. "I can do sad too," he said, promptly affecting a comedy grimace. I was finally treated to an exclusive preview of a new song, "Crack In The Union Jack", which halfway through turned into "A Chas and Dave Britpop special!" with Brett riffing away frantically, repeatedly shouting "Oi!" while headbutting the nearest wall. All this time, Steve Osborne looked on with the bemused air of Tim from *The Office*. Incredibly, he was officially enrolled as Suede's new producer only days later.

With Brett now a text-book junkie, Suede began recording their fourth album on August 10. "Mushrooms was the first drug I really took," reflects Brett. "Mushrooms, acid and dope. I sort of graduated on to Es, then coke, then crack and smack. It's a classic story. It's pathetic isn't it? Fulfilling every cliché in the book!"

Pathetic seems to be the operative word. "I remember we went to the première of that Mike Leigh film, *Career Girls*," says Victor. "They were just a disgrace. Brett was a total, total mess, an obvious junkie, wasted. Really, really bad."

Despite having spent most of the previous few months in bed, Neil Codling was all too aware of what was going on. "Rather than coke he was moving on to crack and to beat the come-down he was doing smack," says Neil. "I was literally on my back for all that time. But when we started recording *Head Music* he was doing heroin and stuff. They were working at Eastcote, just down the road, and I went down there and ended up in Master Rock and Brett…in the same way that I was unable to operate at a certain level, Brett was as well with the smack or whatever."

The rest of the band, meanwhile, were growing increasingly weary of Neil's chronic absenteeism. "Everybody was getting really stressed with him, they weren't understanding at all," says Victor Aroldoss. "I think the view was that these people had worked hard for ten years to achieve what they had and this is someone who's had it all given to him, then he's fucking up. I think it's the same attitude with Richard as well that they had. They'd worked fucking hard, travelled in transit vans, toured their arses off and signed on and stuff. That was the general vibe towards it. Mat and Anissa [Mat's girlfriend] were the only ones there for Neil really. But at the end of the day it was too much. It was on and off and it drew out the recording process and instead of Brett getting frustrated he just did more drugs. I think that was another impetus for him to do more."

Brett's spiralling drug use and Neil's illness seemed to be symbioti-cally linked, as Brett points out: "I was getting fucked up, Neil was getting ill and Richard was losing the plot and feeling sidelined and drinking too much. The only people that were still together were Mat and Simon. But the songwriting team of me, Neil and Richard was completely losing it. I don't really know if it's a chicken and an egg situ-ation. If I hadn't been so fucked up on drugs, maybe Neil might not… I dunno, you can't say. You can't rewrite the past. It felt like all of these things were going on in parallel."

With Neil in bed and Brett off his head, the album recording was a tortuous and torturous time for all concerned. A heavier reliance on loops and samples meant there was less and less for Mat and Simon to do while the two chief songwriters were generally either absent or comatose. For Richard Oakes it was a particularly demoralising period.

"A lot of the time it was just myself and Mat in the studio," he says. "Mat would be in the control room reading the paper and I'd be upstairs in the lounge bit. I got obsessed with the game *Resident Evil 2* on the PlayStation, and this would take up my day and my night. Daytime would be with an ear to what was going on, playing *Resident Evil 2*. Night time would be drinking as much cider as I could."

Despite having come up with "shitloads" of material, Richard found his contributions regularly knocked back in favour of Brett and Neil's electronic experiments. When he did visit the studio he suffered the ignominy of hearing his carefully crafted guitar parts wiped by Steve Osborne in favour of electronic bleeps and squelches.

"Brett would be in and out, often only turn up at 11 o'clock in the evening," continues Richard, "having spent the day scoring, getting high on some drug or other and turn up and lay down the law: 'I've just written a song!' And he'd play these demos incredibly loudly through the studio speakers. No one was allowed to leave the room. 'Listen to this, d'you understand what I'm doing with this? This is how it's got to be!' We never saw Neil. He was really, really ill by that point. Couldn't get out of bed. So it was a bloody miserable time."

Eventually, Richard stopped turning up too and, never a big fan of narcotics, hit the bottle, sitting at home slumped in front of the TV. "It was a genuinely confusing time," he admits. "I still don't know what I felt about everything back then."

It seems that Simon Gilbert got off relatively lightly. "My part of recording *Head Music* was to play a couple of lines of 'Can't Get Enough', copy that, sample that. And that's what it was," says Simon. "Everybody was either out of their heads or ignoring it. I think me and Mat were okay, kind of ignoring it and hoping it would all come out in the wash without someone dying, or someone leaving, or someone exploding!"

The one member of the band who did turn up to the studio every day was Mat Osman, though he was by no means unaffected by what was going on. "I dealt with it in the way I always deal with it, by concentrating on the record. And everyone else dealt with it by staying at home," he says. "When I listen to it now I'm amazed it turned out so well. There were huge swathes of it which were made by Steve Osborne with a thousand samples of the band and a thousand effects pedals, fiddling with stuff and me sitting at the back doing the *Times* crossword and occasionally going, 'Oh that's good.'"

At one point relationships became so strained that Brett called up Charlie demanding that Strangelove's Alex Lee be summoned to the studio immediately, presumably because none of Suede's other members were willing, or able, to show. Alex wouldn't be joining the band just yet, however, and the sessions trundled on at various London studios including Eastcote, Sarm West, Master Rock and Eden. Hours and hours of music were committed to tape, but the end was still nowhere in sight as the year drew to a close. A compilation of the work so far was distributed for everyone to get to grips with over the festive season, dubbed *The Christmas CD* and comprising "Down", "Savoir Faire", "Can't Get Enough", "Indian Strings", "Asbestos", "Fashion", "Stompy", "Union Jack", "Hi-Fi", "He's Gone", "Jubilee", "Electric Riff" and "Shed". Despite some characteristically excellent songwriting, and an encouraging experimentation, there was a worrying lack of consistency. It was trying to be all things to all men but came across as a random hotch-potch, a musical lucky dip. "She's In Fashion" aside, there was also a painfully obvious lack of hits.

"My biggest regret about *Head Music* is that my snowballing love affair with smack and crack restricted it from becoming a great album," reflects Brett. "The album which started out with so much promise mutated into an unfocused shadow of itself as I spent more and more time sat in front of a crack pipe and less time with my eight-track. This lack of respect for my work is something that will never happen again. I suppose I had to almost destroy this beautiful thing I had spent years creating in order to realise how precious it was."

Brett booked another Christmas break to the West Indies, ostensibly to detox. Brett claims he did kick smack on the trip. "I came off it a few times before then and then went back on it like you do. I actually had an operation, they put you under and they give you this thing called Neltrexone. And, basically, if you take that while you're a heroin addict you'll experience the most excruciating pain, because you're expelling all the opiates from your body. So what they do is put you under general anesthetic and then give it to you and this drug just takes you all and gets rid of it. But the problem with that is because you don't have to do anything, it's too easy a fix, so you easily just call up a dealer. The way to do it is do it yourself and I did it on holiday. I did it by reducing. That basically means you take a load of morphine tablets. And the first day you take ten and the next day nine and you do it like that. And I came off heroin Christmas 1998 and I haven't taken it since then."

The problem was that smack wasn't the only drug Brett was addicted too. He was detoxing one drug at a time. "In order to get off of smack I was taking a lot of crack," admits Brett. "Steve was aware I was doing lots of drugs and he really did have a problem with it and rightly so. I wasn't being very professional. He was pissed off with me because I couldn't fucking put a vocal down, my voice was so fucked."

According to Mat, Brett was worse than ever. "The atmosphere just got worse and worse," he says. "Steve had seen it all before with the Happy Mondays. I remember him saying to me, 'I don't mind him doing the brown, it was the crack that killed the Mondays.'"

"I've seen Steve a couple of times since and I've felt really bad about the whole situation because he's seen the worst side of Suede without a doubt," says Brett. "He's seen us as a bunch of selfish, unfocused, weak individuals. It was a shame and I kind of feel embarrassed about the whole situation."

As Brett continued to party like it was 1999, which it now was, the race was on to come up with that crucial come-back single. Brett's personal offering was the title track, "Head Music", a goofy piece of bubblegum fun inspired, like much of the album, by that purple midget, "The Artist Formerly Known As Good". Brett credits Justine as the person who actually came up with the title. "I thought it was a fair swap as she'd nicked plenty off me in the past," he says. "The phrase originally applied to stuff like Eno's *Music For Airports*, which was a bit of a soundtrack at the time."

While the song had a certain naive charm, its jokiness – "Give me head, give me head, give me head...music instead!" – was crassly inapt. "I always said it shouldn't go on," agrees Saul Galpern, "and in fact Steve Osborne wouldn't record it, he refused to record it. So they got Arthur Baker to do a version of it, and it was awful."

Steve Osborne eventually relented. But he wasn't so flexible when it came to Neil's next offering, the contentious "Elephant Man". "Nobody liked that," says Neil, "and Steve Osborne wouldn't produce it." The song was generally taken as an autobiographical exorcism of Neil's medical condition, and the rest of the band were adamant it should be included on the record, if only as a show of solidarity. "Brett thinks it's about my illness or whatever, and that's partly what it's about," says Neil. "But it wasn't a big deal. Everybody writes songs about being in a band. You've got to get it out of your system. It's a fairly stupid situation to be in so that's what it's about. It's like that Electric Six song, 'Gay Bar', it's just kind of a joke song. I always thought it was kind of like that Nuggets compilation, something like that, but everybody thought it was just a joke."

With Steve Osborne still refusing to have anything to do with it, "Elephant Man" was finally recorded at The Church Studios with Bruce Lampcov in late February, as the album release date was pushed further and further back.

In the end it was "Stompy" – verse by Neil, chorus by Brett and Richard – that came to the rescue. Beefed up with a gospel choir and revamped lyrics from Brett, it was now called "Electricity". The song spoke of a relationship "as cold as snow" that got its love "from white, white lines". Gone was the all-embracing ebullience of "Trash", replaced by an icy detachment. It was an all too accurate assessment of the band's fragile constitution.

"Looking back on it now I think it's quite a good album but it's a reflection of a band not together," agrees Victor Aroldoss. "Brett was aloof. When the album came out he got clean and stuff. I think there were trips to the methadone clinic. I remember going to Master Rock when they were finishing off *Head Music*. They were doing "Electricity" – I think Brett was getting clean then. About a month or so ago he'd just come back from Barbados and he was fucked, really fucked. But I saw Richard for the first time and I hadn't seen him for a year and he was just huge, fucking huge. I hardly recognised him."

The album was finally wrapped on March 1. "We finished the record just because it wasn't getting any better and it had to come out," admits Mat Osman. "I hadn't told anyone we were having any problems and I went out to play pool or something with some friends and it totally hit me that I wasn't enjoying a single moment. These were people moaning about their day who worked in shops and stuff. I'm listening to people moaning about their jobs but if I was to start on my day… I personally just thought, 'I'm gonna see how the tour goes, see whether it works, but I'm not doing this again. There's no point in doing this again because it should either be great music or it should be fun.' By the end of it, when we were doing 'Hi-Fi' for the five hundredth time, or especially the track 'Head Music', I was thinking, 'This isn't very good.'"

It was time for Suede, who hadn't performed live for 19 months, to face their public. But the Suede that returned was a pale imitation of the confident world conquerors of *Coming Up*. Instead they were a band perilously close to disintegration.

CHAPTER FOURTEEN
down

ONLY TOO AWARE OF THE mountain they had to climb to regain the ground they'd lost during two years of unfocused mayhem, Suede dipped their toes in the water with a series of invite-only showcases for fanclub members and various media types, kicking off at the Garage in Glasgow on Monday March 22. But the gig very nearly didn't happen at all. After a particularly awkward afternoon press conference, where the assembled hacks' frostiness was rivalled only by the band's haughtiness, Neil dropped the bombshell. He wasn't going on stage.

"This is like the icing on the cake," nods Richard ruefully. "After being through all that shit making the album, spending a good few months wishing I wasn't in the band and just trying to forget about it, and then to top it off Neil was getting iller by the second. So it was like, 'What do we do?' We're trying to come back and do all these fanclub shows and invite the press down and Neil's like, 'I can't go on stage and I've got to have some room-temperature water or I'm gonna die. Can we please open the window, there's no air in here!' I'm not poking fun at him at all, obviously it was genuine...I don't understand it myself, but he wouldn't have bothered doing that for fun. He didn't want to fuck anybody over, but it made our lives so difficult..."

"I was in a situation where I just couldn't operate, couldn't get out of bed," says Neil. "The rest of the band had been great. They said take as long as you want, as long as we can get motoring again, as long as you can operate when it's time to work."

Unfortunately, that time was now, with an expectant crowd of fans and journalists queuing up outside in the pouring Scottish rain. Neil relented literally minutes before show time, but it was a fractious five-piece that took to the stage. "Are you enjoying yourselves?" Brett challenged the crowd, "because I'm not!" This wasn't the right thing to say to an army of journalists, arms folded at the back, waiting to be impressed. "Only joking!" he added, but the damage was done. The reaction to a set of almost exclusively new songs was markedly muted.

Fortunately, the band had cheered up considerably by the time of their Manchester show the next evening when old chum Mike Joyce and fellow ex-Smith Andy Rourke turned up to see them. But by the Saturday, after a quick jaunt to Stockholm to play "Electricity" on Swedish TV, Neil was feeling the strain again. "I was run down and really unable to take touring and take travelling," he says. "I just couldn't...and I think the hardest thing was travelling. It tires you out...at the best of times and I just couldn't deal with it. Whatever anybody says, it was never an attitude or anything. It was just being physically unable to cope with it..."

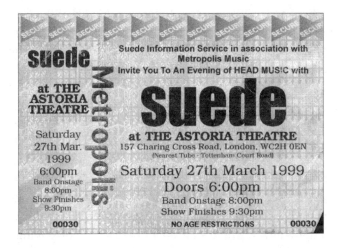

The band were due to play the Astoria that night, their first London show since the legendary Forum appearance almost two years before. With the capital's media in attendance it was a comeback concert of crucial import. They had everything to play for. "Then at the Astoria Neil said he's not doing the gig," says Victor Aroldoss, "and that was really pissing them off. Tempers were frayed. He just kept on doing it. And he might have been ill, but in a way it was like he was holding them to ransom... Everybody felt that he just didn't want to do it any more."

Neil eventually acquiesced on condition that an understudy was hired to stand in for him on the majority of Suede's overseas commitments until such time as he was fully recovered. Despite all these trials and tribulations, the evening was a huge success. Luke Haines's latest project, Black Box Recorder, just signed to Nude, provided a class opening act and the video for "Electricity" was given its worldwide debut during the interval to appreciative cheers from the audience. Fittingly it showed the band performing in the very same urine-soaked alleys around the venue that the audience had been queuing in only an hour before. The band delivered a sterling performance, wisely inter-spersing the new stuff with failsafe crowd pleasers like "Trash", "Beautiful Ones" and, appositely, "Saturday Night", which from this moment on would forever be proceeded with a pantomime act of "What night is it tonight?" whenever it was wheeled out on a Saturday.

From the outside, all seemed rosy. *Melody Maker*, who'd shadowed the band all week yet incredibly missed the drama exploding in their midst, announced boldly: "Suede...emotional, individual, glamorous, sexually ambiguous, timely yet timeless. More relevant, more down-right adorable than ever."

It seemed that it might well be possible to fool all of the people all of the time after all. Brett's dark-bagged eyes stared lifelessly from the cover of every magazine from *Select* to *The Face* while *Uncut* boasted an unprecedented 18-page Suede special. TV appearances included *CD:UK, The O-Zone, Top Of The Pops, TFI Friday, The Pepsi Chart Show, Later With Jools Holland*. The band even played a specially staged concert at Perivale's Asylum for an unimagin-ably dull Channel 4 documentary entitled *Suede Music*.

"There was this big vibe about them and they were everywhere," remembers Victor, "but if they'd looked better and been presented better it might have done them favours. I remember seeing that *CD:UK* performance and Brett looking like fucking fifty. It just wasn't working, there was too much marketing and you can't polish a turd. It just didn't look good. You can all get carried away with the hype, but the essence of the band is that all of them have to be a unit, especially Brett, Mat and Simon. I remember on the way back from Blackburn...Brett being really drunk and trashing the bus going to Simon, 'You and Mat are the most important thing in my life.' Maybe it's a romantic vision I have of the band but that's what the essence is, and when they're not close it shows."

On the back of the supernova success of *Coming Up*, Suede's usual hype machine now had some real financial muscle behind it for pretty much the first time. Virgin Megastore was to be re-branded "Head Music" for the week of release, a *Head Music Magazine* (in reality a flimsy pamphlet) was mailed out to everyone on the band's considerable database and Nude took out a full page ad-cum-pastiche of industry bible *Music Week* on the back of that publication. There was even a *Head Music FM* pirate radio station that some "over-enthusiastic fans" coincidentally started broadcasting at the same time. As with the *Dog Man Star* graffiti, the prank was a carefully contrived marketing ploy.

suede

album launch

Head Music

6 air street
(behind cafe royal)
piccadilly

bank holiday may 3rd 1999
9pm – late

absinthe bar

admits one only

contact 07931 353 2578

nude

The biggest furore, however, began as a joke concerning the album's title. Saul had been bugging Brett for weeks to tell him what it was. Exasperated, Brett announced that he would let him know, but only one letter at a time. He then literally faxed a sheet of paper with nothing but the letter "H" on it to Nude. When we heard about this at Suede's office, we thought this would make an excellent teaser competition for the fanclub: to guess the full title. What we didn't expect was that the rest of the nation's media would jump on it too. The *NME* put it on their front page and the story ran for weeks. Even the *Sun* got in on the act, with their Wildean riposte of "Heap Of Shit". In fact the only person who didn't join in the fun was Brett, who said, "I was really pissed off with the fanclub about that because it sounded like a load of hype."

Still, it seemed to be working. On the day after its April 12 release,

"Electricity" was holding up well at number two, just behind *EastEnder* Martine McCutcheon's latest abomination. It eventually slipped to five, but this was still Suede's sixth top ten single in a row.

On May 3, *Head Music*, like *Coming Up*, was ushered in with a midnight gig at Virgin's flagship megastore on London's Oxford Street. Considering some of the excessive revisionism that's taken place since, it's worth remembering that the album was greeted with almost universal press praise upon its release. *Uncut*'s review was typical: "Suede's best record to date, a transitional yet rampantly audacious vision of a cold, airless pop futurism. It's an album that remains sensual even at its most arid and electronic. It's awesome." "What a much improved band they've become," added *Q*.

The *NME* was far cheekier, and therefore far more accurate than most when they wrote, "Brett Anderson feels real when he's walking like a woman, talking like a Stone Age man. It's true! He feels schizo, ever so psycho. He knows a woman who's as stupid as a mouse and – brilliant – she lives in a house. What's she cooking him? Some crack, of course. Ah yeah, they've got a love that ain't got no name. So three songs into *Head Music*, Suede's fourth album, and the emperor is revealed once more as naked: Brett Anderson had nothing new to say." Nonetheless, they had to admit, "This is hair-raising pop and while Suede may be writing some of the most exciting pop of their career, they're also striking out for new pastures... Ace!" *Melody Maker* would eventually make it their album of the year. "Suede are unmissably, shaggably, outrageously, meteorically the best band in the cosmos."

The album went to number one, but only just. "The hype was all there and the media interest was there but they weren't looking the part," continues Victor. "It was just taken for granted that the midweek for 'Electricity' was number two, and the album went to number one, though it was close. It should have been easily number one but it just scraped number one so it wasn't that great. Signs were showing that things weren't right. So they carried on and gigged. It was still weird. As a fan I felt it just wasn't the same. But even when they're not great they still piss over every other band."

Richard Oakes was well aware that they weren't in for an easy ride this time around. "Some of the fans, they didn't really like the album," he admits. "And when they saw the band and saw Brett looking like he'd had a couple of years on heroin and me looking as though I'd had a couple of years being pissed out of my face and being out of shape, quite rightly they were probably annoyed."

Of even greater concern, however, was Neil's deteriorating condition. "It started to get really fucking impossible for us to try and work the record," says Brett. "I'd sort of accommodated Neil and brought him so much into the picture and made him such an integral part of the band. He wasn't just some guy that sat and played the odd note on the keyboard. He was my co-writer on the record, he wrote more songs than Richard on the record and all of a sudden he was withdrawing and wimping out. That's what it felt like. It didn't seem right. It was really frustrating turning up at the airport and, 'Oh, Neil can't make it.' The whole thing of the condition he had, because it's so intangible, it's not like he's got mumps or whatever, at the back of your mind you're thinking, 'Oh, just fucking pull your socks up.' You are thinking that. I know you shouldn't because it is a medical condition but that kind of made it worse because it wasn't like he had a broken leg or anything. So it was really difficult for the rest of the band to get their heads round. It really wasn't much fun."

Suede still had a secret weapon up their sleeves, however. "She's In Fashion" had long been earmarked as a single and was now scheduled for release on June 21. Almost everyone was convinced it would be a huge hit. "Sumptuous and outrageously poppy," screamed *Heat* "Glorious, summery pop, like the Isley Brothers used to make," added *Select*, while *Attitude* called it "A screamingly obvious summer smash". *NME* hedged their bets by describing it as "A balmy, barmy beaut, shimmering grooves turning a blithe eye to the world", before sticking the boot in with, "as Brett Anderson waxes lyrical balderdash about some wench he spotted pricing spuds in Waitrose".

"I thought 'She's In Fashion' was really good," reflects Neil Codling. "I thought it was kind of what it could have been. I wanted it to be a summery sounding song, so I was quite happy that it sounded quite summery."

Such simple pop perfection didn't come easy, however. "We spent fucking months on that track and just couldn't get it right," remembers Mat Osman. "We must have tried about eight different versions of it. It's just really weird listening to it now because it sounds straight and completely untouched and unforced. It seems ridiculous to go through six months of three studios and eighty attempts to make it as un-studio sounding as that."

Zoe Ball, then presenting Radio 1's *Breakfast Show*, made it her Single

Of The Week and played it to death, presumably associating with the lines, "She's the face on the radio, she's the body on the morning show." It became a huge radio hit.

"It did open us up to a mainstream that we hadn't been open to before," agrees Brett. "Even though the first album was really successful, it was almost like a huge cult album. 'Animal Nitrate' was a huge cult track. And 'She's In Fashion' is probably our most famous song in a funny sort of way."

"'She's In Fashion' was the biggest radio song they ever had," confirms Saul Galpern. "It was a total crossover, what's called an airplay song, but it didn't transfer to sales." Against all the laws of marketing, the single stalled at 13, unlucky for Suede, and the album continued its steady slide out of the charts.

"I think part of the reason is I don't think people trusted the Suede sound," Saul continues. "People liked it but thought, 'It's them isn't it? It's still a bit weird.' Maybe we should have put 'She's In Fashion' out first..."

Herein lies the greatest dichotomy in the history of the band: while Suede always had been inherently a left-of-centre, alternative cult band, they had long harboured the desire to cross over to the mainstream, to become, essentially, ordinary. "We've always said that we wanted to be a pop band," Mat had told *Select* in one of the first interviews after Bernard's departure. "I don't think anyone ever thinks that we mean it, because so many people who say it don't mean it. They don't mean they want to be a pop band, they meant they want to have what a pop band has. But I'm talking about being an ordinary band, that people just listen to your records on the radio and go out and buy them. No prior motive. Not having to wheedle itself in to get people to love it. There is a real desire to become truly ordinary."

"So Young" and "Stay Together" had both been stabs, lyrically at least, at achieving a kind of blankness, when compared to the delightfully perverse playfulness of "Animal Nitrate" and "The Drowners". "The Wild Ones" was perhaps the first obvious example of a song deliberately targeted at the masses, although falling far short of this goal. "Saturday Night", on the other hand, did appeal to those average housewives whom Brett had long championed. Detractors often said the song sounded like a laboratory-produced hybrid of Elton John, Eric Clapton and Chris De Burgh, but far from being an insult it seems this may have been exactly the intention. Almost embarrassingly commercial, "She's In Fashion" now effectively polarised Suede's audience between hardcore fan and casual floating punter. The problem was that Suede had now become far too mainstream for their original fanbase who began to defect in droves. Placebo, with the advantage of a genuine bisexual in their band, and Muse, with, um, blue hair, catered perfectly for the legions of confused and alienated freaks and weirdos who'd previously danced along to "We Are The Pigs", "Trash" and "Beautiful Ones" but for whom "She's in fashion, woo, hoo, hoo!" just didn't cut the mustard. For Joe and Josephine Public, on the other hand, Suede would always be that bunch of polysexual deviants who'd slapped their arses on The Brits. And no amount of crap haircuts or Man At C&A outfits would change that.

"I think Suede never really acknowledged who their fans were," agrees Victor Aroldoss. "They've always hidden away from this gothy thing. And if you look at the bands that have embraced that, like Placebo and Muse, they're doing fine."

In Suede's defence, they were, as ever, simply reflecting where they were at. And if Brett wanted to look like the *Bloke* magazine cover star that *Select* had parodied only six short years ago, then that was surely his prerogative. He was, after all, now a thirty-something near millionaire.

But let's not pretend it was all doom and gloom. *Head Music* also made number one in Denmark, Norway and Sweden and was doing the business admirably in the rest of Europe, notably Germany where a number 26 album was Suede's best performance ever in a country with notoriously bad taste in music. "She's In Fashion" may only have made a small ripple, sales wise, in Britain, but it was a chart topper in places like Singapore and, bizarrely, Peru. Then, in July, Suede played one of the greatest gigs of their career. Well, three of the greatest gigs of their career, to be accurate.

Denmark's Roskilde is Europe's biggest festival, with 100,000 people enjoying subsidised beer which goes for around £1 a pint. Nice. Suede had been there before, in '95 on Richard's first European tour. Then they played the Green tent. Official estimates gave the attendance as 30,000 for a tent meant to hold 18,000. Two years later they returned, on the back of the huge success of *Coming Up*, headlining the big one, the Orange stage. And here in 1999, by now established as Denmark's biggest stars, with only Oasis as serious contenders, they quite literally dominated the festival, playing three different sets on three different stages over three days. After apocalyptic returns to the Green and

Orange stages, they finished with a very special set in the intimate Yellow tent, largely dictated by spins on a custom-built Wheel Of Fortune of b-sides and rarities. "I remember staying up pretty much all night after the second show, just drinking with people, drinking lots of whiskey," says Richard Oakes. "And we were due to go on stage at half past three on the Sunday. Got back to the hotel about midday and I had to squeeze a whole night's sleep and a hangover into like two hours, before turning up to get ready for the show. I felt really dodgy that day."

Suede's big homecoming was as headliners at the two V99 festivals – Saturday August 21 in Staffordshire, and the next night in Chelmsford. These would be Suede's first proper UK appearances since Reading two years before. The handful of British dates since had been semi-secret, low-key fanclub affairs and an *NME* editorial accused them of running scared, of giving up on the UK in favour of their more appreciative continental cousins. But the reason for their long absence from these shores was purely contractual. Saul Galpern faxed the following reply to Steve Sutherland: "As you know, Suede are a great live band and it was always our intention for them to tour the album. They are one of the hardest working bands in the UK and haven't been sitting on their arses. They haven't been off the road since the release of *Head Music* and, in fact, unlike some of their peers they are massive in Europe and South East Asia, where they sell a lot of records. The problem with the UK was we really wanted to play V99 but agreed with the promoters that we would not announce any UK shows prior to this and that is why the UK tour was finally announced this week."

Suede acquitted themselves handsomely, with two stridently confident performances, particularly at Chelmsford where "She's In Fashion" ended in a clapathon reminiscent of Queen's "Radio Gaga", a comparison that would become more and more commonplace. There were some fears, however, that by constantly insisting on headlining, Suede were setting themselves up for a fall. Thanks largely to their huge media profile, and a vague acceptance of their cultural significance, they had always managed to portray themselves as bigger than they actually were. Now, however, the widening gulf between their perceived status and the harsh reality was becoming painfully obvious. In a *Q* "Cash For Questions" article later that year, one reader cheekily asked, "Was it daunting taking the stage at V99 after the Stereophonics, bearing in mind that they are now more successful than you?"

Brett's reply was typically diplomatic. "Not particularly. I didn't have a problem with the Stereophonics. I like their songs and I've spoken to the blokes a couple of times, so it wasn't a big antagonistic thing. I knew they were a popular band and I thought what they were doing was good. But, honestly, I don't think anyone can compare to Suede on a good day."

Brett now remembers the Chelmsford performance as one of the greatest moments in the band's career. "That was really special. The first leg we did at Stafford was okay," he says. "There was that whole thing about the Stereophonics playing under us because they were having a big hit with their album and maybe it should be the other way round. And we played the gig and thought, 'Fuck, maybe they're right!' And then the next night, Chelmsford, I remember being mindblowingly good. That…is one of the gig memories I'll take to my grave, had a real vibe to it."

Morale was indeed relatively buoyant at this point. V99, while not quite the triumphant return that Phoenix had been, was at the very least a great success. Neil seemed to be on the mend and had just helped pen one of the freshest sounding Suede b-sides in aeons. "Let Go" sounded like Crosby, Stills & Nash, largely due to the three-part harmonies from Brett, Neil and Richard. The young Oakes had recently begun adding his tonsil talents to the band's live set up, despite his mum's comment to the local paper that he should stick to the guitar. The story was inevitably picked up by the *NME* resulting in a furious Brett calling up the office with instructions that Mrs Oakes should keep her mouth shut if she had any interest in her son's career.

On September 6, Nude released "Everything Will Flow" as the third single from *Head Music*. A fine song with a pretty melody and a string riff which inadvertently ripped off Duran Duran's "Save A Prayer", it nonetheless fell again into that no man's land between two diametrically opposed audiences. For the first time since anyone could remember, major chains like Woolworths refused to stock it and it was a miracle that it even made it to number 24. It thus gained the distinction of being Suede's least successful single since their "Drowners" debut over seven years before.

Perhaps fortunately, Suede were by this time *en route* to Japan for an extensive tour due to take in South East Asia and, for the first time, Australia. They would soon, however, have far greater disasters to contend with. The tour was an almost comedic catalogue of catastrophes from start to premature finish. "It started off in Jakarata," Brett told *Melody Maker*, "when there was all this stuff happening in East Timor, so we had to cancel Jakarta before we even went there. We went to Japan and I was packing my things to go to Taiwan and our tour manager knocks on the door and says there's been this huge earthquake. So we stayed in Japan for a couple of days."

"Japan was really fun," remembers Victor Aroldoss, who travelled with the band. "They did a cover of 'Bodies' and they did 'Can't Get Enough' with everybody swapping instruments. There was a saving grace that they did bond on tour and they got on really well. But there was always a sense that it was because Brett's other friends weren't there."

Next on the itinerary was Thailand where the band were greeted by the sight of another plane careering off the runway, fire engines racing towards it, just as they landed. "Literally every part of the world we went to, something would happen," says Brett, "either where we'd just been or where we were going. It's the eye-of-the-storm phenomenon. The eye of the storm doesn't get affected, but everything around it does."

The storm manifested itself quite literally as a huge hurricane which swept Japan, almost immediately after which there were typhoon warnings in Hong Kong, their next destination. Before they got there, though, they had a far more immediate problem. Midway through the Bangkok set, Neil walked off stage, provoking an onstage fit from Brett. "I just couldn't stay conscious," explains Neil. "I had to go off stage and lie down in a corner. It was horrendous because you can't expect people to empathise with you." The set was swiftly juggled to accommodate the unexpected four-piece line-up and Brett channelled his fury into the show which was, quite literally, storming.

It was in the Land Of Oz, however, that the shit really hit the fans. After their first antipodean show at the Livid festival in Brisbane, where Offspring were headlining, Neil announced he couldn't go on. "I had horrendous qualms about it," he says, "because we still had some shows to do. If you can't do something, it's not an attitude problem, it really is a physical thing. If you're tired out then you're tired out. It was a terrible thing when we were in Australia, I said to the band, 'I just can't cope with this any more.'" Suede's appearance at Sydney's Glenwood Festival was pulled, radio announcements made, and several hundred refunds handed over.

"I just fucking blew my lid," says Brett. "I felt like punching him in the face. It wasn't a personal thing against him, it was just so frustrating that the universe had dealt me another duff card, d'you know what I mean? Like, 'Fuck sake. Just got everything sorted out and this bastard pulls the rug from underneath me.' It was horrific."

After much coaxing, Neil was persuaded to play two small club dates in Sydney and Melbourne, but the rest of the tour – including what would have been Suede's first shows in Vietnam and Malaysia – was binned, along with their lucrative sponsorship deals.

"Neil was lovely. I tried to help him throughout that whole thing," says Saul Galpern, who flew out to Australia to see the band. "I introduced him to this osteopath guy, who was like an Indian guru. It seemed to work for a bit. Half of me thinks he was scared because he thought he wasn't capable enough and he thought he'd get found out. That's what I think, 'I'm not actually very good at this.' And he wasn't the most talented musician, but you don't have to be the most talented musician in any band. What was great about him was that he really had a total understanding of contemporary music and had some fantastic opinions about music, very leftfield taste, which was a great thing to bring to Suede. Brett needed that. He fed Brett with lots of information and lots of musical ideas which Brett before was only really getting from me. He hadn't had that for a while, a mentor like him that he could associate with and actually get inspired by. And it's a shame that Neil would just zip in and zip out. There was a point where we thought 'Maybe he just won't tour then', like this Howard Hughes kind of character…"

Neil was officially diagnosed with ME, often cruelly referred to as yuppie flu. Doctors advised a lengthy period of rest, and he was sent to bed until the UK tour began a few weeks later on a cold, miserable October evening in Brighton. "Brett bounds and shimmies the Brighton Centre to its knees," raved *Melody Maker*. "It's a blinding retort to the critics who took one listen to *Head Music* and wrote Suede off as the back end of a one-trick pantomime pony."

NME followed the band to Liverpool and couldn't help but notice the striking metamorphosis Suede's singer had gone through. "Looking lithe and healthy, he spends much of the show atop the monitors, insisting Liverpool bellow back the choruses. Long gone is the frilly shirted, arse-slapping Brett, replaced by a sleek, fighting-fit frontman striding about the stage smiling, the troubled fop of old an amusingly tragic memory. They're no longer the litter on the breeze or the misfits sniffing glue in derelict industrial estates. They're a nasty, brutally efficient rock band. You could argue that by diluting their original, striking aesthetic, Suede have sacrificed everything that made them interesting in the first place, but you'd be wrong."

Suede got as far as the cavernous Reading Rivermead Centre before Neil baled out of the rest of the tour. It was hardly a surprise. There had been an unspoken rule that he had to hold out till Reading since it was the last show within easy reach of London and therefore the last likely to be bothered by journalistic flibbertigibbets. Waiting in the wings for this very eventuality was Alex Lee who had kept himself busy since Strangelove's demise in 1998 by lending his talents to the Warm Jets. He had already been substituted for Neil on a number of Suede's European promotional engagements with the unenviable task of mimicking one of the most fancied bits of totty in pop while simultaneously trying to stay as much in the background as possible.

"I had lots and lots of people come up to me saying, 'Neil, I have a picture of you and me here last year. Look, this is me and you,'" laughs Alex. "And I'm going, 'Hmmm...'"

"I think it was pretty hard for him," Neil sympathises. "I remember once when we did *TFI Friday* and I was knackered and he had to go and do the soundcheck and then I rolled up and did the actual thing. He is a consummate professional but doing stuff like that must be soul destroying, to be the *Top Of The Pops* stand-in mouthing Jennifer Lopez's words!"

Alex remains philosophical about his role. "At the time I did a fanzine interview where I compared it to *Being John Malkovich*, because it's the only comparison I could think of. You enter a portal, you go into someone else's world and you live in this bizarre world where you don't sort of really belong. You're in there and then suddenly you're dropped off by a bus at the side of the road. And then, that's the edge of Bristol, that's the M32. It was a difficult time politically. I think everyone wanted to do the right thing by everyone and I was probably at the bottom of their list of priorities and they figured, 'Pay him and he'll do the job.' And as long as it was on those terms I could accept it, but I can't imagine what was going through anybody else's head about it."

He played his first UK Suede show on October 31 at Poole Arts Club, where Richard Oakes had first witnessed the band six years before, just in time for the release of the last single from the album, "Can't Get Enough". Brett's personal "Lust For Life" written during the depths of heroin withdrawal fared slightly better than the previous single, charting one place higher at 23. Interestingly, the Swedes preferred the b-side, Neil's "Let Go", and put that out instead.

From then, Alex completed the rest of the year's UK and European dates, growing more and more confident as the shows went on. "Alex started off replacing Neil and he became Alex," says Brett. "And so many of the arrangements of the songs are so much better live. 'She's In Fashion' sounded shit when we played it with Neil. Once I'd accepted the fact that Neil wasn't going to be on stage...we became a snarling rock band."

For Richard, in particular, Alex's arrival was a godsend. "On some of the old songs like 'So Young' or 'Metal Mickey', he'd bolster them up and it would leave me free to do some more interesting things, and I thought it was great. It made the tour for me," says Richard. "The writing of it was a nightmare, the recording was a nightmare, the campaign was a nightmare. If the touring had been a nightmare as well, that would have been it. You'd probably have never seen me again. Back to Poole!"

The *Head Music* world tour finally came to an end with a sell-out show at the Tel Aviv Cinerama in Israel on January 27, 2000, where they played to over 4,000 fans. "Israel's always brilliant," says Simon. "It's like playing Thailand, but closer. It's quite sinister lying on the beach seeing all these military green helicopters flying past and then doing a radio show and it's full of army kids. But there's something really exciting about it."

At the end of the gig Suede were awarded gold discs for *Coming Up*, which had just been certified as selling over 25,000 copies in Israel, no mean feat in a country of just five million. More importantly, Neil was back on board, having seemingly made a miraculous recovery. Most of the touring party spent a week in Israel, including a day trip to Jerusalem. Not Mr Anderson, however, who had made a New Year's resolution regarding the new Suede record. This time, he vowed, it would be "crack on" rather than "on crack". Almost immediately he holed himself up in a secret hideaway, a cottage in Chipstead, Surrey, free from the distractions and enticements of city life, to begin writing the next album. After the depths of *Head Music*, this one would be about coming back from the brink.

"I isolated myself with books and real instruments. If anything it was born out of a physical need to escape London and its temptations. The place was killing me. Literally. I read *Atomised* by Michel Houllebecq, which directly inspired 'Untitled' and books by Camus, Leonard Cohen, Paul Auster and others. I created a deliberate vacuum so all these influences would flood in. I spent a lot of time walking in the countryside, sometimes for hours and hours, fascinated by nature and its battle with concrete and steel. I was living in *Concrete Island* by J.G. Ballard."

Even by Suede standards, 1999 had been a year that would make Camus's grimmest moments seem like a jolly romp by Jerome K. Jerome. The new millennium promised a clean slate where the band could put the internecine warfare of the past two years behind them and get on with what they were best at: making classic records. In reality, they were about to stumble blindly into yet another chapter of catastrophe verging on high farce.

CHAPTER FIFTEEN
a new morning

SUEDE'S DETERMINED REJUVENATION began promisingly. Clean for the first time in his adult life, Brett entered a period of acute creativity. Blatantly inspired by his new rural locale, one of the first lines he wrote for the next album was "You belong among the wild flowers". The musical origins of the song, soon to be named "Beautiful Loser", came not from any of Suede, but from Alex Lee.

Brett had often talked about writing with people outside the band, but this was the first instance of this idea bearing fruit. "The first thing I sat down and wrote was a thing called 'Left Hand', which became 'Beautiful Loser'. He then rang me up and said, 'I've got an idea for it,' and thrashed out this really brash, trashy version of it down the phone. And I could barely recognise it. But I thought fair enough, I've never really written with people like that before, where they take the raw material and put their own slant on it and I thought it was cool. I thought it was a shame ultimately the song ended up a generic Suede rocker when the original had sounded absolutely nothing like Suede. But it takes time to work out what your musical relationship is."

"Beautiful Loser" was another transparent tribute to that impossibly likeable wastrel, Alan Fisher. The band demoed an inspired rendition of it, along with four other new songs during a week in a residential studio called Parkgate, near Hastings. As well as "Loser" they recorded "Lonely Girls", a kind of female "Young Men" set to a finger-picking folk ditty from Neil, plus "Oceans", "Cheap" and "You Belong To Me". The results were hugely encouraging, being both fresh and melodic, and with a crucial improvement in Brett's lyrics. "Oceans" and "Cheap" in particular seemed to reveal a more honest singer, no longer hiding behind his increasingly worn-out lexicon of Suede clichés. The songs were obvious allusions to his relationship with Sam Cunningham, which had disintegrated in the fall-out of chronic drug addiction. As with Justine, Brett and Sam, while no longer an item, remained close friends and his heartfelt fondness for their time together produced some truly touching material. "You never read Debussy, you never had the time, but everything that you do is wonderful," he sang in "Cheap". And it was clear he meant it, which is more than could be said for the clinical detachment of much of *Head Music*.

The song was co-written by Richard, who was relieved beyond belief that his collaborator was at last back on the same planet as himself. "It affected me when he was a coke-fuelled enthusiastic 'Let's write a pop album!' And then it affected me when he was a heroin-fuelled 'Let's make a synth album!' And it affected me when he had gone off and got clean, which he'd spent the whole tour doing. And then he went off to the cottage to get his head together. He had a load of books and sat typing away on his typewriter, getting his brain working, getting his soul back in gear into his writing, and it was such a relief. Not just that he was paying a lot more attention to what I was doing and was much more in line with my thoughts about the record we should make. It was going to be a really, really folky record at first, all these acoustic demos of things like 'When The Rain Falls'."

Simon Gilbert was similarly relieved that Suede were back to doing what they were best at. "The first of those demos I thought were amazing," says Simon. I was really happy with them because after *Head Music*, which was too electronic, I thought, 'Thank god we're going back to playing rock'n'roll. We're a rock'n'roll band, we should play it rather than press a fucking computer!' I was really pleased we'd gone back to basics playing instruments. And then Saul came back saying they were too retro and I thought, 'You fucking cunt, bollocks, you're full of shit!'"

For Suede's next demo session at Stanbridge in July, Brett invited Alex to join the rest of the band in the studio, primarily to help with the samples on another Anderson-Lee co-write, "Refugees", a stately epic on the heated issue of asylum seekers. The other songs were even more promising, particularly Mat's "Lost In TV", which managed to take the best bits of "The Power" and "Stay Together" and cross them with Richard O'Brien's "Science Fiction Double Feature" – not nearly as hideous as it sounds. Coincidentally, the original piece of music was written on the same day back in '96 as Mat's other masterpiece, "Europe Is Our Playground". If "Where The Rain Falls" was a little too close to

"Still Life" for comfort, and "Untitled" was a little too close to "When The Rain Falls", then no one seemed to mind, if only because it reinforced the feeling that Suede had at last returned to the grand majesty and ambition of the mighty *Dog Man Star*.

So confident were Suede in the strength of their new material that they agreed to take a break from writing to perform at the Iceland Airwaves festival in Reykjavik in October, primarily to try out the new songs as far away from the prying eyes and ears of the media as possible. At least, that was the idea. But with the festival sponsored by Icelandair and Reykjavik Arts Council, Suede unwittingly became Iceland's greatest tourist attraction as the organisers flew in journalists from around the globe to document the band's every move.

It was lucky, then, that the gig turned out to be among the most stunning the band have ever played. All seemed to be back on track. Brett even joked, "Ladies and gentlemen, Neil Codling...back from the dead!"

Suede unveiled no less than nine new songs that night, including most of the songs that had recently been demoed, plus "Simon". This was based around Neil and Richard's effort on the flipside of the shoddy "Chemistry" sketch from years before, and featured one of Brett's most heartfelt lyrics to date. Like "Breakdown" and "He's Gone", the song concerned his close friend Simon Holbrook who, suffering from extreme depression for many years, committed suicide in 1996. "I went to his funeral in Haywards Heath," says Brett, "and was fine until they played "Let It Be", his favourite song, and one that we had listened to together a million times. I erupted into uncontrollable floods of tears."

The concert received unanimously ecstatic plaudits, with the new material gaining most of the accolades. "Anyone who thought that *Head Music* signalled the artistic end of Suede is going to have to think again," raved Julian Marshall in a full-page *NME* review. "The new songs are amazing and arguably the best things they've ever done." Everyone, it seemed, agreed that Suede had entered a creative renaissance.

"I was completely clean and we were writing an album of songs, which has always been our forte," agrees Brett. "Richard was obviously a lot happier and it seemed that Neil was a lot better. Those were the three things that fucked *Head Music* up. And we'd written a couple of songs which I thought were really good – 'Oceans', 'Beautiful Loser' and all those songs – and I felt really inspired and we did that show. And it was another one like Hanover Grand. We did nine new songs and it was great. The crowd really dug it, which was cool, and quite unusual for a festival crowd."

The songs were there. Now all they had to do was record the bloody things. Sadly, this would prove to be easier said than done.

Suede's final obligation of 2000 was recording "Simon" with Sigur Rós producer Ken Thomas, who they had met in Iceland. The result was damn near perfect, save for an ever so slightly cringeworthy hint of "It's raining, it's pouring, the old man is snoring," during the chorus. Tragically, the song was destined not for Suede's next album, but as part of a soundtrack for an arthouse movie by underground director C.S. Leigh, who was something of an untried quantity. Neil was closely involved with the rest of the soundtrack, reinforcing suspicions that he was planning to establish himself as the new Brian Wilson. The session was also a chance for the band to assess Ken Thomas's suitability as producer for the album proper. Their criticism was that although he had made a sterling job of recording the song as it was, he had brought precious little new to the proceedings. It was this blinkered quest for the intangible that would pave the way for disaster.

In February 2001 the band took up residency at the famous Rockfield Studios in Monmouth, Wales, for a three-week trial run with Beck collaborator Tony Hoffer. Brett and Mat in particular were huge fans of Beck's *Midnite Vultures*. "When I heard it, I was so jealous for the next couple of weeks," says Brett. "It was exactly what I wanted *Head Music* to be like. It was a little bit pastiche Princey in places, but when we played it in the dressing room, as soon as you heard it, you knew that you were gonna love these songs."

It turned out that Tony was a fan of the band too. "I remember buying a copy of 'The Drowners' because it had a picture of a naked girl on the cover whose suit was painted on her body," says Tony. "It reminded me of a record I might like – Pink Floyd, Scorpions, ELO? – so I bought it and thought it was pretty good. The funny thing is, I thought the girl on the cover was named Suede and she was singing the songs. Then in 1995 Jesse from the Chemical Brothers told me it was just some guys who look like girls."

Saul Galpern arranged a meeting with Tony while he was in Paris mixing the second Air album. "So I flew to London and we hit it off right away," Tony explains. "The main thing I wanted to get across was that, as a fan and potential producer, the next Suede album would have to take a credible creative turn. With bands like Radiohead and Blur tearing into creative realms, it seemed like the band's very survival depended on it."

With Tony, the band recorded reworkings of "Beautiful Loser", "Untitled" and "When The Rain Falls", plus a jam called "Pish Posh". Tony had certainly brought something new to the mix. The versions were radically different from the original demos. Whether they were actually any good or not was an entirely different matter. Charlie described them as "Sonically interesting" – whatever that means. Hearing what they'd done to "Beautiful Loser", Alex Lee diplomatically stated that it was "Stripped back and experimental, but ultimately too slow and laborious".

Simon Gilbert was decidedly less understanding. "Tony had this drum machine and was trying to get me to play 'Beautiful Loser' along to this awful messy hip hop loop he had worked out. I was getting more pissed off every time we played it and I thought, 'This is not how our songs should sound.' The next morning I had to say I thought it sounded like shit and we shouldn't be working with this guy."

Simon wasn't the only one with strong opinions on the results of the Rockfield session. "I was into it when we were doing it " admits Richard, "but we got back to London and everybody went, 'What a lot of fucking shit!' This is true. Saul and Charlie and half the band!"

It seems fair at this juncture to raise the question, why on earth did they decide to record the album with Tony after such a disastrous trial run? "I don't really know actually," ponders Brett. "I think we were all fucking mad. We were so fucking keen to get a new sound. There were things that Tony was doing that were interesting. We approached the session very differently. We were trying to find the song in the recording. We were working on this song called 'Pish Posh'. It had one really great element, this great riff, and a really good verse and we were basically trying to write while we were recording, which was a dreadful mistake."

Unsurprisingly, Tony's own recollections of the time at Rockfield are decidedly different from the band's. "There was a very creative spirit in the air throughout the sessions," he says. "We were all working together to help the band develop this electrifying new sound. Neil Codling and I spent a lot of time together, trying to come up with synth lines that sounded warm and organic."

Tony considered Neil to be Suede's secret weapon. "He had joined the band after its initial flash of fame, so he had no sentimental attachment to the past. He was well educated in music theory and had a keen knowledge of all different genres, making it easy for him to guide Suede into several different directions at once. With the results we were getting, everyone really got involved in the effort to freak the songs out."

It appears that one of the main factors in choosing to record the album with Tony, who they described as "A cross between Beck and Woody Allen", was that the band genuinely got on with him so well. "The best thing about him, because he does hip hop stuff and he lives in LA, is the way he talks about our records," said Mat, shortly after they began working with him. "The thing I most enjoy about playing with him is he'll say, '"Electricity"? Yeah, man, I love that jam!' And 'You should drop some postcodes 'n' shit on this track to represent where you're coming from like W10 or 0207 969…' I've never heard our music being described as 'phat' or 'dope' before. Like me and Simon will be doing something like this song 'Untitled', which is pretty pastoral, and for some reason he got into the groove of it, and we're playing this folky thing, and at the end he said, 'At this point I'm seeing cars in the video, bouncing up and down!'"

At last it looked like Suede were all set to begin recording their fifth album. It was all systems are go. For one member, however, the reality of what a new record and its accompanying promotional treadmill would actually entail began to sink in. For Neil Codling, it was all systems are stop.

"I came back from Rockfield then I had to do this soundtrack for that *Far From China* film and I couldn't physically get out of bed," says Neil, "I just realised that if we had to do a big tour then I wouldn't be able to do it, that after a couple of weeks I'd just be physically exhausted. And that's a very difficult thing to expect people to empathise with… And they say, 'Well, we've all done it before, we've all been ill and we've all been on stage. We've all been professional about it.' If it's a perpetual thing and it's constant and physically exhausting there's not much you can say except, 'I can't do it.' And it was such a hard thing to do. But I knew I had to because I'd just be letting people down again and again."

On March 13 Neil called Charlie and told him the news. "We went round to Brett's and I just told him and that was that," says Neil. "It was really quick and curt and to the point. It was fairly clinical, a nasty thing to do."

For Brett, who had cleaned up his act and was now more focused than ever on putting everything into the next album, this was not what he wanted to hear at all. "He was really pissed off," confirms Neil, "but I didn't get half his anger at all. He was like, 'Are you sure? Right.' And I left. Crap thing to do and I didn't want to do it but I had to do it. And that was it."

"I'd sort of convinced myself that he was better," says Brett. "I'd see Neil socially, we were going out drinking and he seemed to be okay. He was a little bit wobbly occasionally but a lot better. And he turned up here with Charlie one day and he goes, 'I'm leaving the band.' I didn't say anything and he walked out and got a taxi home. It was beyond the point of reasoning. So he went and I called Alex up about ten minutes later."

Having gone from being an unemployed drama student living in a shoebox to becoming a *Top Of The Pops* regular and *Smash Hits* cover star in less than a year, it's easy to surmise that Neil's condition was at least partly due to the pressures of fame, that after the whirlwind of success and all its attendant temptations he was simply burnt out.

Someone who'd become pretty close to being a rock'n'roll casualty herself was Justine Frischmann. She'd noticed early on that Neil was struggling. "It was pretty obvious that Neil was really not very well," she says. "But I think it was really difficult on both Richard and Neil walking straight into a big band with all its history and all the pressures that go with it. It's one thing to have always wanted it and to get on to a slow climb. Zero to 60 in ten seconds, it's probably too much to expect from anyone. There's a lot of debate about ME. Whether or not it is psychological. There's a lot of people that take a lot of anti-depressants and miraculously it goes away. But all illness comes from the body and the mind, so what comes first, the chicken or the egg?"

Neil insists that his condition had nothing to do with fame, burn-out, or simply having too good a time. "I don't think I'm any different from Richard," he says. "There's thousands of people in bands and they cope with it. People leave bands for various reasons. I had to leave. It was hard but I couldn't put the band through it again. I couldn't wait till we were on tour again and expect them to put up with it again."

Alan Fisher's opinion probably betrays some of the less sympathetic thoughts in the Anderson household. "He was ill wasn't he?" says Alan. "Neil's a great guy but, yeah, he'd see a schedule, you know Brett would show him the itinerary and all of a sudden he'd go, 'Oh I feel ill now.' It's not as if he had to do much. He just sat there on stage. He'd play a couple of notes, smoke a lot of cigarettes, look around. It wasn't exactly the hardest job in the world, was it? Really, I was quite amazed how he could leave. He'd only been doing it, what, two years?"

As far as Neil is concerned, though, if there was any way he could have stayed, then he would have done. There was simply no other choice. "There's no reason why you'd want to give it up. There's nothing better than touring and playing these songs, fantastic stuff. It was a very difficult thing, nobody believed I would do it."

"To be honest I sort of felt betrayed by Neil," reflects Brett. "That's my gut feeling, even though I know he wasn't in control of his decisions. I appreciate it's a medical condition. It's a shame. I think Neil could've been a great popstar and a really great artist as well. He had that little spark that great pop music has to have, that little bit of creativity and little bit of stupidity in the right amounts. He really had it. There were a couple of things he did musically, like the music to 'She's In Fashion' is just so perfect. It's such a shame."

While most people would blanch at a key member quitting on the eve of recording a new record, Suede on this occasion had an obvious substitute sitting on the reserve benches. "When Neil decided he had to leave, there was only one phone call I made," says Brett. Alex Lee was now a full-time member of Suede. "When we were on tour with Strangelove, apart from getting on with him really well, it was also really obvious that he was a bit of a whiz-kid," continues Brett. "I mean, he can play anything. He's one of these people that you can stick a euphonium in front of him and he'll go 'toot-toot-toot'. He was the main musical and songwriting guy in Strangelove. Alex was the Johnny Marr of Strangelove."

And so Suede, now in something like their eighth incarnation, descended on Parkgate Studios on May 28 to begin work on their next album. Farcically, the recording was immediately delayed by two days due to a lack of the "correct" tape. It was a worrying portent of what was to come.

On paper the sessions progressed well. In less than a month there were rough mixes of "One Hit To The Body", "Lonely Girls", "You Belong To Me", "Shout" and, the song Brett was particularly excited about, "Positivity", in the can. "Positivity", one of the very last songs written with Neil and which materialised almost fully formed in rehearsal one day, was officially inspired by the film *Amelie*, but with a fairly obvious nod to Brett's recent ex Sam's stoic recovery from crack and smack addiction. The song exemplified Brett's newfound *joie de vivre*. "There's been a kind of new shot in the arm with Alex joining," he said at the time, "and the songs have got very kind of celebratory and jubilant. The only way I can describe the phase I'm going through at the moment is a kind of…unity. This force of human life." This lust for life even manifested itself physically. He had ditched the traditional black barnet in favour of shiny happy golden locks.

As if to confirm the confident progress the band were making in their country retreat, Brett trod the boards for the first time that year at the Royal Festival Hall on June 24 as part of the annual Meltdown festival, this year compered by Robert Wyatt, most famous for his rendition of "Shipbuilding", which Suede had so ably covered a few years back.

Brett took the opportunity to introduce Suede's latest recruit, Alex Lee, on guitar, and that other "Magic Alex", Tony Hoffer, looking every inch the madcap scientist, fiddling with what appeared to be a Tardis control console. Typical of Tony's kooky style, he explained, "We heard Robert Wyatt is homeless and living in a shopping cart behind Safeway, so we wanted to make one of his songs to make him some money and give him a second chance. But then we heard that's a different Robert Wyatt. But by then we already liked the song we were working on, so everything's good now."

Over a weird, hypnotic groove, Brett belted out a supremely assured version of Wyatt's "Sea Song", made all the more impressive by its starkness and brevity. "If tonight's performance is anything to go by, there's magic in store for us," enthused Ali Lush, a lifelong Suede fan, in one of her regular pertinent contributions to the band's fanclub mag. "To use Mr Wyatt's words, we're 'seasonal beasts' and our season is about to begin."

Sadly, this would prove to be a somewhat optimistic prognosis. By September, Suede were in a different studio, with a different producer. Something had gone horribly wrong.

"It was a shame because we get on so well," says Brett. "That was probably part of the problem. He was a really funny guy and a really nice guy to be around. It wasn't a professional enough relationship. We pissed around a lot. I genuinely wish him well. Sometimes it works and sometimes it doesn't, the chemistry between band and producer. I listen to the album he did with Supergrass and it sounds good. I don't know if he learned a lot from our session, but their chemistry worked and ours didn't, it's just one of those things. It was no one's fault."

"Tony had some great ideas for the band," says Alex Lee. "I thought the principle of not making a Suede-sounding record was a good one, with him bringing his own set of influences. But unfortunately the chemistry wasn't there and it ended up with lots and lots of arguments and bickering, and he wasn't great at defusing any confrontation and it just turned into a banging your head against the wall session rather than a recording session. I wasn't exactly a massive help because I didn't know exactly where I stood and was just watching the sessions dissolve into arguments and bad experiments, thinking, 'What have I got myself into?' We would literally spend days outside because it was lovely weather, doing something else while he would fiddle on his computer."

For all their initial enthusiasm it had soon become patently obvious that the inherent rustic feel of the songs sat uncomfortably with Tony's futuristic noodlings.

"It was a little hard not having Neil around," says Tony. "Brett also lost a bit of his initial appetite and his singing seemed a little half-hearted compared to the earlier sessions."

Neither side was getting the results they desired from the relationship. Tony cites interference from Saul as the final straw. "He asked if it would be possible for Brett to write a few singles in the mould of *Coming Up*, the band's most successful album. Brett seemed genuinely down about this strange request. He felt he was a completely different person then and wanted the new material to reflect his musical and mental growth in the intervening years."

According to Tony, Saul's diffidence completely sapped his and the band's collective enthusiasm for the project. "We started chasing our tails," says Tony. "We second-guessed the original idea of making an electronic-folk record and tried to recreate an album the band had already made six years earlier. Then one day Brett came into the studio with a copy of Nelly Furtado's 'I'm Like A Bird' and asked me if we could adopt the sound and feel of it for 'Positivity'. The death knell was ringing."

Tony eventually returned to the US, leaving behind almost an entire album of unused material. "I was sad the experiment we attempted was not seen as a success in the band's or the label's eyes," sums up Tony. "On the other hand, I was grateful to break out of the tangled web the band, management and label had built around itself over the years. The funny thing is, I would kill to work with Suede again. I'm still a huge fan and think Brett has one of the most distinctive voices in British music since Bowie. I think together we still have the potential to set the world aflame."

As it was, of the Hoffer tracks, only "Hard Candy" was released – as a b-side – which might have been charming had it not been such a blatant steal of Bowie's "Boys Keep Swinging". Its throwaway nature was understandable, however, as Brett had originally written the song as a theme tune for Sam's band of the same name. "When they inevitably didn't get their shit together, I took it back."

Sam would shortly emigrate to India on a mission of self-discovery but stayed long enough to celebrate Brett's thirty-third birthday at the Cobden club in Notting Hill. The marvellous *Popbitch* website reported that Brett was spotted in the early hours of the morning, shouting "I've got the best cocaine in the whole of London!" from his balcony. Whether that's true or not, an eyewitness observed a scene of post-mayhem *chez* Anderson with vintage Suede videos playing downstairs and the band's latest recordings blasting from the stereo upstairs. At least someone was still an unshakable fan of the band.

Floundering in a creative wilderness, Suede hoped to get back on track by recording two of their strongest numbers with fabled Stone Roses producer John Leckie. The versions of "Beautiful Loser" and "Positivity" were certainly promising, but other commitments for the producer meant this was ultimately another blind alley. It was time to go back to the drawing board, or in Brett's case, a writing room in Harlesden. The window looked out over a huge billboard for So Solid Crew's album, which directly influenced the more urban themes of "Obsessions" and particularly "Streetlife".

Before the band returned to the studio, however, there were another couple of interesting diversions. October 14 saw Brett officially acknowledged as a poet when he appeared at the Bristol Poetry Festival, rather nervously rattling off a handful of his better lyrics. His choice of songs spoke volumes about the varying quality of his wordsmithery over the years. "Killing Of A Flash Boy", "Introducing The Band", "Heroine" and "Daddy's Speeding" all came from the exalted *Dog Man Star* period. "Trash" and "Beautiful Ones" were concessions to *Coming Up* but there was nothing from "Head Music". Perhaps encouragingly, though, Brett did preview two sparkling new sonnets, "Simon" and "Refugees", signalling an upturn in his lyrical prowess. Of far greater significance was his encore of three actual songs. Accompanied only by an acoustic guitar, he thrilled the awed crowd with stunning interpretations of Suede classics from throughout the ages. "Indian Strings", "Oceans" and "The Living Dead" proved beyond a doubt that while the timbre of his words might fluctuate, his music, at its best, remained consistently excellent. "Tonight," noted Ali Lush, "Brett has proved he's a musician first, not a poet. But there's no denying that where the lyrics can also stand as poetry, as with 'Living Dead', the combination of the two is devastating in its emotional impact." Amen.

A fortnight later, Suede performed their only gig of the year at a student festival in Coimbra, Portugal, playing it safe with only two new songs, "Beautiful Loser" and "Positivity". It was a perfectly respectable affair, but would have been a crushing disappointment to anyone who had witnessed the majesty of their Iceland show only a year before. If anything the band seemed to have regressed rather than progressed.

Keenly aware of this the band locked themselves in 2khz Studios for the rest of the year. The results were impressive. Three of the songs they came up with would make it on to the new album, one of them a single. "The actual song ["Obsessions"] was written in a really productive time at the end of that year," confirms Brett. "It was kind of like when we got our shit together again and 'Obsessions' was one of the ones we wrote when we thought, 'Oh, it's going really well now.' And it is about what it's about...obsession."

A close relative of both "Trash" and "Electricity", "Obsessions" bore all the hallmarks of a Richard Oakes classic. "I went home and hit myself over the head and said, 'Write a fucking single, you have to do it!' I had to kick myself to do it. And then I did 'Obsessions', which I know has echoes of other Suede singles...but sometimes you have to just pull out the stops and do something with a bit of energy and a bit of a vibe to it."

The two other principle newbies stemmed from a Mr A. Lee of Bristol. "Streetlife" stemmed from a demo of Alex's called "Motorway". "It started off as a kind of Krautrock drone jam," remembers Mat. "Literally, it was just a riff for about 12 hours. It was good though."

"When we were at Parkgate I faced a three-hour cross-country dash every Saturday night to make it back for last orders in Bristol by car," says Alex. "So I did myself a compilation tape of as much foot-to-the-floor music as I had – stuff like Neu, Iggy's *Raw Power* – and I did an extended instrumental version of 'Motorway', which was based around a relentless drum loop, the acoustic guitar riff and Richard's electric guitar riff and a few experimental synthesizer squelches. At this point it wasn't really thought of as an album contender as everything else we were working on was very song-based and much gentler. But as time went by it became clear that we needed some more up-tempo rock'n'roll stuff. Brett came up with a vocal idea and 'Motorway' was pruned into 'Streetlife' in rehearsal and kept as short as possible 'cause Simon and

Mat found it so knackering to play. It's not the best song on the album but it's great for driving." The song turned up on *Top Gear* shortly afterward.

"It's kind of inspired lyrically by UK garage," adds Brett. "I was trying to do something in the verse like Oxide & Neutrino, that's the idea, but obviously my completely inaccurate version of it, a kind of pastiche of More Fire Crew and stuff like that."

The idea of Brett wigging out with the UK Garage Massive might conjure up hilarious images of Ali G, but much as with his clumsy attempts to replicate Prince in songs like "Savoir Faire", his enthusiasm for the music was completely genuine, even if the results were decidedly suspect. The press inevitably took the piss, though Oxide & Neutrino were gracious enough to respect the compliment – with the painful kiss off that they'd never even heard of Suede.

In far more comfortable territory, "Astrogirl" was one of the last songs written for the album and although probably the most complex and mature song musically, it was one of the simplest and quickest to do. "It just fell out of the piano one night pretty much fully formed," says Alex. "I demoed it and played it to Brett who responded really quickly with the vocal melodies and words, all pretty much within a week of its conception – unbelievably fast by 'A New Morning' standards. As we'd gone round the houses with some other songs which had been worked on for nearly two years it was quite a relief to have a song that was really quick and instinctive to work on."

The working title was "Slow UFO" because the words for the chorus originally referred to UFOs, but as the band were also working on a fast "UFO" song Brett kept the cosmic theme and changed it to "Astrogirl".

"["Astrogirl"] is a real throwaway…it's not a big, deep, meaningful thing," admits Brett. "People probably don't wanna know it but when you're writing songs and you've written 15,000 songs, occasionally one of them is like, 'Oh fuck, what am I gonna write about now?' And that was one of them to be honest. The title's ripped off from a friend of mine who runs a clothes design company and one of the designs is called 'Astrogirl'."

Despite this cavalier approach to the lyrics, the song has all the hallmarks of a timeless Suede classic. "It's one of Al's but in a way it sounds a lot more old Suede than a lot of stuff on the album," agrees Mat. "There's mellotron strings on it and it's quite grand and quite stately."

To remind the rest of the world that they still existed, Suede released a retrospective DVD of their videos in time for Christmas. The compilation was bolstered by a generous helping of extras, including the opening sequence of *Far From China*, which was soundtracked by the song "Simon". The film itself was premièred on November 19 at the Royal Court Theatre in Sloane Square – an event which saw Brett and Neil in the same room for the first time since March – before promptly disappearing up its own backside. "Fucking hell, they could have warned us it was gonna be two hours long," laughs Alan Fisher.

Suede's DVD, titled *Lost In TV* as a hint to the future, was a far more entertaining proposition, particularly the "On The Couch" feature, which saw the band mercilessly pillorying their unwanted alternate career as filmstars. "The best thing you can say about this one is that everyone looks more of a knob than us," observed Mat. But while such candid commentary was revealing, there was a nagging sense that the band were deliberately sabotaging the mystique which made them so alluring in the first place. Suede may finally have begun to convince people that "It's all about the music, maaan", but brilliant as it was, anyone who truly believed that the Suede phenomenon – or indeed any great pop act – was purely about the music was clearly deluding themselves.

Nevertheless, it was with some confidence that Suede entered the studio in January 2002 to begin work – again – on their fifth album. The producer baton had now been passed to Stephen Street. "When Stephen came along I thought, 'Wow, fucking fantastic, old school producer, huge history behind him,'" says Simon Gilbert. "He knew exactly what to do. He was absolutely brilliant. The sounds on the album I thought were brilliant, it sounds like Suede."

The sessions were completed in just nine weeks, light-speed by Suede standards. "Even I felt relief and I'd missed the first year and a half of it," says Alex. "But I was used to working with smaller budgets and bands who worked a hell of a lot quicker and that Tony Hoffer session was like pulling teeth – and about as musical."

After two years, four producers and nigh on a whole album in the bin, *A New Morning* was finally completed on March 23, 2002. There was an enormous sense of relief for all concerned and Brett was effusive in his praise for the man who had finally cajoled Suede into getting their act together. "Stephen has just turned this whole album around, he really has. Every song he's just taken and done something special with... From the millions of other sessions we've done for this album, there's just no comparison."

The sad truth of the matter, however, was that this collection of indisputably first-class songs had been pored over, analysed and re-recorded to death. Even Brett admits a certain disappointment with the finished product. "I think it's got a couple of great moments, but I think it's weak," he says. "Writing the album, I'm not sure I was at my sharpest mentally. Didn't really quite know where I wanted to go. I don't think it was extreme enough. I think it maybe would have been better and much cooler if it had just been an album of acoustic songs."

"I think the lacklustre, Street-produced version of *A New Morning* speaks for itself," says Tony Hoffer. "To me it sounds like a band going through the motions, a band cast adrift with self-doubt and muddled goals. It does not represent Suede at its best. Perhaps all the band wanted to do was re-record its demos in a bigger studio."

Ironically, after all the sonic experimentation, Stephen Street's production and arrangements mirrored the earliest demos almost identically. It's interesting to compare the finished results with those very first demos from Parkgate in the spring of 2000. The stunning "Oceans", relegated to the album's hidden (read wasted) track, was in fact the very same recording with a little tinkering from Mr Street. "Cheap" – possibly the greatest Anderson-Oakes composition ever – was also the exact same version, and its demotion to b-side status quite frankly beggars belief. "Lonely Girls", "Beautiful Loser" and "You Belong To Me" were all re-recorded, but follow the original blueprints almost note for note, adding only a whiff of stale malaise to the sprightly originals. One can't help hypothesise that had Suede simply packaged those five Parkgate demos with the best bits from Stanbridge – let's say "Lost In TV", "Instant Sunshine", "Refugees" and "Untitled", plus Ken Thomas's "Simon" – then things might have turned out very differently indeed.

Mat Osman agrees: "We should have just done it like we ended up doing and not bothered with the experimentation and got it out quickly," he says. "And we shouldn't have tried to tart it up. It ended up like 12-year-olds in make-up and high heels. We should have done it smaller and quickly and kept true to the sentiments. And we also shouldn't have gone to the countryside because you just go mental. We didn't even notice that it wasn't working. It was only when we got back to the city and played it to people and they were saying, 'Are you sure?' It's a shame we didn't go straight in and do it with Stephen because that's how it should have sounded anyway. But it ended up taking so long and costing so much money that people expected it to be something it wasn't."

At the very least, the album would have arrived a year earlier, before the Stalinist purge of anything remotely resembling Britpop in favour of anybody with a pair of Converse trainers and a copy of *Marquee Moon*, and preferably from the New York or Detroit area. As it was, Suede emerged from their protective bubble into an almost unrecognisably alien landscape. Stalwart champions like *Select, Vox* and *Melody Maker* had all bitten the dust while Pulp, perhaps Suede's closest contemporary comparison, had just announced early retirement after the lacklustre performance of their excellent and critically revered *We Love Life* album. Things couldn't possibly get any worse. Or could they?

Of course they could. How about their accountant pilfering nigh on half a million pounds from the band's coffers? Or Nude Records, the band's staunchest ally over the last decade, going under? Nude had been on the skids for some time but started the year encouragingly with a new deal with Zomba just around the corner. Or so they thought. At the eleventh hour, the rug was pulled leaving Nude without a home for the label, its artists or its staff. Suede were actually the least affected by this disaster, being signed to Sony for the rest of the world, where unlike most UK bands they sold most of their records. Nevertheless, it certainly wasn't going to help the suspicion that Suede were regressing from dangerously cool art pioneers into workaday corporate muppets. Suede were shunted on to Epic, home of the Manics, who hadn't done too badly since the interesting one had disappeared and given them the opportunity to fit words with the correct number of syllables into their artisan anthems.

Suede popped their head above the parapet with a carefully contrived showcase for the most devoted fanclub members. Under the ruse of a Suede-themed party to celebrate ten years of "The Drowners", two busloads of the faithful were ferried up to the band's rehearsal studios at The Depot in North London where they bashed out storming versions of the best bits of the new album along with old faves like "The Drowners" and "Flashboy".

The revelry continued at the Sahara Nights club in Kings Cross, where the band mingled amicably with the thrilled fans. Brett could be spotted enjoying himself enormously with a gaggle of cackling fans in the corner where anyone paying close attention would notice that his public announcement to have packed in drugs completely wasn't strictly true. One punter, Ricky Coffey, took the opportunity to ask this particularly perky Brett a question he'd always wanted to ask. His chance came at the urinals.

"You know how you said you were a bisexual who'd never had a homosexual experience. Have you managed to rectify that yet?"

"Nah," sniffed Brett, "I fancy birds too much."

Suede's comeback proper took place at the Royal Festival Hall in June, where they were special invitees of Dame David Bowie, that year's curator at *Meltdown*. Well aware of the sterile nature of the venue, the band did their best to spice up the proceedings by bringing a ten-piece orchestra with them, and having archly ironic punk slut Peaches provide support. Brett had been turned on to Peaches by Justine Frischmann who credited her as the principle reason for the dissolution of Elastica. Having toured America with two double deckers and a fleet of artics, Justine found Peaches' minimal beatbox-in-the-back-of-a-cab modernism hugely refreshing.

Peaches was by all accounts fairly chuffed to be picked for the job. "I used to love Suede. When they first came out they were really avant garde. It was an honour to play for them. I don't think their crowd liked me much, though!"

Suede might have shot themselves in the foot with such a brave choice of opening act, however. Peaches was so painfully hip that the star turns were in danger of exposing themselves as woefully outmoded in comparison. Writing in the *Guardian*, Caroline Sullivan discussed this conundrum: "The last time Suede had a single in the chart, the world was preoccupied by the Millennium bug and the Spice Girls were a going concern. Pop has since trundled on, leaving the band held to be the architects of Britpop in a pickle: too arty to chime with the mainstream, too mainstream to find a niche alongside confrontationalists such as Peaches. Indeed, it seemed this modish Canadian rapper would run away with the show. After Peaches, Suede sounded as conventional as Kylie."

If only they sounded half as contemporary as Kylie. Nevertheless, Suede accredited themselves with aplomb, delivering an assured set of extreme confidence and some dignity, helped in no small measure by the string section, as David Sinclair agreed in the *Times*, "Suede have used strings before, but on this occasion, when combined with the mellifluous quality of new songs such as 'Positivity', 'Lost In TV' and 'When The Rain Falls', the orchestral touches tended to steer the whole direction of the show away from the group's rock'n'roll roots into territory that felt a lot more melodically-driven and generally grown-up."

"Suede's return reveals just how impoverished English pop has been without bands of their calibre," continued Sullivan's *Guardian* piece. "This was an exceptional example of the fact that their music still has glamour and potency. The middle section of Suede staples, including 'Trash' and the clangorously seedy 'Metal Mickey', was possibly the best twenty minutes of live music performed this year."

After such generous positivity, the review ended on a note of caution "Can they rebrand in a sufficiently noughties way to ensure a fourth number one album?"

Aye, there was the rub.

CHAPTER SIXTEEN
attitude

THE SUMMER OF 2002 WAS spent mostly at festivals, taking in Sweden, Turkey, Finland, Latvia, Spain, Denmark, France, Japan and plucky little Belgium. These passed largely without incident, though there was a minor drama when Brett's bag was lost somewhere between Copenhagen and Charles De Gaulle airports. Richard Kiernan, from the band's management office, acting as assistant tour manager, had the joy of relaying the news. "We'd travelled all through the night and were fucking knackered coming back from Skandebourg," remembers Richard. "We're stuck in Charles De Gaulle airport where we've just found out there's not enough seats on the plane to the gig at St Malo and Brett's bag's gone missing on the plane from Copenhagen. When I told him he said, 'If I don't get the bag I'm not doing the gig. It's got my make-up and my lucky trousers in it.'" Eventually, the bag did turn up at Charles de Gaulle. "So we had to get a fucking express cab for about 500 quid to zoom this bag halfway across France so Brett could get his mascara and lucky trousers in time to play the shittiest stage in Europe!"

In the UK they played Manchester's Move festival, again at the invitation of David Bowie. It was an excellent show despite the oddly portentous thunderstorm as the band sang of how "The birds sing for you and the sunshine is free" during slightly anticipated forthcoming single, "Positivity".

"The rain just came at us, horizontal and I thought I was going to explode," remembers Alex Lee. "And then David Bowie came on stage and the sun came out for him, which just goes to show he is in league with the Devil." Despite Suede's valiant performance, there was a tangible sense that Mr Bowie no longer saw Brett & Co. as a threat to his "Queen of Space-Glam Pop" crown.

"Positivity", Suede's first single for almost three years, was finally released on September 16. The choice of lead-off single had been a topic of heated debate for some time and is still something of touchy subject in Suede circles. Although by no means a bad song, "Positivity" had neither the dark rocking seduction of the likes of Suede outsider anthems like "Trash" nor the winning mainstream hooks of "She's In Fashion" or "Saturday Night". It was, in all honesty, bland, something Suede, for all their faults, could rarely have been accused of in the past. They had finally leapfrogged out of the indie ghetto they had always faintly despised, but now found themselves in Radio Two land, where they were still tarnished with enough weirdness to put Ken Bruce and Wogan's listeners off their *Crunchy Nut Cornflakes*. Suede heard the midweek while on the train to perform the song on *Pop Factory*, an excellent Welsh music show set in an old lemonade works deep in the valleys. "Positivity" was holding at number 11, not too bad at all, but the fact that the band were on their way to an obscure regional TV programme, rather than *Top Of The Pops*, spoke volumes about their standing at the time. That the busloads of school kids who made up the audience obviously had no idea who Suede were can't have been much of a morale booster either.

"'Positivity' is a funny one," concedes Brett. "I know Suede fans hate it with a passion but I still quite believe in the song. I know that the decision for that to be the single contributed towards the fuck up of that album, I'm aware of that, but there's something I still feel is quite beautiful about the song. I don't wanna write it again, I don't wanna go down there again. But the whole thing about *A New Morning* was coming back from the horror that I'd been in with *Head Music* and a lot of it was almost a personal need to write something that was simpler and less fucked up. It was almost the first Suede album that we'd done for ourselves. I wanted to experience reality and purity rather than paranoia and all that shit and write about it. And I feel totally justified because I was expressing how I was feeling at the time. I felt quite strongly that 'Positivity' expressed what I wanted to say, even if it didn't make as much sense commercially. I felt justified artistically."

The single made it to a still-respectable-but-only-just 16. This, however, was a staggering victory compared to the cataclysmic disaster that awaited. Reviews tended to be generally sympathetic, if hardly ecstatic. "When Suede are good, they're great," said the *NME*, awarding the album seven out of ten – the same mark they'd given to *Suede* and *Head Music*. "'Astrogirl' has shades of the almighty 'The Asphalt World', 'When The Rain Falls' is as mournful as 'The Big Time'. Ironically, it's when they try their hardest to be Suede that things go haywire. 'Beautiful Loser' is a hamfisted attempt to recreate 'Metal Mickey'. It's almost as if Brett feels compelled to exit his Notting Hill pad now and then trawl through the graffiti ridden subways of Basingstoke. Why bother? At its best, *A New Morning* sees Suede show off their vulnerable side again. It won't attract any new admirers but old fans will love them more for it."

Q magazine came to a similar conclusion. "Suede have settled for cult status. Their fifth album's a holding pattern, a circling of wagons that, perhaps wisely, was unveiled at a couple of mostly fan-only London shows. The faithful will be overjoyed."

If only that were the case. The fans, it transpired, were even less interested than the media. Released on September 30, *A New Morning* limped into the album charts at number 24.

"We were utterly, utterly shocked and horrified," admits Brett. "I couldn't believe it, and just couldn't work out what had happened. I thought there had been some fuck up with the barcodes or something, It's just bizarre. We've had three number one albums and a number three album, and then this one went in at 24. I kind of know what it is. We've not had the media support that we've normally had. People have turned their backs on us, which is fair enough. I almost think that our fanbase deliberately decided not to go out and buy the album, and that has a lot to do with the choice of the first single. We actually alienated a lot of our fan base, who decided that we shouldn't come out with upbeat songs like 'Positivity'."

"It was difficult," says Mat Osman. "We knew the kind of record we made and we knew it was out of step with the times. I don't think any of us were expecting it to be number one, but we weren't expecting it to do that badly. I think it's partly down to choosing a single that was almost deliberately chosen to alienate everyone who'd ever been into the band. And that's what it came down to. The feeling in the band was we should release it because everyone says we shouldn't. There's logic there. That sounds like we're just being contrary but we're not. I think Brett personally wanted to change who he was and one of the ways of doing that is saying things you don't expect from him. I don't feel we went absolutely mad, because 'Positivity' was one of the very few number one singles we've had in the rest of the world. I think we've had three now. In a lot of places it's the biggest ever Suede single. It's really bizarre."

Alex Lee believes that *A New Morning* will be viewed more kindly in the future than it was at the time. "I think people were expecting another big Suede statement album and the fact that the band had spent three years doing it [meant that] there was inevitably going to be some disappointment unless it was a *magnum opus*, which it wasn't. It was quite an understated, heartfelt record and I can see why people were expecting more from it. I don't think it's perfect at all but I think there's some really good songs on it."

Suede's first gig after hearing the news was another in-store at Virgin Megastore. Brett was evidently extremely pissed off, and his curmudgeonly petulance would have done little to win over the support of any waverers in the audience. Spitting, swearing and showering the audience with water, Brett asked for requests then replied "Tough shit!" before belly-flopping into "Positivity".

"To be honest I was sort of angry with the audience because I felt as if it was their negativity about 'Positivity' that had put us in the slot," he says. "I felt as if the feedback from the fans was so bad I almost felt a bit betrayed by them, which is probably me overreacting. I've done enough good work in my life to be given a bit of faith and...I didn't think [it] warranted a complete lack of confidence. You don't like one song, fair enough, it's not the end of the world. And that was probably quite irrational but that's the reason why I was so angry."

Tempers had calmed slightly when Suede invited fans to appear in the video shoot for their next single, "Obsessions", a couple of days later. The shoot took place at the new Marquee, a sterile box in the Angel shopping centre which bore absolutely no resemblance to the legendary original. Fortunately, Suede still managed to rock, Brett channelling his recent disappointments into an animalistic performance that conjured up memories of some of the classic gigs of old.

Spirits were even higher when the band returned to their adopted second home, Denmark. Hard to imagine as it might be, "Positivity" was a number one smash there, while the album had just entered the top five. Here at least they were still kings, as *Q* was surprised to discover. "It's rare that an established band earns the biggest cheers of the night with its new songs. Yet with the single 'Positivity' residing at number one and their three Copenhagen shows selling out in a record-breaking 26 minutes Suede are Denmark's current big draw. A lithe, muscular Brett Anderson shimmies and poses like he's lost ten years from his age, twirls his mic in outrageous arcs, and indulges in the corniest banter this side of a Run-DMC revival. 'Wave your hands in the air. Bounce! Bounce!' he yelps, causing floorboards to give under the weight of 1,500 feet. When they're brought back to the stage for a third time, the rapturous reception of 'The Wild Ones' is a pertinent reminder that its parent album, 1994's *Dog Man Star*, led to Suede's temporary dismissal as Britpop underdogs. As tonight's performance displays, if ever there was a band that kicks vigorously against the pricks, it's Suede."

The reviewer took the opportunity to quiz Mat and Brett about the abysmal sales of the album in their home country. "We wanted to make something straight and immediate and honest and a million words you wouldn't really associate with Suede," replied Mat. "We kind of knew a lot of people wouldn't like it but we've never done anything for fashion or profile's sake."

Brett did his best not to sound bitter. "Because it's kind of naive and simple and the guitars aren't as loud they're cynical about it, so fuck 'em. How successful it is depends where you go. The UK's fucked up, but everywhere else… I'm not going to sit here and moan about it. I'd just sound fucking sad."

"It was very strange that little period," considers Brett now. "The British media had completely turned their backs on us and it was number one in Denmark and number two in Japan and we were doing quite good business abroad. I felt this new found vigour. A lot of it was to do with being really fit, after years and years of taking drugs. I felt I could express the songs the way they were meant to be. I feel when we play now we're better than we've ever been. There's an energy and a passion to every gig we do."

Nevertheless, it must have been fairly demoralising to return to the UK to play the same venues they'd played in as long ago as 1994, only now to slightly fewer people. The band put a brave face on it, however, and the gigs were generally excellent, particularly a trio of sold-out nights at London's Shepherd's Bush Empire. Outside the world of the Suede fan, however, the band might as well have not existed. The *NME* and whatever else was left of the UK music press didn't even bother to review the shows. All in the Suede camp had been well aware of this eventuality and some frantic head-scratching had taken place to see if anything could be done to generate some media interest. One suggestion was the possibility of inviting McAlmont & Butler to be very special guests on the tour, or at least one of the London shows – a Suede & Butler reunion of sorts. While it may seem unlikely that Bernard would ever deign to stoop as low as supporting his estranged colleagues, there were indications that some burying of hatchets might be in the offing.

In an interview with the *Daily Record* to promote the recently reunited McAlmont & Butler's latest offering, the patchily brilliant *Bring It Back*, Bernard was quizzed on his departure from Suede. "When I left Suede I didn't do it because I fell out with people," he was quoted as saying. "I did it because I didn't want the producer we had to mix an album. It was a case of 'call my bluff'. It was him or me. It was a stupid mistake. I was stupid enough to go for it. It shouldn't have gone that far, but the band said they weren't sacking the producer, so I had to go. They did sack him a year later and have complained about him ever since."

Brett voiced similar nostalgic regret in an interview with *Boyz*. "I think it was such a wrong thing to do, such a mistake, and such a tragedy for music, and this is the thing I find slightly upsetting about the whole thing, that now – eight years down the line – we couldn't just pick up where we left off. It's just impossible. And I think it's a shame that only now Bernard is realising that a) we made some great music together, and b) Suede were a precious thing that shouldn't have been tampered with so early. It's a difficult thing to talk about, and I'm not saying it was all his fault, because there was a lot of shit from me. I was turning into a bit of a lunatic. But everything I ever did was never just for Brett Anderson, it was always for Suede and it did turn into a situation where it was Bernard Butler against the rest of us, which was a shame. But again, I have no problem with Bernard, and like he says, we just literally haven't bumped into one another. I have no problem with him at all, and I wish him well. I mean that genuinely."

Not everyone was quite so readily eager to kiss and make up, however. Alex Lee remembers the McAlmont & Butler proposal receiving short shrift from certain quarters. "Simon nearly blew his top. He literally had steam coming out of his ears, I've never seen anything like it!"

Almost apologetically, Suede signed off their British tour by releasing "Obsessions" as a second single from the album on November 17. The staunch loyalty of their British fanbase was demonstrated by the single's number 29 placing, but it was clear that few others in the UK were interested and the band took refuge in a second European tour for the rest of the year.

Perhaps the most bizarre engagement of the year was as part of the star-studded Nobel Peace Prize Concert in Oslo on December 11, honouring former US president, Jimmy Carter. Hosted by Jessica Lange and Anthony Hopkins, other performers included Jennifer Lopez, Santana, Willie Nelson and Hall & Oates. Suede's two-song slot, however, was almost cancelled when Brett refused to take part in the Band Aid-style ensemble finale of "Give Peace A Chance". Eventually a compromise was reached and he consented to standing on stage looking grumpy as long as he didn't have to sing.

A holiday was probably in order and most of the band set off for New Year breaks in Thailand, though Richard spent a romantic Christmas break in New York with his girlfriend, before they all met up in Hong Kong for an ambitious tour of South East Asia.

Suede became the first western act to perform on Hong Kong's prestigious RTHK Radio Awards, played a blinding show in Taipei, then visited Shanghai as the first western act on the *Chinese Music Awards* (170 million viewers!). After Shanghai they head back to Hong Kong to collect a gold award for *A New Morning* and played another blinder before finally making it to Indonesia, three years after they were first due to play there. Despite official warnings from the UK Foreign Office against travelling to Indonesia in light of the Bali bombings, the 5,000-capacity show was thankfully free from strife. The 86 photographers and umpteen TV crews give some indication as to how warmly Suede were welcomed for having the courage to visit this troubled country.

"Decent gigs are rare, mainly because only dancing pop acts sell down here," attests Claudia Pramono from respected fan site, *Essential Suede*. "Things got worse as our country become more and more unsafe – many gigs are cancelled for security reasons. So I couldn't help preparing myself for the worst when I heard Suede were coming. You get used to it if you live here. But in the end, I had to salute them and be grateful that I'm a fan of this particular band, because unlike others, they didn't give up on their fans."

Among the many highlights for the band was watching Missy Elliot at the *MTV Awards* in Singapore, where Brett presented the award for best local act. At the band's Singapore gig the next evening the promoter was arrested because Brett took his shirt off, contravening one of the country's many draconian rules which also apparently include the right to push in front of people with long hair in queues.

After a typically ecstatic reaction in Japan, where the band continued their tradition of ending their Nipponese tour with a cover version, in this case Blondie's "Union City Blue", the band headed to the People's Republic Of China. Other than Wham!, Elton John and Jean Michel Jarre, Suede were the first western act ever to play this Communist super-power, and certainly the first alternative rock band. No one knew quite what to expect.

Suede arrived just in time for the dawning of the Year Of The Goat and a spectacular eight-hour fireworks display over Beijing. On their day off they were treated to a whirlwind tourist tour, taking in the Great Wall Of China, the Forbidden City and Tiananmen Square – site of the 1989 massacre, a vaguely sinister reminder that this was a totalitarian regime where normal rules did not apply.

"China was an amazing place to go," says Richard Oakes. "I'm really glad we went there. For a lot of the kids it was their first ever rock show...you didn't see the Beatles in 1966 but you can see a Suede show in 2003! The gigs were really funny, the police were all lined up, it's still quite oppressive. They don't like the idea of kids rebelling and rock-'n'roll is all pure rebellion. So there were police lined up, holding kids back. 'You mustn't shout to the audience to come to the front of the stage or they'll pull the plug!' So all we can do is play the songs really well. So we did, we were giving it everything. And when we got halfway through 'Trash' they did manage to break through the police lines and run to the front of the stage, 2,500 Chinese kids, which isn't bad. It was their first ever rock show and they experienced rock'n'roll madness, and we inspired that."

Suede returned to the UK on February 10 and almost immediately began working on new material, primarily with the aim of producing two new tracks to go with that classic contractual obligation, the greatest hits album, due for release at the end of 2003. They unveiled the first of their new compositions at two sweaty club shows in Arhus, Denmark, in April.

Suede kicked off both nights with the track titled "Love The Way You Love", a hard, relentless, almost electronic number, belying the sentimental title. They followed up with two very different but equally impressive sets. The Friday night show saw the band revisit some lesser known gems from their back catalogue. "Cool Thing", "Cheap" and "Daddy's Speeding" all received their live debuts, while classics like "To The Birds" and "The Next Life" were dusted down and performed live for the first time in many years. Saturday night saw the band go into overdrive with a hits-all-the-way set that wowed even the most jaded of spectators. The band made another nod to their rich heritage during the encores with a stunning rendition of "The Asphalt World", a song not played since 1995 and sounding better than ever with the addition of Alex on keyboards and second guitar. After all the recent disappointments and disasters, it seemed the band were back on track at last.

Brett took the time to chat with fans on the band's official website to discuss some of the new tracks. "Most of the new material is more aggressive and less song-based than *A New Morning*. We're spending a lot of time working on tracks that sound nothing like traditional Suede. There's a kind of electronic reggae thing called 'Attitude', an insane metallic robot march called 'Golden Gun' and a punky thrash called 'I Don't Need A High'. I needed to write something as soulful as *A New Morning* at the time but now that's out of my system and it's time to release the beast."

At a sweltering outdoor show in Thessalonika, Greece, in June, the band road-tested no less than six of the tracks they'd been working on. In addition to "Love The Way You Love", "Attitude" and "Golden Gun" they debuted "Teenage Rose", which Brett described as "a song about masturbation", a typical Suede ballad called "Oxygen" and, most promising of all, "Quiet/Loud", which was largely based around a looped sample of "Music like sex we like to have sex to music like sex…", which was almost ridiculously catchy. Many of the songs were so new that Brett read the lyrics from a sheet of paper. "Love The Way You Love", in particular, went down a storm. It seemed their recent drubbing had done them the power of good.

Tensions boiled to the surface the next night in Athens when a series of technical hitches, including the intro tape being played too early and the backdrop having to be set loose mid-gig when gale-force winds threatened to topple the entire stage, led to much screaming and shouting in the dressing room afterwards. They were still not in the best of moods when they made what should have been a triumphant return to Glastonbury, ten years since they had last played the mother of all festivals. This time they were on the main stage, but third from the top. They had the uncommon experience of playing in daylight to an early evening crowd and the reaction, while by no means bad, wasn't the ecstatic response they'd been becoming reacquainted with in Europe and Asia. They returned to the womb-like comforts of Denmark shortly after for the seven date Gron Tour, a kind of travelling festival principally of Danish bands but with Suede being guests of honour as honorary Danes.

The gigs got better and better, culminating in a huge show in Copenhagen in front of almost 100,000 people and – Roskilde aside – probably one of the largest crowds they'd ever played to. Among the throng were two Finnish fans, Elina and Sirje, who'd made a special pilgrimage to follow the band throughout the whole tour. For the encore, they decided to have a little poke at Brett's somewhat predictable between-song banter.

"Brett asked his usual Saturday night question, 'What night is it tonight?'" says Elina. "Having heard it quite a few times recently, we decided to answer him with a banner. The banner did not have 'Saturday Night' written on it, but 'Monday Morning!' instead. Alex, Mat and Simon burst out laughing. We guess no one other than the band actually saw our banner, as we didn't hold it up for long enough to get it shown on the screen. The reason for this was that Brett was soon carried to us sitting on a sofa and so we gave it to his lap and the poor guy had to sing most of the song with it. The sofa was the security staff's idea. Brett was just going to go for his usual walk down in front of the first row when they pushed him to sit on a portable sofa they had brought as a surprise. A good one!"

Suede immediately travelled on to Sweden to record "Love The Way You Love" in Malmo with Cardigans producer Tore Johansson. At the time of writing it looks like being one of two new tracks on the greatest hits album, to be titled simply, *Singles*.

"It's a singles collection, not a 'Best of...'," points out Brett. "If it was a best of it would have to include album tracks and b-sides and stuff like that. But it's a pretty good piece of work."

The 21-track compilation is indeed an extraordinary body of work including some of the greatest pop moments of the last decade and beyond. But perhaps the most extraordinary thing about it is that Suede managed to stay together this long at all. They have suffered the slings and arrows of misfortune a darned sight more than most, yet have still always come up fighting. And it is this refusal to throw in the towel, this triumph over adversity, no matter how high the odds are stacked against them, that is part of their enduring appeal and goes some way to explaining the near fanatical devotion they inspire among their supporters. For many people Suede are, or at least were, a way of life, a huge inspiration that went way beyond the already impressive achievement of simply encouraging people to pick up guitars and start bands of their own.

"I don't want the next record to take three years. I don't think we can afford it to be honest," says Richard Oakes. "But it's just not fun keeping the fans waiting because there's such a community. They live in a Suede world. They do all these polls – which Suede member would you most like to punch in the face? I nearly won that poll! I was a couple of per cent behind Brett."

Suede turned guitar music around for the decade. They started a movement in pop music that laid the foundations for '90s music. As Brett once put it, "The reason we stood out when we started was we were the first alternative band to write a fucking tune for four years. Now everyone writes pop songs. We got teenage girls interested in guitar bands again. We made bands think about image again. We reintroduced lyrics about everyday life. Even vocal affectations: every record you hear now has one, but when I sang 'The Drowners' everyone was totally shocked."

That "Best New Band In Britain" piece described Suede as "the most audacious, mysterious, sexy, absurd, perverse, glamorous, hilarious, honest, cocky, melodramatic, mesmerising band you're ever likely to fall in love with". While they may no longer be quite as mysterious, sexy or glamorous as they once were, they're certainly one of the most honest and in turns absurd, perverse, hilarious, cocky and melodramatic too. At their very best, they can still be mesmerising. Their recent live gigs have been phenomenal.

"I think the most important thing about Suede is that they're a fantastic live band and they've never been able to quite put something on record that blows you away like they do live," believes Neil Codling, "and if they'd been able to do that things would be very different. I always thought that Suede got a bad press for the wrong reasons. You'd go abroad on tour and read these seven-word reviews, 'De da de da de da, Ziggy Stardust, eight out of ten'. Whenever a Pet Shop Boys album comes out nobody says, 'Oh my god, he still sounds exactly like Al Stewart, why does he get off trying to sound like Al Stewart?' And the poor bloke must have an iron will to be able to carry on, he really must."

Brett's stoic determination is undeniable, built on the firm foundations of a heritage of which he remains fiercely proud. "For years I think Suede were the only intelligent working-class voice in music," he says. "We were the first band for ages who actually talked about real life and who addressed uncomfortable and not particularly pop-friendly issues. I've always tried to reflect life as I've seen it, even when it's not so pretty. Songs like 'Sleeping Pills', 'Animal Nitrate', 'Trash' and the rest were born of a burning desire to talk about MY life, not the handed down experiences of Jimi Hendrix or John Lennon. We talked about sex, obsession, poverty, sadness and death and presented them in a pop format which infiltrated the mainstream. Even the ultimately conservative, safe and tasteful indie ghetto felt threatened by a band confronting sexuality and doing it with style and drama. I also believe that Suede set the blueprint for what was to become the '90s guitar band. Our sense of ambition and belief and our re-introduction of classic songwriting was shockingly new in 1992, but became the norm afterwards. I genuinely feel as though we redirected pop music, we're a fork in the road, which is a big thing to do."

Their original manager Jon Eydmann agrees wholeheartedly. "I get a bit confused to how they could possibly be so overlooked in terms of how important they were at the time," he says. "Because I don't see how anyone could deny that, they made the blueprint for me. I don't understand how anyone could miss that. Blur were already there, they weren't really a Britpop band, they were baggy. And 'There's No Other Way', somebody had put some awfully baggy reverb on those drums hadn't they? That was baggy-tastic! Whatever happens in the future to Suede or whatever goes on, I think they should be credited for what they achieved. And I do think they achieved the start of a new kind of musical genre."

Of course, with a back catalogue like Suede's it would be very easy for them to rest on their laurels. Critics have already made mutterings of Suede turning into a cabaret act, eternally wheeling out the greatest hits. It's a trap that Mat Osman is eager to avoid and he remains cautiously optimistic about the band's future. "It's obviously a low time for the band but those have always kind of been the best for us," he says. "The stuff we did for the *Singles* album, I think is probably as different from the one before as anything we've ever done. The one good thing is, it's a completely new start, it kind of leaves you at ground zero. Of the six new tracks we've done there's a couple of things that are completely different from anything we've done before and as good as anything we've done before, so I'm quietly confident. And I really, really don't ever want to spend three years making a record again. Less fucking touring and more making records."

But perhaps the most miraculous aspect of the Suede story is the fact that they have come this far without anyone dying or ending up in prison. That *"Fear & Loathing* re-written by Machiavelli" comparison doesn't come close to depicting the carnage and chaos, drama and disaster of their fantastic voyage. Suede's history is not so much the "crazy rollercoaster ride" of most rock'n'roll memoirs, more a Wheel of Death featuring crack-addled Uzi-toting clowns armed with live ammunition. Far from ending up in a ditch with hypodermics protruding from their posteriors, Richard, Mat and Alex all have happy long-term relationships with girlfriends who quite frankly deserve medals. Simon has moved to the country, where he lives in a beautiful house with his golden labrador, George. Justine Frischmann is enjoying a successful second career as a television presenter. Justin Welch is happily married to Mew from Elastica and living drug-free in Devon. Bernard Butler, extricating himself from what must have been a truly horrendous last couple of years with the band, is now the proud father of two children as well as having a glorious musical CV. Brett Anderson, meanwhile, is one of the few true, classic British pop icons of recent history, a national treasure.

"The last couple of years are the first when me and Brett have been totally straight," reflects his best friend, Alan Fisher. "And it's like before you die, the whole of your life flashes before you. Every day, memories are coming back to me now. It's funny how it all comes back to you as all the chemicals come out of your body. I've got these videos I've been watching recently and thinking, 'Fucking hell, did we really do that!' Going off to score crack at two in the morning, carrying ridiculous amounts of drugs on us at five in the morning, you know, big deals… It's a wonder we never got pulled over. I really can't believe we never got busted."

For Brett's longest-running musical side-kick, the last 13 odd years have been absolutely nothing like he could ever have imagined. "I expected it to be a glorious plateau of success," says Mat Osman. "I expected it to be good and get better. It just doesn't occur to you. It's a day-dream, you can't be expected to fill it with ups and downs. But it's been far more up and down than I expected. And I've almost got used to the idea of living in perpetual crisis. There's always a crisis. And it's always a different one, just in case you think you're prepared. The band is always on the verge of splitting into a million tiny pieces and I've kind of got used to that. I suddenly realised that's how life is, or that's how life in Suede is."

The only predictable thing about Suede's future is that it will be utterly unpredictable. But whatever happens next, there's no denying that Suede have, at various points in their career, been one of the most important and exciting bands ever to walk the planet. "I think we changed things," declares Brett. "I think we made a difference."

And I want "Still Life" played at my funeral. See you in the next life.

suede official uk discography

This lists all the commercially available Suede records released in the UK. For imports, promos and rarities I would recommend David Gejlimo's exhaustive discography site, www.suedestation.com

THE DROWNERS
NUD1CD

Tracks:

"The Drowners"
"To The Birds"
"My Insatiable One"

Released: May 11, 1992
Highest chart position: 48

METAL MICKEY
NUD3CD

Tracks:

"Metal Mickey"
"Where The Pigs Don't Fly"
"He's Dead"

Released: September 14, 1992
Highest chart position: 17

ANIMAL NITRATE
NUD4CD

Tracks:

"Animal Nitrate"
"Painted People"
"The Big Time"

Released: February 22, 1993
Highest chart position: 7

SUEDE
NUDE1CD

Tracks:

"So Young"
"Animal Nitrate"
"She's Not Dead"
"Moving"
"Pantomime Horse"
"The Drowners"
"Sleeping Pills"
"Breakdown"
"Metal Mickey"
"Animal Lover"
"The Next Life"

Released: March 29, 1993
Highest chart position: 1

SO YOUNG
NUD 5CD

Tracks:

"So Young"
"Dolly"
"High Rising"

Released: May 17, 1993
Highest chart position: 22

STAY TOGETHER
NUD9CD

Tracks:

"Stay Together" (edit)
"The Living Dead"
"My Dark Star"
"Stay Together"

Released: February 14, 1994
Highest chart position: 3

WE ARE THE PIGS
NUD10CD

Tracks:

"We Are The Pigs"
"Killing Of A Flash Boy"
"Whipsnade"

Released: September 12, 1994
Highest chart position: 18

DOG MAN STAR
NUDE3CD

Tracks:

"Introducing The Band"
"We Are The Pigs"
"Heroine"
"The Wild Ones"
"Daddy's Speeding"
"The Power"
"New Generation"
"This Hollywood Life"
"The 2 Of Us"
"Black Or Blue"
"The Asphalt World"
"Still Life"

Released: October 10, 1994
Highest chart position: 3

THE WILD ONES
NUD11CD1

Tracks:

"The Wild Ones"
"Modern Boys"
"This World Needs A Father"

NUD11CD2

Tracks:

"The Wild Ones"
"Eno's Introducing The Band"
"Asda Town"

Released: November 14, 1994
Highest chart position: 18

NEW GENERATION
NUD12CD1

Tracks:

"New Generation"
"Together"
"Bentswood Boys"

NUD12CD2

Tracks:

"New Generation"
"Animal Nitrate" (live)
"The Wild Ones" (live)
"Pantomime Horse" (live)

Released: CD1 January 30, 1995, CD2
February 6, 1995
Highest chart position: 21

TRASH
NUD21CD1

Tracks:

"Trash"

"Europe Is Our Playground"
"Every Monday Morning Comes"

NUD21CD2

Tracks:

"Trash"
"Have You Ever Been This Low"
"Another No One"

Released: July 29, 1996
Highest chart position: 3

COMING UP
NUDE6CD

Tracks:

"Trash"
"Filmstar"
"Lazy"
"By The Sea"
"She"
"Beautiful Ones"
"Starcrazy"
"Picnic By The Motorway"
"The Chemistry Between Us"
"Saturday Night"

Released: September 2, 1996
Highest chart position: 1

BEAUTIFUL ONES
NUD23CD1

Tracks:

"Beautiful Ones"
"Young Men"
"The Sound Of The Streets"

NUD23CD2

Tracks:

"Beautiful Ones"

"Money"
"Sam"

Released: October 14, 1996
Highest chart position: 8

SATURDAY NIGHT
NUD24CD1

Tracks:

"Saturday Night"
"W.S.D."
"Jumble Sale Mums"

NUD24CD2

Tracks:

"Saturday Night"
"This Time"
"Saturday Night" (original demo)

Released: January 13, 1997
Highest chart position: 6

LAZY
NUD27CD1

Tracks:

"Lazy"
"These Are The Sad Songs"
"Feel"

NUD27CD2

Tracks:

"Lazy"
"Sadie"
"Digging A Hole"

Released: April 7, 1997
Highest chart position: 9

FILMSTAR
NUD30CD1

Tracks:

"Filmstar"
"Graffiti Women"
"Duchess"

NUD30CD2

Tracks:

"Filmstar"
"Rent" (live)
"Saturday Night" (live)

Released: August 11, 1997
Highest chart position: 9

SCI-FI LULLABIES
NUDE9CD

Tracks:

"My Insatiable One"
"To The Birds"
"Where The Pigs Don't Fly"
"He's Dead"
"The Big Time"
"High Rising"
"The Living Dead"
"My Dark Star"
"Killing Of A Flash Boy"
"Whipsnade"
"Modern Boys"
"Together"
"Bentswood Boys"
"Europe Is Our Playground" (new version)
"Every Monday Morning Comes"
"Have You Ever Been This Low"
"Another No One"
"Young Men"
"The Sound Of The Streets"
"Money"

"W.S.D."
"This Time"
"Jumble Sale Mums"
"These Are The Sad Songs"
"Sadie"
"Graffiti Women"
"Duchess"

Released: October 6, 1997
Highest chart position: 9

ELECTRICITY
NUD43CD1

Tracks:

"Electricity"
"Popstar"
"Killer"

NUD43CD2

Tracks:

"Electricity"
"See That Girl"
"Waterloo"

Released: April 12, 1999
Highest chart position: 5

HEAD MUSIC
NUDE14CD

Tracks:

"Electricity"
"Savoir Faire"
"Can't Get Enough"
"Everything Will Flow"
"Down"
"She's In Fashion"
"Asbestos"
"Head Music"
"Elephant Man"
"Hi-Fi"

"Indian Strings"
"He's Gone"
"Crack In The Union Jack"

Released: May 3, 1999
Highest chart position: 1

SHE'S IN FASHION
NUD44CD1

Tracks:

"She's In Fashion"
"Bored"
"Pieces Of My Mind"

NUD44CD2

Tracks:

"She's In Fashion"
"Jubilee"
"God's Gift"

Released: June 21, 1999
Highest chart position: 13

EVERYTHING WILL FLOW
NUD45CD1

Tracks:

"Everything Will Flow"
"Weight Of The World"
"Leaving"

NUD45CD2

Tracks:

"Everything Will Flow"
"Crackhead"
"Seascape"

Released: September 6, 1999
Highest chart position 24

CAN'T GET ENOUGH
NUD47CD1

Tracks:

"Can't Get Enough"
"Let Go"
"Since You Went Away"

NUD47CD2

Tracks:

"Can't Get Enough"
"Situations"
"Read My Mind"

NUD47CD3

Tracks:

"Can't Get Enough"
"Everything Will Flow" (Rollo's vocal mix)
"She's In Fashion" (Lironi version)
"Can't Get Enough" (CD-ROM video)

Released: November 8, 1999
Highest chart position: 23

POSITIVITY
EPIC672949 2 (CD1)

Tracks:

"Positivity"
"One Love"
"Simon"

EPIC672949 5 (CD2)

Tracks:

"Positivity"
"Superstar"
"Cheap"

EPIC672949 9 (DVD)

Tracks:

"Positivity"

"Colours"
"Campfire Song"

Released: September 16, 2002
Highest chart position: 16

A NEW MORNING
EPIC5089569

Tracks:

"Positivity"
"Obsessions"
"Lonely Girls"
"Lost In TV"
"Beautiful Loser"
"Streetlife"
"Astrogirl"
"Untitled"
"Morning"
"One Hit To The Body"
"When The Rain Falls"
"You Belong To Me" (limited edition bonus track)
"Oceans" (hidden track)

Released: September 30, 2002
Highest chart position: 24

OBSESSIONS
EPIC673294 2 (CD1)

Tracks:

"Obsessions"
"Cool Thing"
"Instant Sunshine"

EPIC673294 5 (CD2)

Tracks:

"Obsessions"
"UFO"
"Rainy Day Girl"

EPIC673294 9 (DVD)

Tracks:

"Obsessions"
"Hard Candy"
"ABC Song"

Released: November 18, 2002
Highest chart position: 29

ATTITUDE
SONY MUSIC UK
674 358 2 (CD1)

Tracks:

"Attitude"
"Golden Gun"
"Oxygen"

674 358 5 (CD2)

Tracks:

"Attitude"
"Just A Girl"
"Heroin"

674 358 9 (DVD)

Tracks:

"Attitude"
"We're So Disco"
"Head Music (Arthur Baker Remix)"

Released: October 6, 2003

SINGLES
SONY MUSIC UK 513 604 2

Tracks:

"Beautiful Ones"
"Animal Nitrate"
"Trash"
"Metal Mickey"
"So Young"
"The Wild Ones"
"Obsessions"

"Filmstar"

"Can't Get Enough"

"Everything Will Flow"

"Stay Together"

"Love The Way You Love"

"The Drowners"

"New Generation"

"Lazy"

"She's In Fashion"

"Attitude"

"Electricity"

"We Are The Pigs"

"Positivity"

"Saturday Night"

Released: October 20, 2003

suede timeline

1989

28.10.89   Brett Anderson, Justine Frischmann and Mat Osman advertise for "Young
            guitar player" in *NME*. Bernard Butler joins. Justine christens band "Suede".

1990

10.3.90   Suede play first ever gig, at the White Horse, West Hampstead. London
12.4.90   London Rock Garden
3.5.90   London Kentish Town Bull & Gate
21.5.90   Shepherd's Bush Opera on the Green
6.6.90   London Kentish Town Bull & Gate
24.6.90   London Kentish Town Bull & Gate
21.7.90   Suede's first live review appears in *Melody Maker*
24.7.90   London Kentish Town Bull & Gate
22.8.90   London Camden Falcon
13.10.90   London Queen Margaret's Uni
16.10.90   Brighton Zap Club (supporting Blur)
11.12.90   Justin Welch joins band, records "Be My God" and others, leaves band

1991

21.2.91   Suede rehearse with Mike Joyce on drums, he agrees to help out with
            recording
10.3.91   Suede record "Art" and others with Mike Joyce
21.3.91   Simon Gilbert auditions for Suede, joins band
30.4.91   London Rock Garden – Simon Gilbert's first gig with the band
29.5.91   London Camden Falcon
19.6.91   Cambridge University Ball
17.7.91   London ULU supporting Teenage Fanclub and Groovy Little Numbers
29.7.91   London Subterrania
2.8.91   London Camden Falcon
12.9.91   London Moonlight Club
15.10.91   London The Borderline
26.10.91   London The Venue
30.10.91   London ULU – Justine Frischmann's final gig with the band
4.12.91   London Camden Underworld
5.12.91   Queen Mary's College
12.12.91   London Camden Falcon

1992

3.1.92	London New Cross Venue
24.1.92	Camden Underworld
25.1.92	New Cross Venue
1.2.92	London Hampstead White Horse
6.2.92	Islington Powerhaus
12.2.92	London New Cross Amersham Arms
14.2.92	Mean Fiddler
20.2.92	London Hampstead White Horse
21.2.92	London New Cross Venue
28.2.92	London Camden Falcon
11.3.92	London The Powerhaus
12.3.92	Marquee
3.4.92	Tunbridge Wells Rumble Club
4.4.92	Mark Goodier Session
10.4.92	London ULU
17.4.92	Portsmouth
25.4.92	Suede appear on the cover of *Melody Maker* with the headline "The Best New Band In Britain"
28.4.92	London Africa Centre
8.5.92	Glasgow (supporting the Fall)
11.5.92	**"The Drowners" released**
20.5.92	*The Late Show* – first ever TV appearance
19.5.92	Folkestone Metronome
20.5.92	Brighton The Event (supporting the Fall)
21.5.92	London Town & Country
23.5.92	Nottingham Trent Poly
24.5.92	Northampton Road Menders
25.5.92	Birmingham Institute
26.5.92	Reading University
28.5.92	Newcastle Riverside
3.6.92	London Underworld
8.6.92	Manchester Boardwalk (broadcast on *New Sessions* TV show, 24.7.92)
10.6.92	Windsor Old Trout
11.6.92	Southampton The Joiners
12.6.92	Bath Moles
13.6.92	Aldershot
14.6.92	Leicester Princess Charltotte
15.6.92	Leeds Duchess of York
16.6.92	London Camden Palace
23.7.92	Gimme Shelter, T&C (with Blur)
29.8.92	Reading Festival – first performance of "Animal Nitrate"
5.9.92	London Hampstead White Horse
12.9.92	Aldershot Buzz Club

14.9.92	**"Metal Mickey" released**
15.9.92	London 100 Club
16.9.92	Manchester Virgin Megastore
16.9.92	Manchester University (live on 1FM)
24.9.92	*Top of The Pops* – performing "Metal Mickey" (single is at No.17)
2.10.92	Bradford Queens Hall
3.10.92	Sheffield Leadmill
5.10.92	Glasgow King Tuts
6.10.92	Edinburgh Venue
7.10.92	Newcastle University
8.10.92	Cleveland University
10.10.92	Nottingham Polytechnic
12.10.92	Norwich Waterfront
13.10.92	Leicester University
14.10.92	Birmingham Edwards
15.10.92	Liverpool Krazy House
16.10.92	Staffs University
18.10.92	Bristol Bierkeller
19.10.92	London Victoria SW1 Club
7.11.92	*The Word* – perform "Brass In Pocket"

1993

28.1.93	Paris, Bernard Lenoir's *Black Session*
29.1.93	Nantes Olympic
16.2.93	*Brit Awards*, Alexandra Palace
22.2.93	**"Animal Nitrate" released**
24.2.93	Southsea Portsmouth Pyramids Centre
25.2.93	Exeter Lemon Grove
27.2.93	Sheffield Leadmill
28.2.93	Coventry Main Hall
1.3.93	Cambridge Junction
9.3.93	"Animal Nitrate" on *The Beat*
21.3.93	*Kroq* interview
27.3.93	Dublin Tivoli
28.3.93	Belfast Limelight
29.3.93	***Suede* released**
30.3.93	*The Beat*
31.3.93	Newcastle Mayfair
1.4.93	Glasgow The Plaza
2.4.93	Hull University
4.4.93	London Town & Country
6.4.93	Manchester Academy
7.4.93	Birmingham Hummingbird
10.4.93	Bristol Victoria Rooms
11.4.93	Brighton Event

19.4.93	Helsinki Tavastia Club
21.4.93	Stockholm The Melody
22.4.93	Oslo Alaska
24.4.93	Copenhagen Pumpenhuset
25.4.93	Hamburg Logo
27.4.93	Amsterdam Paradiso
28.4.93	Brussels VK Club
1.5.93	Cologne Luxor
2.5.93	Frankfurt Batschkapp
3.5.93	*CFNY* interview
5.5.93	Vienna Szene Wien
6.5.93	Milan Shocking Club
7.5.93	Zurich Albisriederhaus
10.5.93	Barcelona Estandard
11.5.93	Madrid Revolver
13.5.93	Paris La Cigale
13.5.93	*Top of the Pops* – "So Young"
16.5.93	London Brixton Academy
17.5.93	**"So Young" released**
18.5.93	Birmingham Hummingbird
19.5.93	Brighton The Event
21.5.93	Poole Arts Centre
22.5.93	Newport Centre
23.5.93	Liverpool Royal Court Theatre
25.5.93	Brixton Academy
1.6.93	Washington DC 9.30 Club
2.6.93	New York Irving Plaza
3.6.93	Boston Paradise
4.6.93	*Later With Jools* Holland broadcast
5.6.93	Toronto Opera House
6.6.93	Detroit St Andrews Hall
7.6.93	Chicago Metro Club
8.6.93	*Tonight Show* in LA – "Metal Mickey"
10.6.93	San Francisco Slim's
11.6.93	Los Angeles Hollywood Colonade
12.6.93	Los Angeles *Kroq* Festival
14.6.93	San Diego Backdoor
15.6.93	Phoenix The Roxy
17.6.93	Dallas Trees
25.6.93	Glastonbury Festival
30.6.93	Tokyo Nippon Seinankan
2.7.93	Kawasaki Club Citta
3.7.93	Kawasaki Club Citta
5.7.93	Tokyo Shibuya Kokaido
6.7.93	Osaka Sankei Hall

8.7.93	Nagoya Club Quattro
12.7.93	London Clapham Grand featuring Siouxsie Sioux & Chrissie Hynde
16.8.93	"Drowners" US video shoot, Ealing, London
20.8.93	*Naked City* TV – "Still Life"
4.9.93	Channel 4 *Opening Shots* documentary
8.9.93	Suede win Mercury Music Prize at Savoy Hotel, donate £25,000 to Cancer Research.
10.9.93	Live 105 session
13.9.93	**"The Drowners" US release**
22.9.93	Seattle Rekeudy
23.9.93	Vancouver BC Town Pump
24.9.93	San Francisco Tower Records
25.9.93	San Fransisco Warfield Theatre
28.9.93	Las Vegas The Huntridge
29.9.93	Phoenix Club Rios
1.10.93	Los Angeles, Hollywood Palace
2.10.93	Los Angeles
4.10.93	Santa Fe, Luna
6.10.93	Dallas Deep Ellum Liv
7.10.93	Houston Numbers
9.10.93	New Orleans Tipitanas
10.10.93	Atlanta Masquerade
12.10.93	Washington Radio Music Hall
13.10.93	Boston Avalon Ballroom
14.10.93	*MTV 120 minutes*
14.10.93	New York HMV acoustic set
15.10.93	*Conan O'Brien Show*, NBC studios
15.10.93	New York Academy
25.10.93	London cinema – premiere of *Love & Poison*
25.10.93	"Still Life" originally scheduled as a single for this date
15.11.93	***Love & Poison* released** directed by Wiz, starring Suzanne Bull as Angel
25.11.93	Toulouse Salle Potet
26.11.93	Tours Salle de Fetes
27.11.93	Paris Casino de Paris
2.12.93	Rennes Transmusicales
4.12.93	London LA2
24.12.93	London The Forum – XFM Christmas show

1994

16.1.94	Simon as guest speaker at House of Commons
7.2.94	"Stay Together" on *The Beat*
8.2.94	Worthing Pier Pavilion
10.2.94	"Stay Together" on *Top Of The Pops*, recorded the night before
10.2.94	Mark Radcliffe Session for 1FM
11.2.94	Blackpool Tower Ballroom

12.2.94	Edinburgh Queen's Hall – Bernard's last gig with Suede
14.2.94	**"Stay Together" released**
24.2.94	"Stay Together" on *Top of the Pops*
15.3.94	*MTV Most Wanted*
22.3.94	Suede enter the studio to record their second album
26.4.94	"Stay Together" US release
19.7.94	Bernard's departure announced on 1FM *Evening Session*
26.7.94	Final mixing of the album is completed
27.7.94	*Melody Maker* ad for new guitarist
22.8.94	Brett on *Evening Session* to promote new single, "We Are The Pigs"
7-10.9.94	US promo visit
12.9.94	**"We Are The Pigs" released**
22.9.94	Richard's worldwide debut, "We Are The Pigs" on *Top of the Pops*
9.94	"The Wild Ones" video is shot in Dartford.
4.10.94	Paris, *Black Session*, France
6.10.94	Paris, *Top Gear* radio show
7.10.94	Paris, Passage du Nord Ouest
10.10.94	**Dog Man Star released**, Richard's UK debut at Raw Club
12.10.94	Radio One, live session
26.10.94	Preston Guildhall
28.10.94	Hull City Hall
29.10.94	Sheffield Octagon
31.10.94	Manchester Free Trade Hall
1.11.94	Wolverhampton Civic Hall
3.11.94	Brighton The Dome
4.11.94	Cambridge Corn Exchange
7.11.94	**"The Wild Ones" released**, Frankfurt Batschkapp
8.11.94	Geneva Salles des Fetes du Lignon
10.11.94	Modena Vox Club
12.11.94	Pordenone Rototom Club
13.11.94	Milan Rolling Stone
15.11.94	Madrid Aqualung
17.11.94	Valencia Arena
18.11.94	Barcelona Chic Studio
19.11.94	Montpellier Rockstore
21.11.94	Lyon Transbordeur
22.11.94	Paris Bataclan
24.11.94	Amsterdam Paradiso
25.11.94	Gent Vooruit
27.11.94	Copenhagen Pumpenehuset
28.11.94	Oslo Rockefeler
29.11.94	Stockhom Cirkus
1.12.94	Hamburg Zillo
2.12.94	Berlin Loft
3.12.94	Cologne Kantine

4.12.94	Munich Charterhalle
13.12.94	Aberdeen Music Hall
14.12.94	Middlesbrough Town Hall
15.12.94	Glasgow Barrowlands
17.12.94	London Heaven
19.12.94	Southampton Guildhall
20.12.94	Newport Centre
21.12.94	Bradford St Georges Hall

1995

11.1.95	Belfast Ulster Hall
12.1.95	Dublin SFX
13.1.95	Cork City Hall
19.1.95	Bremen, Germany
24.1.95	Oxford Apollo
25.1.95	Norwich University of East Anglia
27.1.95	Bristol Colston Hall
28.1.95	Liverpool Royal Court Theatre
30.1.95	**"New Generation" released**, Ipswich Regent
31.1.95	Leicester de Montfort Hall
2.2.95	Hanley Victoria Hall
3.2.95	Watford Colosseum
5.2.95	Exeter University
6.2.95	London Hammersmith Palais, "New Generation" CD2 released
7.2.95	London Hammersmith Palais
10.2.95	Washington DC Wust Music Hall
11.2.95	Philadelphi Theatre of Living Arts
12.2.95	Providence Lupos
14.2.95	New York Manhatten Centre
15.2.95	Boston Axis
16.2.95	HMV Acoustic Session
17.2.95	Toronto Warehouse
18.2.95	Montreal Club Soda
20.2.95	Detroit St Andrews
21.2.95	Chicago Metro
22.2.95	St Louis The Other World
24.2.95	Atlanta Masquerade
26.2.95	Houston Numbers
27.2.95	Dallas Trees
2/3.95	"Sam" and "Have You Ever Been This Low" recorded in Los Angeles.
2.3.95	Los Angeles American Legion
5.3.95	San Fransisco, The Fillmore Theatre, USA
8.3.95	Tokyo NHK Hall
9.3.95	Nagoya Diamond Hall
10.3.95	Osaka Koseinenkin Hall

12.3.95	Sendai Denryoku Hall
13.3.95	Niigata Phase
14.3.95	Tokyo Gotanda U-Port
15.3.95	Tokyo Gotanda U-Port
17.3.95	Tokyo Liquid Rooms
19.3.95	Hong Kong Queen Elizabeth Hall
21.3.95	Bangkok MBK Hall
1.4.95	Amiens Cirque Municipal
3.4.95	Paris La Cigale
5.4.95	Strasbourg La Laiterie
7.4.95	Hamburg Grosse Freiheit
8.4.95	Lund Olympen
10.4.95	Stockholm Cirkus
11.4.95	Stockholm Cirkus
14.4.95	Groningen Oosterpoort
15.4.95	Brussels La Luna
16.4.95	Utrecht Tivoli
20.4.95	Bristol Sound City Anson Rooms
1.5.95	Berlin Huxleys Neu Welt
2.5.95	Stuttgart Longhorn
3.5.95	Dusseldorf Tor 3
5.5.95	Cesena Vidia
6.5.95	Florence Auditorium Flog
7.5.95	Padova Extra Exra
11.5.95	Barcelona Zeleste II
12.5.95	Valencia Arena
13.5.95	Granada Jardines de Nettuno
15.5.95	Madrid Aqualung
16.5.95	Zaragoza Sala Multiusos
19.5.95	Blackpool Empress Ballroom
21.5.95	London Royal Albert Hall
10.6.95	Provinssirock Festival
12.6.95	***Introducing The Band*** **concert video released**
15.6.95	Saloncia, Mylos Arena
16.6.95	Athens Viron Amphiteater
23.6.95	Skelleftea Festival
24.6.95	Oslo, Isle of Calf Festival
25.6.95	Israel radio show – acoustic session
26.6.95	Tel Aviv Cinerama Theatre
27.6.95	Haifa Tower records
29.6.95	Haifa Airport Festival
1.7.95	Roskilde Festival, Denmark
8.7.95	Lummen Zwemdokrockfestival
9.7.95	Dour Festival
14.7.95	Phoenix Festival, UK

25.8.95	Church Studios
28.8.95	*Introducing the Band* video screened at the NFT
4.9.95	Olympic Studios – recording of "Shipbuilding" for *Help* album
3.12.95	Recording of third album begins at Townhouse studios

1996

27.1.96	London Hanover Grand – Neil Codling's worldwide debut
5.7.96	Midtfyns Festival, Denmark
8&9.7.96	"Trash" video shoot
12.7.96	Doctor Music Festival, Spain
22.7.96	VH1 Hamburg
24.7.96	*Top Of The Pops* "Trash"
28.7.96	Big Site, Tokyo, Japan
29.7.96	**"Trash" released**
1.8.96	*White Room* TV
5.8.96	Stockholm Water Festival
7.8.96	"Trash" on *Top Of The Pops*
13.8.96	*Black Session* album preview
16.8.96	St Malo Festival
28.8.96	*Evening Session*
1.9.96	London Virgin Megastore
2.9.96	***Coming Up* released**
5.6.96	French TV
6.9.96	Arhus Denmark
7.9.96	Oslo, Norway
8.9.96	Bergen, Roekeriet USF, Norway
10.9.96	Dublin, Tivoli Theatre
12.9.96	"Beautiful Ones" video
13.9.96	NRK TV Norway
14.9.96	Trondheim Norway
16.9.96	Hamburg album launch
19.9.96	Belgium festival
20.9.96	Italian TV, Boulogne
21.9.96	Helsinki, Finland
30.9.96	Aberdeen Music Hall
1.10.96	Glasgow Barrowland
3.10.96	Sheffield Octagon Centre
4.10.96	Leicester de Montford Hall
5.10.96	Hanley Victoria Hall
7.10.96	Leeds T&C
8.10.96	Hull City Hall
10.10.96	London Kilburn
11.10.96	London Kilburn (+ *TFI Friday* – "Beautiful Ones")
13.10.96	Norwich UEA
14.10.96	**"Beautiful Ones" released**, Birmingham Que Club

17.10.96	Frankfurt Germany
18.10.96	Forum Nurnberg Germany
20.10.96	Amsterdam, Paradiso
21.10.96	E-Werk Cologne, Germany
23.10.96	*Top of the Pops* – "Beautiful Ones"
24.10.96	Markthalle Hamburg
25.10.96	KB Hallen, Copenhagen
26.10.96	Gothenburg Sweden
28.10.96	Stockholm Sweden
30.10.96	Huxleys Berlin
31.10.96	Babylon Munich
9.11.96	Zeleste Barcelona
10.11.96	Madrid, La Riviera
12.11.96	Grenoble France
14.11.96	Bataclan Paris
15.11.96	Salle d'Allones, le Mans
16.11.96	Krakatoa Bordeaux
18.11.96	La Laiterie Strasbourg
19.11.96	Geneva
20.11.96	Milan
22.11.96	*TFI Friday* – "Filmstar"
24.11.96	"Saturday Night" video shoot
26.11.96	Manchester Apollo
27.11.96	Liverpool Royal Court
28.11.96	Wolverhampton Civic Hall
30.11.96	Newcastle City Hall
1.12.96	*Smash Hits* – "Trash" mime
2.12.96	Capital Radio session
3.12.96	*Later With Jools Holland*
5.12.96	Southend Cliffs Pavillion
6.12.96	Derby Assembly Rooms
7.12.96	Bristol Colston Hal
9.12.96	Newport Centre
10.12.96	Southampton Guildhall
11.12.96	Oxford Apollo
13.12.96	London Roundhouse
14.12.96	London Roundhouse
15.12.96	London Roundhouse, featuring Neil Tennant

1997

15.1.97	French TV
13.1.97	**"Saturday Night" released**
18.1.97	Gran Canaria
22.1.96	*Top Of The Pops* – "Saturday Night"
26.1.97	Bradford St Georges Hall

27.1.97	Poole Arts Centre
28.1.97	Guildford Civic
30.1.97	Cambridge Corn Exchange
1-2.2.97	Danish Grammies
3.2.97	Brighton Centre
4.2.97	Folkestone Leas Cliff Hall
5.2.97	Reading Rivermead
7.2.97	Plymouth Pavilions
8.2.97	Watford Coliseum
11.2.97	Middlesbrough Town Hall
13.2.97	Edinburgh Meadowbank
14.2.97	Carlisle Sands Centre
15.2.97	Blackburn King Georges
25.2.97	Osaka Imp Hall
26.2.97	Fukuoka Logos
27.2.97	Nagoya Diamond Hall
1.3.97	Tokyo Blitz
2.3.97	Tokyo Blitz
3.3.97	Tokyo Blitz
7.3.97	Singapore, Harbour Pavillion
3.97	Radio Station, Singapore
8.3.97	Bangkok
10.3.97	Hong Kong
11.3.97	Hong Kong
15.3.97	"Lazy" video
27.3.97	Munich TV
29.3.97	Stuttgart SDR3 Radio
30.3.97	Dusseldorf, Rocknacht
5.4.97	London, The Forum – b-sides gig
7.4.97	**"Lazy" released**
8.4.97	***Coming Up* US release**
11.4.97	TFI Friday
13.4.97	York Barbican
14.4.97	Doncaster Dome
15.4.97	Braintree Arena, with Justine on 'Implement Yeah"
17.4.97	Bourges, France
20.4.97	Spain, acoustic radio
21.4.97	Utrecht Music Centre
23.4.97	Modena Vox Club
24.4.97	Rome Horus Club
25.4.97	Pistoia Auditorium
4.5.97	Dublin The Castle
5.5.97	Belfast Point
9.5.97	Toronto Warehouse
10.5.97	Ottawa Barrymore Theatre

11.5.97	Montreal Spectrum
14.5.97	New York Supper Club
15.5.97	New York Supper Club
17.5.97	Boston Paradise, Suede's equipment is stolen after show
18.5.97	Boston Paradise (acoustic set)
21.5.97	Los Angeles El Rey Theatre
22.5.97	Los Angeles El Rey Theatre (acoustic set)
23.5.97	San Francisco Filmore
25.5.97	San Francisco Live 105
6.6.97	Tel Aviv Bitan II
7.6.97	Israel Radio acoustic session
7.6.97	Tel Aviv Bitan II
13.6.97	Hultsfred Festival
14.6.97	Provinssirock Finland
25.6.97	"Filmstar" video shoot
27.6.97	Roskilde
2.7.97	Quart Festival
4.7.97	Torhout Belgium
5.7.97	Werchter Belgium
6.7.97	Belfort
11-12.7.97	Mayfair Studios, recording "Poor Little Rich Girl"
21.7.97	**"Filmstar" released in Europe**
30.7.97	MTV special
1.8.97	Ostersund
8.8.97	Paul Ross show
9.8.97	Benicasim festival
10.8.97	Sudoeste Portugal
11.8.97	**"Filmstar" UK & German release**
14.8.97	Top Of The Pops – "Filmstar"
22.8.97	Reading Festival
28.8.97	*Mercury Music Awards*
24.9.97	Danish TV
6.10.97	***Sci-Fi Lullabies* released**

1998

15.1.98	*Red Hot & Blue* TV mime of "Poor Little Rich Girl"
10-15.6.98	Trial session with Steve Osborne at Mayfair Studios
10.8.98	Suede begin recording fourth album with Steve Osborne at Eastcote Studios

1999

8&9.2.99	Alternate version of "Head Music" recorded with Arthur Baker at Mayfair Studios
1.3.99	Final mixing completed.
10.3.99	Shoot video for "Electricity"
22.3.99	Fanclub show at Glasgow Garage

23.3.99	Fanclub show at Manchester University Main Debating Hall
25.3.99	Swedish TV show, performing "Electricity"
27.3.99	Free fanclub show at London Astoria
31.3.99	Milan TV show
9.4.99	"Electricity" live on *TFI Friday*
12.4.99	**"Electricity" released**
13.4.99	Recording "Electricity" and "She's In Fashion" for *Pepsi Chart Show*
15.4.99	Record "Electricity" for *Top of The Pops*
16.4.99	Film special concert for Suede Music TV show at Perivale, West London
17.4.99	Perform "Electricity" on *CD:UK*
18.4.99	"Electricity" enters UK charts at number 5, Suede's sixth consecutive top ten hit
22.4.99	Shoot video for "She's In Fashion"
24.4.99	Concert for MTV Milan
27.4.99	Swedish fanclub concert at Stockholm Klubben
28.4.99	Norwegian fanclub concert at Oslo John Dee club
30.4.99	Danish fanclub show at Copenhagen Pumpehuset
2.5.99	In-store performance and signing session at Virgin Megastore
3.5.99	***Head Music* released.** Brett takes part in Jo Whiley TV show
5.3.99	Spanish fanclub show in Madrid
7.3.99	French fanclub show in Paris
9.5.99	MTV concert at London Shepherd's Bush Empire

Head Music enters the UK album charts at number 1

11.5.99	Perform three songs for *Later With Jools Holland*
13.5.99	French TV show in Cannes
16.5.99	TV in Milan
19.5.99	Libro festival in Vienna
21.5.99	Rock Im Park Germany
22.5.99	Rock Am Ring Germany
31.5.99	*Black Session* live concert for French radio
4.6.99	*TFI Friday*, first live performance of "She's In Fashion"
6.6.99	Norwegian Wood festival, Oslo
8.6.99	Acoustic radio session in Amsterdam
12.6.99	*CD:UK* TV show
15.6.99	*All Back To Mine* radio interview, Neil records "Weight of the World"
17.6.99	Suede support REM in Lisbon
18.6.99	Mime "She's In Fashion" for Italian TV
19.6.99	Hultsfred festival, Sweden
20.6.99	Provinssirock festival, Finland
21.6.99	"She's In Fashion" single released
22.6.99	1FM radio session
24.6.99	"She's In Fashion" on *Top Of The Pops*
26.6.99	German support tour with REM begins in Oberhausen
27.6.99	Frankfurt. "She's In Fashion" enters UK charts at number 13
29.6.99	Hannover

30.6.99	Berlin
3-4.7.99	Suede headline three nights at the Roskilde festival in Denmark.
7-8.7.99	Film video for "Everything Will Flow"
9.7.99	Acoustic radio session in Brussels
10.7.99	Italian TV show
11.7.99	Support REM in Bologna
24.7.99	St Nolff festival, France
4.8.99	Budapest Island Festival, Hungary
7.8.99	Benicassim festival, Spain
9.8.99	Live concert at Sound Republic for XFM
10.8.99	Record eight songs for VH1
11.8.99	Mime two songs for Radio 1's *Eclipse Roadshow*
12.8.99	Rock Oz'Arenes festival, Switzerland
14.8.99	Paredes de Coura festival, Portugal
16.8.99	Acoustic session for Steve Lamacq
21.8.99	V99 Staffordshire
22.8.99	V99 Chelmsford
27.8.99	Lowlands festival, Holland
28.8.99	Pukkelpop festival, Belgium
6.9.99	**"Everything Will Flow" released**, record "She's In Fashion" for NPA TV, Paris
8.9.99	Record "Everything Will Flow" live for *Top Of The Pops* in Nottingham
11.9.99	Perform "She's In Fashion" and "Everything Will Flow" for Norwegian TV
15.9.99	Japanese tour begins at Drum Logos, Fukuoka
16.9.99	Osaka Imp Hall
17.9.99	Nagoya Diamond Hall
19-21.9.99	Tokyo Akasaka Blitz
23.9.99	South East Asian tour begins at Taipei Gymnastic Hall, Taiwan
25.9.99	Dance Fever Bangkok, Thailand
28.9.99	Hong Kong Convention & Exhibition Centre
30.9.99	Singapore Harbour Pavilion
2.10.99	Suede's first tour of Australia begins at the Livid Festival in Brisbane
4.10.99	Metro Theatre, Sydney
6.10.99	Forum, Melbourne
16.10.99	RTL radio session, Paris
22.10.99	Brighton Centre
23.10.99	Newport Centre
24.10.99	Liverpool Royal Court
26.10.99	Doncaster Dome
27.10.99	Manchester Apollo
28.10.99	Wolverhampton Civic Hall
30.10.99	Reading Rivermead
31.10.99	Poole Arts Centre
1.11.99	St Austell Colliseum
3.11.99	Glasgow Barrowlands

4.11.99	Dublin Olympia, Ireland
5.11.99	Dublin Olympia, Ireland
8.11.99	**"Can't Get Enough" released**
12.11.99	Danish TV show
17.11.99	European tour begins at Lille Aeronef, France
18.11.99	Paris Olympia, France
19.11.99	Strasbourg La Laiterie, France
21.11.99	Hamburg Grosse Freiheit, Germany
22.11.99	Copenhagen Valby Hallen, Denmark
23.11.99	Lund Olympen, Sweden
25.11.99	Gothenburg Lisebeghallsen, Sweden
26.11.99	Oslo Spektrum, Norway
27.11.99	Stockholm Hovet, Sweden
29.11.99	Arhus SCC, Denmark
30.11.99	Berlin Columbiahalle, Germany
2.12.99	Brussels Halles de Schaarbeek, Belgium
3.12.99	Utrecht Music Centre, Netherlands
4.12.99	Cologne E-Werk, Germany
6.12.99	Stuttgart Longhorn, Germany
7.12.99	Munich Babylon, Germany
8.12.99	Neu Isenburg Hugenottenhalle, Germany
10.12.99	Rome Palacisalfa, Italy
11.12.99	Modena Vox Club, Italy
12.12.99	Milan Alcatraz, Italy
14.12.99	Barcelona Zeleste, Spain
15.12.99	Madrid Riviera, Spain

2000

25.1.00	IDF radio session, Tel Aviv, Israel
27.1.00	Cinerama, Tel Aviv, Israel
10.3.00	White Horse fanclub party
10.00	Brett records "Trainsurfing" and "Keen Yellow Planet" with Stina Nordenstam
21.10.00	Iceland Airwaves Festival, Laugardalsholl, Reykjavik
11.00	Record "Simon" with Ken Thomas

2001

2.01	Record three demos with Tony Hoffer at Rockfield Studios
13.3.01	Neil Codling leaves the band, Alex Lee joins
28.5.01	Recording begins at Parkgate studios with Tony Hoffer
24.6.01	Brett, Alex and Tony Hoffer perform "Seasong" at Royal Festival Hall
11-18.9.01	Record two tracks at RAK with John Leckie
14.10.01	Brett reads lyrics and performs three songs at Bristol Poetry Slam
27.10.01	Coimbra University Pavilion, Portugal
26.11.01	***Lost In TV* DVD collection released**

2002

14.1.02– 23.3.02	Recording *A New Morning* at Townhouse with Stephen Street
25.4.02	Belfast *Hot Press Awards*, perform "Positivity"
4.5.02	"The Drowners" party & secret gig at The Depot
23.5.02	Perform "Astrogirl" on Dom Jolly
25.5.02	*Re:covered* TV – "Beautiful Loser" & "Union City Blue"
14.6.02	Hultsfred Festival
23.6.02	Meltdown, Royal Festival Hall with 10-piece orchestra
3.7.02	H-2000 Turkey
6.7.02	Mardi Gras
10.7.02	Move Festival Manchester
13.7.02	Finland
16.7.02	Electric Ballroom fanclub gig
25.7.02	Shoot video for "Positivity"
28.7.02	Latvian festival
4.8.02	Benicassim festival, Spain
7-8.8.02	Working on "You Belong To Me" in Wessex studios
10.8.02	Smukfest festival, Denmark
11.8.02	St Malo festival, France
15.8.02	Acoustic performance for Singapore radio
17.8.02	Summersonic, Tokyo, Japan
18.8.02	Summersonic, Osaka, Japan
22.8.02	Perform "Positivity" on Ralph Little show
24.8.02	Pukkelpop festival, Belgium
2.9.02	Edinburgh Liquid Rooms
3.9.02	London Scala
5.9.02	Cardiff Coal Exchange
6.9.02	Pilton
16.9.02	**"Positivity" released**
17.9.02	Virgin Radio Session
18.9.02	XFM radio session
22.9.02	Belfast Radio 2 Show
30.9.02	*A New Morning* **released**
10.10.02	Copenhagen Vega
11.10.02	Copenhagen Vega
12.10.02	Copenhagen Vega
14.10.02	Brussels Ancienne Belgique
15.10.02	Amsterdam Paradiso
17.10.02	Hamburg Markthalle
18.10.02	Berlin Universal Hall
20.10.02	Oslo Rockefeller
21.10.02	Stockholm Circus
22.10.02	Stockholm Circus

30.10.02	Glasgow Barrowlands
31.10.02	Aberdeen Music Hall
2.11.02	Liverpool Royal Court
3.11.02	Manchester Academy
4.11.02	Leeds University
6.11.02	Northumbria University
7.11.02	Birmingham Academy
8.11.02	Norwich UEA
10.11.02	Bristol Academy
11.11.02	Cambridge Corn Exchange
12.11.02	Southampton Guildhall
14.11.02	London Shepherd's Bush Empire
15.11.02	London Shepherd's Bush Empire
16.11.02	London Shepherd's Bush Empire
18.11.02	**"Obsessions" released**

2003

17.1.03	Hong Kong RTHK awards
18.1.03	Taipei University Taiwan
19.1.03	Shanghai Channel V Awards
20.1.03	Hong Kong acoustic show
23.1.03	Jakarta Indonesia
24.1.03	*MTV Awards* Singapore
25.1.03	Singapore Fort Canning
28.1.03	Tokyo Akasaka Blitz
29.1.03	Tokyo Ax
30.1.03	Osaka On Air
3.2.03	Chao Yang Gym Beijing, China
4.2.03	Chao Yang Gym Beijing, China
7.2.03	Chaing Mai Thailand
9.2.03	Bangkok Thailand
4.4.03	Arhus Train Denmark
5.4.03	Arhus Train Denmark
23.6.03	Thesolonika Greece
25.6.03	Athens Greece
27.6.03	Glastonbury
11.7.03	Esbjerg Denmark
12.7.03	Odense Denmark
10.7.03	Arhus Denmark
17.7.03	Blokhus Denmark
18.7.03	Borkop Denmark
19.7.03	Naestved Denmark
20.7.03	Copenhagen Denmark
8.8.03	Sudoeste Portugal
10.8.03	Benicassim Spain

29.8.03	Pukkelpop Belgium
30.8.03	Terremoto Germany
31.8.03	Lowlands Holland
6.9.03	Rock & Coke Turkey
22.9.03	ICA
23.9.03	ICA
25.9.03	ICA
26.9.03	ICA
27.9.03	ICA
6.10.03	**"Attitude" released**
20.10.03	***Singles* album released**
1.11.03	Festival do Norte Santiago Spain
18.11.03	Vitoria Spain
20.11.03	Barcelona Spain
21.11.03	Vencia Spain
22.11.03	Madrid La Riviera Spain
7.12.03	Glasgow Academy
8.12.03	Bristol Academy
11.12.03	Birmingham Academy
12.12.03	Brixton Academy

index